Welcome to Everytown

A Journey into the English Mind

Julian Baggini

Granta Books

London

Granta Publications, 2/3 Hanover Yard, Noel Road, London N1 8BE

First published in Great Britain by Granta Books, 2007

A CIP catalogue record for this book
is available from the British Library.

1 3 5 7 9 10 8 6 4 2

ISBN 978-1-86207-921-2

Typeset by M Rules

Acknowledgements

I would like to thank the many people of Rotherham who helped make my stay there so enjoyable, including Alan, Alf, Ann and Andy, Barry, Colin, Dave, Harry, Ian, Jack, Paul and Carol, Pete, Ray and Tractor Dave from The Travellers; Keith, Adrian and Teresa Bury from Maltby; Alex, Tina, Andy and Debbie, Elaine and Shane (splitters!) from The Ball; Dave and Ernest, Alan, Arthur, Mavis and Pat from The Transport Club; Dave Brennan and his band, Jim, Dot and their two friends whose names I shamefully don't recall from The Horseshoes; Phil and Stuart from Philip Howard Books; neighbours Rachel and Steve, Bob and Kath and their kids; Councillor Shaukat Ali and his team at MAARI; Dearne Valley Ramblers too many to mention without offending the names I inevitably forget; Jim and Brian from Maltby Tennis Club; Trevor Potts and all the fabulous singers from The Stockyard; wonder mechanic Kenny Melling; Amanda from Rotherlets and Darren the landlord. Apologies to any others I have not mentioned but should have.

In addition I'd like to thank Yasmin Alibhai-Brown, Alessandra Buonfino, Nicholas Fearn, Justin Irwin, Fiona Measham, Roderick Graham and Huw Thomas for various help tracking down information. Special thanks to Patrick Tate at CACI for providing information on ACORN profiles that enabled me to select S66 as my Everytown. Any lack of wisdom in this choice is entirely down to me.

As ever, numerous thanks to those at Granta, especially my editor George Miller, who with his partner Katharine Reeve also went beyond the call of duty and helped move me to Bramley. A big hand also to Louise Campbell, Frances Hollingdale, Gail Lynch, Leonie Taylor – all gone but not forgotten, plus Sajidah 'just one more query' Ahmad, Julio Ferrandis, Sara Holloway, Angela 'record-breaker' Rose, Pru Rowlandson, Bella Shand, Sarah Wasley, Cathie Game and all the splendid sales team working so hard to get my books onto the shelves. Thanks also to the ever-loyal and supportive Lizzy Kremer.

A Note on Names

Since people did not talk to me on the understanding I would expose them to the nation, most names have been changed. In addition, the regulars at The Travellers have been mixed up, boiled and distilled into rather fewer composite, fictionalized individuals (Andy, Johnny, Neil, Pete and Reg). I have included only true words and descriptions of these people, but not necessarily in the true order. Where real names are used, surnames are usually included, except in the case of Tractor Dave, which is a real name I couldn't bear to change.

Contents

Prologue

Finding Everytown

Welcome

Few impressions are as vivid as those of arriving in a strange place for the first time: the scrum of imploring bodies jostling for your custom in Nairobi, the chaos and disorder of Athens, the unrelenting reminders of the past penetrating the present in Rome, the just-arrived-on-a-film-set unreality of New York. People travel all over the world searching for such experiences of the world made new. But none of my own arrivals into foreign lands unsettled me as much as when I stepped off the bus and first set foot in Everytown. Here on Braithwell Road I had a curious sense of being somewhere that was at once entirely familiar, and at the same time utterly alien. And absurdly, these confused emotions were being stirred in Rotherham, South Yorkshire.

I was here in June 2005 to find somewhere to live for six months, as part of my attempt to understand the English mind: what we think, what we believe, what we want and what we value. I wasn't in search of the elusive 'national character' or the 'essence of Englishness'. Rather, I was looking to describe and examine the national 'folk philosophy', the set of beliefs and assumptions that informs how we live and how we think.

The English care little for philosophy in the formal sense. I laughed when spoof chat show host Alan Partridge named his favourite philosopher, but I didn't realize how insightful the joke was until I read a letter in the *Yorkshire Post* which quoted him more or less verbatim, talking of 'the late actor, writer and philosopher, Peter Ustinov'. But although people may not know much about philosophy, they know what they like. I'm always amazed at how many people profess to be 'a bit of a philosopher myself'. One person I met gave me a short pamphlet he had written claiming to prove the existence of God. Another, a retired rambler had similar ideas and had been trying to get his work published for years. He believed that we had perverted the true teachings of Jesus and that nature would heal everything if we left it alone.

But the English philosophy I was looking for was implicit rather than explicit. Most people aren't able to tell you what their metaphysical framework is, for example, not least because few English schools believe that their students (or teachers) have any need to know what 'metaphysics' means. Nevertheless, everyone carries around with them a set of assumptions about the fundamental nature of the world: whether it is purely physical or partly spiritual; whether things just happen or whether everything has a purpose; whether we are locked in the present or whether we can see into the future or past. Likewise we all operate according to an implicit value system, a sense of what the good life entails, and an idea of how the laws and institutions of the country should be arranged. What I wanted to do was to identify what the dominant philosophy of England added up to, and whether it was sustainable.

To uncover this underlying belief system, I wanted to rely on facts, not just my personal opinions and perceptions. In his book about the English, A. A. Gill ventured that 'facts are what pedantic, dull people have instead of opinions'. I would counter that facts are what boorish, bigoted people lack to back up their opinions. But facts alone cannot tell you everything. C. P. Snow was only half-right when he said that 'Comment is free, but facts are sacred.' Facts need to be dissected and analysed if they are to tell us anything of use.

Finding pertinent facts is difficult enough in any country, but is even more complicated in one in which identity is shared between England, Great Britain and the United Kingdom – an entity that, perhaps uniquely among nations, lacks its own adjective to describe the things and people which belong to it. Ulster Unionists have to rely on the geographically and politically inaccurate term 'British' to express their loyalty. Most facts I would discover would be drawn from the nation as a whole, and not just England. Why then is this not a journey into the British mind? The reason is that England dominates the UK, accounting for nearly 85% of its population. Facts about the British are therefore mainly facts about the English: any differences in Wales, Scotland and Northern Ireland are diluted and lost. In many cases these differences are slight, and so a lot of what I would be looking at would concern the whole of the United Kingdom, as well as England. But it is also the case that many of the beliefs and opinions are common to even larger units: northern Europe, Anglo-Saxon nations, the developed West, and in some cases perhaps human nature. So it should not be assumed that what I say about the English folk philosophy applies only to the English. The purpose is to describe the English mind accurately, and if as a result we are able to differentiate it from the minds of others, that is a bonus.

I was not short of facts about what the English think. A bewildering number of opinion polls and surveys are carried out every year, and the government produces a number of weighty annual tomes revealing the state of the nation. People are very mistrustful of opinion polls, but when conducted properly they are at least indicative of general opinion. The knack is to avoid spurious self-selecting polls, or those with heavily leading questions. The polls I quote from may not be 100% accurate, but their findings do tell us things worth knowing.

Stated boldly, however, mere facts and polls leave us with more questions than answers. For instance, what does it mean that shortly after the 7/7 London bombings, 51% of Britons did not think that the UK Muslim community did enough to stop British Islamists supporting terrorism? After all, it is possible to reach this conclusion for a number of reasons. You might think that we have all become too tolerant or complacent about a militant

Muslim minority; or that British Muslims had simply failed to understand the extent of radicalism in their community; or that Muslims are generally murderous extremists. Which of these best explains the fact revealed by the opinion poll? Does it reflect thought-through, rational concern or knee-jerk prejudice?

To answer questions like that, I needed to look beyond the mere facts and see how they reflected the people whose thoughts they described. The trouble is that there is no one place I could go to find out what the typical English person thinks. Everywhere has its own particularities and nowhere is a perfect microcosm of the country as a whole. Nevertheless, some places are more representative of the nation than others. My Everytown would therefore be as typical an area as is possible, but could function as no more than a sounding board, a kind of community-wide focus group in which abstract facts would be tested against organic reality.

What kind of town would meet these requirements? Typically, the media look to the average when they're looking for England in miniature. That would take you to Milton Keynes or Reading, and having already lived in Reading once, I was in no hurry to repeat the experience. But fortunately for me, this method of identifying the typical is misleading anyway. The average is the blurred-out middle. It does not represent the true variety of the English people but a rather untypical, bland blend. What I wanted was somewhere that contained all types of the English.

To find it, I turned to CACI Ltd, whose ACORN demographic profiles power the uncannily accurate neighbourhood information found on upmystreet.com. You type in your postcode and read what people in your area typically eat, read, drive, watch and do, and you find that, to your horror, you fit the stereotype all too closely. The question I put to them was: which postcode area has the closest match of household types to the country as a whole? In other words, where in England has the most typical mix of wealthy pensioners, struggling families, aspiring singles and so on? The answer was S66, on the outskirts of Rotherham, South Yorkshire, with a 93% match with the national data set. The fact that the neighbouring S25 was the fourth closest match clinched it.

So it was that I set out from Bristol on 8 June 2005, heading for 'Everytown' to find a place to live.

In order to absorb as much normal life as possible I set myself a few rules. I would read only the most popular newspapers, watch the highest-rating television programmes and listen to the nation's favourite radio stations. I'd take the kind of holiday most people take and eat what they eat. If I had time to spare, I would not do what I'd do back home, but use it as an opportunity to try something as mainstream as possible. I didn't see the point of going to Everytown if I was going to stand aloof from what went on there.

On the train, I jotted down a list of values and characteristics I expected to find, making no attempt to mask my prejudices. I thought there would be toleration for difference, but no real love for it, and only as long as it is not perceived as threatening. There would be provincialism. People's aspirations would be modest, or else for superficial things like fame or wealth. The best life would be comfortable and fun. People would think religion was for weirdos and philosophy for boffins. Anti-intellectualism would be rife. People would have their philosophies of life, which would be simple, but true: be thankful for what you've got, make the most of what you have; time waits for no man. Although in behaviour most people would be sexually liberal, most still want to be married and think that children deserve two married parents. There would be a thin line between having some youthful fun and being a slag. Homophobia would be normal. Despite the talk of a national culinary renaissance, people would still eat badly and the 'best restaurant around' would be rubbish. People would have several fears which are just not founded in their actual experience. Crime, the youth of today and so forth will worry people, even though S66 is probably a fairly quiet area. There would be cynicism, especially about politicians. They would say the television is full of trash but they'd still watch it all the time. They would have a sense of who they were and what their kind were, and would be keen to differentiate themselves. The much-heralded decline of identity would turn out to be overstated. But overall most people would be pleasant and decent.

Reading that list back now, three things strike me. The first is how critical and condescending a lot of it sounds. The second is nonetheless how little turned out to be totally wide of the mark. The dissonance is a result of the fact that beliefs can be true, but mislead because they are but part of a wider or deeper truth. Consider how getting to know a people can be like getting to know a person. What you first notice are often features that the person really has: she might be boisterous, tall, opinionated, witty, clever but unreflective. If you don't get to know her any better, you will always have a set of true opinions about her, but it will also be the case that you don't really know her. To do that you need to understand how all these obvious characteristics relate to the less evident ones. Only then do you progress from having a mental sketch to a full psychological portrait. In the same way, my perceptions of the English were accurate, but didn't go deep enough. My caricature was a good likeness, but it was still just a caricature.

But the third thing to strike me about these observations helps explain further why they add up to a mere caricature: they don't really reveal anything about the national philosophy. This is why the numerous attempts to describe 'Britishness' or the English national character are generally so unsatisfactory. They teach us how to spot an English person, but they don't explain the dominant implicit belief system that makes people act in such recognizably English ways. We fail to look into the national philosophy, all we get by describing the idiosyncrasies of the English is a better and more detailed sketch, never the full picture. Perhaps, I thought as my train headed north, I was foolish to attempt to paint this more revealing portrait.

Fortunately, I did not have time to dwell on these worries. Laptop packed away, tea and KitKat consumed, I switched from the gleaming Virgin Voyager at Sheffield onto the more utilitarian branch line for the final short leg of my journey. The approach to Rotherham was not promising. I passed industrial site after industrial site, so that when we pulled into Rotherham Central Station, I had seen very little evidence that people actually lived here at all. The omens continued to be bleak as I trudged along the walkway exit from the station, assaulted by the smell of something vaguely unpleasant I was glad I couldn't put my finger on.

But these signs were misleading. The gleaming new 'Transport Interchange', as bus stations are now called, was as bright and pleasant a terminus as I had ever seen. And far from being an oppressive industrial wasteland, the bus ride out of town took me through streets and suburbs, past fields and parks, no more or less unattractive as anywhere else in the country. At least it looked as if I was in Everytown.

Yet most people whom I had told about my project could not believe that anywhere in Yorkshire could be at all typical. Of course, everywhere has its quirks, and this part of the world has more than its fair share. You used to see graffiti all over the region saying 'The Socialist Republic of South Yorkshire' and there is certainly a fierce regional identity: the *Yorkshire Post* is the county's 'National Newspaper'. Yet behind these visible differences, the way of life here is much like it is in any English town. Someone from my birth town of Dover, on the south Kent coast, would find S66 much more familiar than London or Oxford.

When challenged to explain why S66 could not possibly be typical, no one ever gave me a better answer than that, basically, normal is defined in relation either to London, which is absurd, or the south, which is false. Anyone who thinks Surrey reflects typical England should either get out more or stay in for good.

If you're not convinced that Rotherham reflects the full range of English life, then take part in the annual round walk: a 25-mile circuit of the town. I just managed to do it on the hottest day of the year, soon after I moved up. Rotherham, like England, is much less urban than you might think. Around 70% of the town is rural, compared to 79% of the country as a whole. The round walk takes you from the neglected, often spectral, town centre, past allotments, along industrial canals, through comfortable but undistinguished housing estates of red brick semis and terraces, and then into the grounds of Wentworth House, with the widest frontage (600 feet) of any stately home in Britain. Then there are more fields of corn and rape, leading to a hamlet called Street, comprising little more than a pretty row of half a dozen cottages. After a sequence of fields, cobbled paths and villages, you suddenly confront the uglier side of modern England: the Parkgate Retail Park and the largest of the region's few remaining steelworks, in the shadow of which I saw some children fishing near a weir. The rural idyll was replaced by urban reality, when a fat kid of about ten asked me if I had a light. Past an Asda and a McDonald's, you head along the Valley Road, flanked by postwar council estates, with houses more generously sized and spaced than more recent developments. Through Valley Park, with its mowed lawns and tennis courts, you are taken into the suburbs – or villages as they are often called – of Brecks, Listerdale and then along the Bawtry Road to Wickersley – into S66 itself. Then the route becomes more rural again, passing through farms and stables, gardens with pigs and chickens, and fields of horses. A series of paths across yet more fields and through woods would be much more scenic if it weren't for the views of a large electricity substation and the M1 carving the countryside in two and providing a constant soundtrack of tyre on tarmac. A path through another wood at Treeton takes you to Boston Castle, one of Rotherham's posher areas, which wouldn't look out of place in a salubrious corner of Oxford or Edinburgh. Finally, you descend the urban arterial street of Moorgate into the town centre. The itinerary is not exactly John Major's cricket pitches and maids on bicycles, but is surely a more accurate reflection of how England really is.

But the full variety of Rotherham wasn't evident to me when I first arrived because, like most of us most of the time, my view of it was entirely from the roads that linked where I had arrived to where I wanted to go to. My main impression of S66 was of a series of suburban villages, all cut in two by the Bawtry Road, the main eastern passage in and out of Rotherham. In Wickersley, the more affluent end of the postcode district, two rows of shops stood divided on opposite sides of a dual carriageway. This struck me at first as a kind of social vandalism, but I soon realized that since for many these villages had become dormitories rather than centres of life, the proximity to a major road was for most an advantage, not a problem.

Then the bus moved on into Bramley, a more mixed area. The traditional village has been annexed by relentless developments over recent decades, to the extent that Bramley is now two places in one: a core of people who have lived here all their lives and newcomers who rarely integrate. Here, I spied a seventies semi flying a St George's cross so tattered that only half of it still fluttered. I noted that the house next to it was for rent.

At last, I entered Maltby, the poorer end of S66, a former pit village which has never fully recovered from the economic shock of the mine closures. Yet many good cars were parked in drives, white UPVC front doors and double glazing were almost universal, and ornaments graced many windowsills, framed by net curtains. Rotherham's last pit is still here, but it only employs about 200 people, very few of whom are local men.

What I had not yet seen were the large country piles scattered between and around these villages where the real money resides. You need to add those into the equation to see that S66 really did contain a genuine cross-section of society.

It was in Maltby that things started to feel weird. As a Man of Kent, the source of my unease might have been a report on the *Rotherham Advertiser's* website of a Kentish family who had moved to Maltby, and claimed they were forced to move five times by hostile locals who persecuted them for their allegedly snooty ways. 'We just try to maintain standards,' they protested, which made me suspect the locals might have had a point. But this wasn't the explanation for my confused state. It was that Addison Road seemed oddly familiar. It reminded me of Dover's Buckland estate in the 1970s, a vast collection of council houses, only smartened up. For the city-dweller I had become, such areas seem dull and lifeless. There is little to do and the streets are devoid of life. But people live contentedly here, more affluent than their counterparts in the seventies. So if it was so familiar, why did I feel so strange?

My feelings were contradictory and confused because of the dissonance between, on the one hand, recognizing completely the kind of place where I was and, on the other, sensing that I ceased to belong here years ago. My discomfort embarrassed me. To find unusual that which was completely normal said a lot about how far removed from the typical life of my compatriots and upbringing I had become. But, of course, I was not alone. This world is rarely written about, because people in the national media and the arts don't live here and don't come here, even if they come from here. For them, 'getting real' means the extreme poverty of the inner cities. The mundanity of the typical life passes them by. As Michael Collins put it in his biography of the working class, 'Middle-class authors who took the working-class as their subject were writing of the exceptional rather than the typical.' The norm lies somewhere between the Home Counties image of twee Middle England and the cliché of the struggling urban poor.

I felt confident I wasn't going to make that mistake. But there was another trap Collins described which I could not avoid falling into. Quoting G. K. Chesterton on 'slum fiction', he wrote, 'These books are not a record of the psychology of normality. They are a record of the psychology of educated, liberal urbanism when brought into contact with normality.' Like it or not, my study would say as much about me, and those like me, as it would about the English mind I was investigating. I was not sure I liked that idea. For, if I am honest, my relationship with England is somewhat strained. 'England' for me stands for my home town of Folkestone or my birth town of Dover, the types of places I have avoided all my adult life. I lived for many years in London, which is a world city in a class of its own, unlike the rest of the country. For example, in London 29% of the population is from an ethnic minority, whereas in England as a whole that number is a mere 8%. I liked London precisely because it was everything small towns like Folkestone were not. You live with a sense of endless possibilities and a constant flow of people, rather than the end of all possibilities and the same old faces. You can see how this jaundiced view would make life in suburban Rotherham something of a challenge.

From the perspective of a naive boy from Folkestone, there were only two social classes in England, and neither attracted me. In the homes of the 'working-class' families I saw, the fathers were usually shadowy presences to be feared, while the overworked mothers were always shouting. Meals were based around baked beans and chips, and the kids were sent out onto the street, to keep them from under the feet of the parents. The *Sun* or the

Mirror would lie folded on the arm of father's worn, nicotine-infused armchair, with the television permanently on and tuned to ITV. Even worse were the aspiring 'middle classes', in whose homes I felt suffocated under the oppressive veneer of respectability. In many ways, these homes were rather like the ones on the council estate, which is not surprising, for they had the same cultural roots. Father was also a little feared, only they called it respect and his superiority was not expressed through profane shouting. Mother also did all the household work, but with fewer kids and more money, she was not so much harassed as bored and frustrated. Dad also had his somewhat plusher chair, and here too the television was almost always on – only this time tuned to the BBC. But as on the estates, the new Channel 4 was only for left-wing homosexuals.

Of course, these were stereotypes born from limited experience, and they didn't stop me liking many individuals of all classes. But they did leave me feeling that the characteristics people shared, and hence identified them as members of their class, were all ones I disliked. Nor did I become more enamoured of my country as I grew older. I never wanted to be one of the lads, I hated the drinking culture; going out with a gang of guys and gals for a big night was my idea of hell.

These childhood impressions reveal more about me than the English. They reflect someone who stands somewhat outside of mainstream life and therefore doesn't get what people see in it. They expose the fact that I may be intellectually committed to giving people the benefit of the doubt but am temperamentally inclined not to. They are the views of someone who is not so much anti-social as asocial, able to go without company quite gladly. I once went on a week's holiday to Athens by myself. On the last day I reflected on what a good time I'd had, only to realize I hadn't had a proper conversation with anyone the whole time I had been there.

My sense of being not quite English is partly explained by my father being Italian, even though I have lived in England all my life. I have always had two cultural influences, and this would perhaps give me an advantage, in that it could help me look at my country's philosophy almost as an outsider. But that would only work if I could get beyond my prejudices and preconceptions to see things from the inside.

Despite these unsettling emotions and personal obstacles, I felt quite optimistic during the two days I spent in Maltby looking for somewhere to live in S66. It almost felt like a second chance to discover England. We take it for granted that we know what normal means in England, and so fail to see that we are as weird and wonderful as any people in the world. Looking at what surrounds you every day with new eyes is often more delightfully surprising than seeing something completely new. That was just as well, because Maltby is always going to have a hard job selling itself as a tourist destination. I stayed at the village's only bed and breakfast, which was comfortable enough, though the traffic on the A road passed right by the window. There was only one place I could find to sit down for an evening meal in the village, an Indian restaurant. It had a silver award from Quality Food Online, whose resident food critic gave a rave review to Domino's delivery pizza chain, praising the quality of their chicken. For a drink, I was advised to avoid The Queen's, since other strangers who had tried it had felt as if they'd walked into a saloon in the wild west. When I later passed it I realized there was no need for the warning: I'd never go alone into such a large pub with so few windows.

Two days later I left Maltby believing I had secured a house in Wickersley. Finding something suitable was difficult, since there was very little rented accommodation to be found, and without a young, mobile professional population, what little there is tends to be houses, not flats. I found mine through a local small business owner I just happened to get talking to, a woman who made

Coronation Street's Bet Lynch look like a triumph of understated style. I'm not sure if her tan was fake, but it certainly took unnatural means to get it that particular shade of orange. As for her hair, it looked like a cross between a Grenadier Guard's bearskin helmet and a lampshade, dyed blonde. My landlady at the b. & b. knew of her and said she was 'what my mother would call a brassy blonde, disapprovingly'. (In case you think this is disrespectful, let me say that I believe we're all quite ridiculous, including myself, so I'm not going to confer on anyone I talk about more dignity than they do actually possess.)

But only a week before I was due to move in, I still hadn't received the signed contract from her. Nor had my deposit cheque been cashed. I rang her up. 'Ah, Julian. Yes. I'm sorry, love, they're selling it.' 'They' were the people who actually owned the house, which I had thought was hers. I protested that I was due there in one week and new tenants were already signed up for my place. She apologized, and then said I might be able to move in later, which didn't seem to fit the first story. It wouldn't work. People may be nice and full of good intentions, but it's their thoughtlessness and incompetence that screws you over. So after a few frantic phone calls to letting agencies, I ended up with a place in Bramley instead. It was the house next door to the tattered St George's cross. Not for the last time, I smiled and thought, you couldn't make this up.

1

Working-class Roots

Ray Beecher, Bramley, Rotherham

On 1 July I moved into a three-bedroom semi-detached house on Bramley's ironically named Flash Lane. The house was modern and clean with a fitted kitchen, fitted carpets throughout but for the wood laminate in the living room, a shower *and* a bath (though in the same room), gas central heating, a burglar alarm (like a quarter of homes in England), UPVC double glazing and patio doors at the back. It's the kind of home many dismiss as a characterless, identikit box, with a lack of 'period features'. But for people with limited budgets who need somewhere comfortable and pleasant to live – which is almost everyone – it was as good a home as one could hope for.

The main problem as far as I was concerned was that it was just off a dual carriageway. I thought this would make it virtually unsellable, which was interesting because it had a FOR SALE board in the front garden. Having been let down at short notice by Bet, I had taken the house out of desperation, even though I had been told it might well be sold before my six months were up. I had to take a chance, and in any case, who'd want to buy a house blighted by the constant noise of a major road? I already had the answer to that: lots of people. The house on the Bawtry Road with two Mercedes parked on the drive was no aberration. People with the money to live anywhere would actually opt for some-where right on the A road. Perhaps the rumble of traffic was now as natural to many as the sound of tweeting birds, or more so. To me it wasn't. My sleep was disturbed for many weeks. Although it was summer, I had to sleep with the windows shut to minimize the noise.

Strolls to Morrisons supermarket and the local shops in between unpacking revealed an area in which nothing stood out and everything seemed nice enough. At school, English teachers would go crazy if you ever used that word, claiming it told you absolutely nothing. On the contrary, I think it describes something quite specific and common. England is full of nice things, the unexceptional but agreeable, that which pleases but doesn't excite. Tea is nice, people are nice, barbecues are nice, cheese-and-onion crisps are nice. Perhaps the reason English teachers hate the word is that they feel oppressed by the omnipresence of the nice and yearn for something less bland.

I was looking forward to getting to know this place better. One thing did bother me though. Despite the signs of increasing affluence, this area seemed to be working class in character. But isn't England supposed to be more middle class now? Maybe demographics lie and S66 was no Everytown after all.

For instance, Rotherham has numerous working men's clubs. Most WMCs are affiliated to the CIU: the Working Mens Club and Institute Union, which was founded in 1862. While 4,000 clubs were affiliated to it in the seventies, that has now declined to 2,500. If this continues there will be none at all by 2025. It would seem that just as the traditional idea of the working class is passing into history, so working men's clubs are going the same way. As Lee, the builder, put it as he delivered the second-hand washing machine I'd bought from him, the clubs are 'a step back in time'.

Look a little closer, however, and this supposed past has more of a present life than might be supposed. Although the CIU may be well past its heyday, with two million members, it can still claim to be the 'largest non-profit-making social entertainment and leisure organisation in the UK'. Many of its affiliated clubs are still going strong. Indeed, Lee's sidekick goes to one which is still very popular. 'They pay turns £1,000 a night down there, real quality acts,' he says.

The builder who thought the clubs were history not only has a mate who goes to one, he also has a Peter Kay ringtone. At the time, Kay was pretty much the most popular comic in England, and up north he seemed even more popular than anywhere else. His award-winning series *Phoenix Nights* is set in a Bolton working men's club, and is an affectionate, gently mocking portrait of a world that has its roots in a bygone age. Yet when the protagonist Brian Potter says that 'Clubland will never die', he's expressing the thoughts of his creator. For Kay is firmly rooted in the tradition of the club comic, and his popularity among both young and old is testament to the continuities between the generations. Look at the audiences at his live shows and you'll see every age group.

The popularity of Peter Kay is one clue among many that, despite received opinion to the contrary, England's culture remains predominantly working class. Talk of embourgoisement is grossly exaggerated. Increased affluence has not made people change the fundamentals of their outlook, it has simply given them more money and better houses. Since you cannot understand a nation's philosophy without understanding the social context from which it springs, any such investigation into the national mind needs to start with the working-class culture that shaped it.

There was no better place to start than clubland. *Phoenix Nights* reinforced the impression that WMCs are a northern phenomenon, but in fact the CIU has more affiliated clubs in the southern metropolitan regions than in the north east. Their greatest concentration is, however, in the north with the Rotherham area being a particular hot spot – a relic of the steel and coal industries. The local paper regularly has one and a half pages of 'clubscene' adverts which describe the entertainments in terms which pay no heed to fashions. I could go to the Rotherham Trades Club to see 'Top clubland group' Sensation; or try 'dancing to Steve, Derek and Barry' at Greasebro' WMC, or even 'Bingo and open the box' on Friday night, a grand start to the weekend, at the Thrybergh WMC.

Since I'm told it's probably best to go the first time with a member, I make my trial visit to a club that is actively courting outsiders through its flyers at the Rotherham Visitor Centre. The Transport Club's no-nonsense A4 leaflet sets the standard for plain English. Of 'The New Dizzy Club', it says 'Their last visit was enjoyed by everyone who attended', while the 'Jim Wilkes Stompers' provided an 'excellent night on their last visit to the club'. I like a bit of jazz, so off I go.

The flyer indicates an 8 p.m. start, but since I have never been to a jazz gig that started remotely close to the advertised starting time, I don't roll up until 8.30. But when I arrive I can hear from the outside that the band ('Martyn "Kid" Boyd Band, from York – their last gig was excellent') have already started. The function room is more church hall than Ronnie Scott's. Everyone is seated at tables attentively watching the band with their pints, gins or juices in front of them. It's a mixed crowd of men and women, but I seem to be the only one under 50, let alone 40. Since I stand out even more than the lone Asian guy, I can't help feeling a little self-conscious.

I get a pint of Stones Bitter and find an empty table. The band supports the builder's mate's claim that the clubs book quality turns. Not surprisingly, it's traditional jazz. But even though the set is straight as an arrow, the inclusion of a couple of not exactly far-out South African tunes seems to make it pretty daring. After 'Soweto Circle', people turn to their friends, raise their eyebrows and I hear people mutter the word 'different', with begrudging approval. It becomes a refrain. At the end of the first set (there are three), the garish strip lighting is turned on, before we are sent to the bar and given notice that the 'open the box' raffle tickets will be on sale during the break. Even the genial, rotund host comments on how that was 'a little different', as though qualifying his praise, lest they push it even further in the second set. And in the gents as I leave, one guy says to me, 'That were a good night tonight. A bit different.' I'm reminded of the scene in *The Blues Brothers* when a bar owner says, 'We like all kinds of music here – country *and* western.'

But you don't just get almost three hours of quality jazz for less than a fiver. You also get the 'open the box' raffle. Inside the box sits the prize fund, which accumulates week by week until it is won. Tonight it stands at nearly £400, the announcement of which cues a ritualistic 'Woooooo!' You buy tickets (3 for 50p, 7 for £1) and near the end of the second set, an electronic number picker is set in motion. Then in the second break, the owner of the winning ticket comes up to collect £20 – 'yours to keep'. They also have the chance to pick one of an ever-decreasing number of containers with a key in it. If your key opens the box, it lights up and buzzes and you walk away with the booty.

When I buy my ticket from the even more corpulent co-host, I suggest that I'd get lynched if I won, walking in here for the first time, and he replies, 'You've paid your money, so tonight, you're a member.' This is typical of the club's friendliness. Yes, I did stand out like a sore thumb, but that only made people more keen to make me feel at home. On my second visit, the host even noticed that a tray of dripping sandwiches that was being circulated had passed me by, and he made a point of telling me I should help myself.

Tonight's winner fails to open the box, and the host then tries the other two keys and opens it, just to show the right key was in there. Then there's another draw for a bottle of Liebfraumilch and free entry for next week, which a woman wins, to some groans. She always wins. It is all very Peter Kay, except that instead of the rubbish Les Alanos, the act is actually very good.

The Transport Club might seem to tell against my thesis that England remains rooted in the working-class culture of the past, not support it. After all, it sounds like 'a step back in time'. But look more closely and the continuities between a top night at a

WMC and a big night in the pub or an evening in front of the telly are closer than you might think. The most popular pub in S66 with young drinkers is The Masons Arms, known to all as The Masons. It has built its success on the same formula as the WMCs: almost every night of the week it has entertainment, but instead of jazz and country and western, it's a disco, a quiz night or a karaoke. Live Sky Sports also features regularly. Like their grandparents, the younger generation has a good time by dancing, drinking or playing a game in an unpretentious environment with their friends.

As they get older, the regulars at The Masons will probably start going to quieter pubs, but what they are looking for will be the same. The music they will be listening to when they are retired will seem just as quaint to the youth of tomorrow as old-time rock 'n' roll or traditional jazz does to the youth of today. They probably won't graduate to the WMCs though, unless the clubs themselves change. There is a formality to the clubs which is out of kilter with modern times, and to which it is unlikely we will ever revert. At the heart of each club is the committee, which the builder told me the members fear more than going to prison, because it has the power to take away membership for life, if you break the club's rules. When pubs offer much the same as clubs, only, as the builder put it, at the latter 'there are old fuddy-duddies at the door saying you can't do owt', people are going to choose the pubs. One club advert even states: 'Strictly no standing in the concert room on concert nights.'

The clubs are also not keeping up with changes in sexual equality. In 2006, the CIU's annual conference once again failed to get the two-thirds majority required to give women members the same rights as men to visit clubs other than their own, much to the embarrassment of the General Secretary. Nor can women be elected to the branch or National Executive committees.

However, the basic template for a grand night out is still the same as that offered by the WMCs. You can see this reflected in other aspects of British life. In the 1970s, people tuned in to ITV to see the likes of Lenny Henry, Victoria Wood, Showaddywaddy and Les Dennis compete on the talent show *New Faces*, facing the harsh judgement of TV's-own Mr Mean, Tony Hatch. Now people tune in to ITV to see the likes of Shayne Ward and others we have already forgotten compete on the talent show *The X Factor*, facing the harsh judgement of TV's-own Mr Mean, Simon Cowell. The production is more glitzy, but the formula is the same. The most popular television shows reflect working-class culture, whether they are soaps about it, or quizzes and entertainments which follow a template that is straight out of clubland. And this has hardly changed over decades. The top four television programmes on Christmas day 2005 were *EastEnders*, *Dr Who*, *Coronation Street* and *The Two Ronnies*. It could have been 1985. Two of the top three programmes started their runs in the sixties.

Working-class culture, however, runs deeper in England than simply our preferences for TV and a good night out. It is at the heart of what people think themselves to be. The British Social Attitudes survey, for instance, shows that the proportion of the population who identify themselves as working class has remained more or less constant at around 60% since 1955, despite the fact that the number of people defined as working class by more objective standards has declined. In fact, you could say this persistence has been in defiance of attempts to take traditional notions of working and middle class out of circulation, by use, for example, of the A, B, C1, C2, D, E classifications of social class.

One reason why we don't acknowledge the dominance of working-class culture is that we have too narrow a conception of what working class means and too economic a conception of what being middle class means. Michael Collins, for example, in *The Likes of Us*, discusses the working class only in the context of the urban poor. So, for instance, he claims that there is more racial intermarriage among the working classes than the middle classes. But this seems to be based on his perceptions of inner city London, which is exceptional in how far ethnic groups mix. A black and white couple would certainly stand out in S66. The urban poor are just one part of a working class that is as at home in the suburbs as it is in the cities.

In contrast, we think of being middle class in strictly economic terms. Yet as historian Tristram Hunt sees it, the middle classes actually arose during the industrial revolution as a new merchant class, between landowners and the wage-earning working class. Their natural home was the cities and with their money they sought social improvement, civic life and culture. Only gradually was this abandoned, as the growth of the cities forced them to the suburbs and they broke their ties with the urban centres. Then, the signs of their class became purely material. What Hunt doesn't say, but I think is true, is that we have since come to mistake these material signs for the distinct class they were once associated with. So, as the working classes have acquired more of this material wealth, we have come to think of them as being more middle class. In reality, the majority of those who fit their houses with en suite bathrooms and drive bigger and better cars are, in their values and beliefs, as resolutely working class as they ever were. And in financial terms, working-class earnings are often higher than many of those in the middle class. I met several working families done well who had been or were looking to buy properties in Spain or Portugal.

The exception that proves the rule that working-class culture still dominates comes in the shape of the most overtly middle-class institution England has: the *Daily Mail*. The *Mail* trumpets its credentials as the defender of the middle classes as often and as loudly as it can. However, if you look at the values it actually promotes, they are remarkably similar to those of the resolutely working-class *Sun*. You could express it like this: the *Sun* + money + fear = the *Daily Mail*.

Take the *Sun*'s values first. It is defiantly patriotic and is keen to defend Britain's values and way of life. It is anti-intellectual, anti-liberal, anti-political correctness and anti-immigration. It is also pro-family, which may seem odd when it revels so much in sexual peccadilloes. Take, for instance, the famous advice column Dear Deidre, which covers almost identical problems again and again (sex is over too quickly, women can't orgasm, someone's having an affair or has shagged their girlfriend's mother), leading one to suspect it's there more for titillation than counselling. Yet celebrating 25 years of the now daily column, Deidre Sanders summed up her approach by saying, 'My advice is always about maintaining the family if at all possible. You should work your absolute hardest in a good relationship for the sake of the children.'

Despite the alleged decline of the family, it remains a very important institution for mainstream England. A teacher from Sheffield explained to me that even though many kids at his school, which served a deprived area, had parents who were divorced or separated, the family remained very adaptable and resilient. He told me about one kid who, when asked to give a note to his dad, ran through his complicated custody schedule out loud to work out when it would be possible to do so. The working-class clans you see portrayed in soaps like *EastEnders*, where being a Mitchell or a Slater matters above all else, reflects the genuine importance family life holds for the English.

The *Daily Mail* middle classes are not that different. Like *Sun* readers they are defiantly patriotic, keen to defend Britain's values and way of life, pro-family, anti-intellectual, anti-liberal, anti-political correctness and anti-immigration. Look at what they stand for and the split between the officially middle-class *Mail* and the working-class *Sun* is a schism within the same group. The only real difference is simply one of anxiety. The *Sun*, as its name suggests, has an optimistic, up-beat tone, reflecting the attitude of those who are comfortable with who they are and don't feel their position in society is too threatened. The *Mail*, however, is virtually paranoid. A typical headline, which goes beyond parody, once accompanied a Quentin Letts column: 'I am white, middle-class, love my wife and adore traditional TV sitcoms. So why does the BBC hate me?'

Whereas I found I liked the *Sun* more than I expected to, I came to loathe the *Mail* more than I could imagine. Its main purpose seems to be to inspire fear. The reason for this is that it serves a segment of the population that wants to maintain its middle-class status yet is only one step removed from the traditional working class. No one who was truly secure in their middle-class status would be so anxious to proclaim it so loudly and feel it was under such a threat. Just look at the token-collect offers running through October, for instance. They were all for things which proclaim the middle-classness of their possessors so transparently you cannot but feel that is precisely their attraction: a Spode Christmas plate, Janet Reger earrings, a Royal Doulton crystal glass set and a spa break at Champneys.

I came across many examples of such *Daily Mail* families when I was growing up. I remember one in particular who, like many, both emphasized their humble working-class backgrounds and revelled in their acquired middle-class status. They remembered what it was like to not have very much and so what they wanted more than anything was security and respectability, and they looked to their children to cement both. They wanted their offspring to go to university so they could acquire wealth and standing. They didn't believe in higher education for its own sake and would pour scorn on any suggestion that their kids might choose a subject they loved but which didn't meet their often warped perceptions about what would be useful. They thought they were a cut above the working classes, but all they had really acquired to differentiate themselves was money and a new-found social anxiety about their precarious position.

The idea that England's culture remains predominantly working class goes against the grain, for almost everyone thinks that things ain't what they used to be. That rarely means that they have got better. The national myth of perpetual decline is one that all classes sign up to. And of all the things that are not as they once were, the pub is number one. Pubs are still at the centre of many communities. When Shelley Rudman took up skeleton sledding, it was her pub, The Moonraker in Pewsey, which raised money for her, supported her, and was the focus of celebrations when she won a silver medal at the 2006 Winter Olympics. But pubs packed with old-fashioned regulars are a dying breed. Most are not as full as they used to be, and the shift from landlords to managers has also changed their character, as the latter don't live and breathe the pub as their predecessors did. Think of the cellarman, like *Coronation Street*'s Jack Duckworth, once a linchpin of pubs and now increasingly a rarity. The cellarman would have a full-time job changing barrels, keeping bottles topped up and so on. Yet Darren, caretaker manager of Ye Olde King Henry, a pub I could see from my bedroom window, hadn't worked in a pub with a cellarman for thirteen years. For all the talk of binge drinking, pubs aren't selling the ale quickly enough to warrant one any more.

One notable exception in S66 is the legendary Stockyard, known to all simply as the truck stop, which is what it actually is. But despite that, and the fact that it is located in the middle of an industrial estate, half an hour's walk from the nearest house, local people flock to it, especially on singers' nights, which are like karaoke with class: people can sing, they know the words, and there's a live keyboard player.

The landlord, Trevor, is of the old school. Everyone knows him, he makes you feel like a welcome guest to his home. Trevor is the first landlord I've ever known to buy me a drink the first time I went into his pub, and that was before he found out I was a journalist. Trevor is from Maltby and he used to be a butcher before he fitted out The Stockyard with entirely reclaimed materials, from church pews and old desks to old light fittings. 'I wouldn't want to be anywhere else,' he told me, and why would he when he is so much a part of local life?

It was inevitable, then, that one of my first tasks in Everytown was to find a pub to be the focus for my social life. Over three-quarters of the UK adult population go to pubs, and over one-third of us are regulars, going at least once a week. Among younger age groups, that proportion rises closer to two-thirds. I had a choice of two. Although Ye Olde King Henry was closest to me, I had already popped in when I was house hunting and discovered its recent transformation into a smart, modern pub, complete with sofas and low tables, had left it underfrequented. So I ventured a few minutes down the road to The Traveller's Rest, known to all as The Travellers. The pub had a saloon bar and a lounge, but the saloon entrance was around the side, so when I walked in the front in the early evening, I was taken directly into the lounge. Three or four small groups of mainly middle-aged men were sitting around the dark wood tables in the low-ceilinged, sparingly lit bar, in a scene that is familiar to anyone who has spent any time in this country. Although generally more of a wine drinker, I did the decent thing and ordered a pint, and sat down at an empty table with a copy of the *Yorkshire Post*. I wouldn't call it going undercover, just trying not to stand out. The attempt was futile, however. Reading here was an odd thing to do: you came to be social and people saw the paper not as a sign that I wanted to be left alone (which I didn't) but that I was by myself and should be talked to.

After a brief chat with a guy known to all as Tractor Dave – because his name is Dave and he drives tractors – I got talking to Reg, who had recently retired after a lifetime down pits, in steel-works and, after both industries had been ripped to shreds, in distribution. Reg looked like he could be a gurning champion and his default facial expression was of dour discontent, but when he laughed or smiled, which he often did, he looked as if he didn't have a care in the world. The contrast summed up his personality. He found plenty to complain about, but at the same time counted his blessings and thought himself lucky. In that he was perhaps a true working English man.

On my third visit, Reg saw me again and introduced me to a group of men who would form the nucleus of my drinking companions throughout my stay and, I hope, a bunch of friends I'd have for life. The oldest was Johnny, a cantankerous, sharp and slightly deaf Yorkshireman through and through. He would usually turn up ten minutes before closing and order two pints of John Smith's to take him through to chucking-out time. He was a big man whose body had slowed down considerably more than his mind. Pete was younger, but had already taken early retirement and his trim white beard and beer belly made him look older. His voice and face were youthfully animated, however, and he lived a quiet but active life, playing golf and looking after his garden. He came down The Travellers almost every night, though, like most of them, not until around ten. These were drinkers of the old school, who took their ale regularly and drank it swiftly, but were rarely drunk. Andy was short and lean, in his fifties, still working, with children who had been through university. He was in the pub less often than the others, but drank faster to make up for it. His slow manner and constant puffing on Hamlet cigars, however, gave him an air of quiet thoughtfulness. He also went fishing with Neil, who was around the same age and the only one of them not to have at least one prominent tattoo, though his shaven head fitted his reputation as the most right-wing of the group by a long shot. In The Travellers, the old regulars such as these made it clear to the staff that they were the kings of the pub, not the people who ran it, and that was more or less accepted.

That this was an all-male group says something about the way we live but also about the limitations of my immersion in Everytown. The facts about England which I have drawn on are of course about both sexes, but it would not be possible for me to have talked equally to men and women without resorting to highly artificial means. I don't apologize for this, because I never relied on my observations to provide the objective measure of the English mind. The people I met did not represent the whole country, but they were good examples of how its citizens talk and think.

Among these men, decline was a recurring topic of conversation. Pete would fix me with his intent stare as though he was talking about it for the first time, lament in a tone of indignant disbelief that 'The gardens around the estate all used to be immaculate. *Immaculate*. But now people just let them run to seed.' Johnny remembered how there used to be plenty of well-kept tennis courts and bowling greens but now they were being ruined by a minority of no-good-uns. If I expressed the view that maybe it wasn't all bad, he'd say, 'You haven't been around as long as I have, Justin.' He never got my name right. Reg would talk about how murder used to be so rare, that if there was one it would be in the news for weeks. Now there's one every day. Such tales of decline were told by others I met. Another local man said that if you asked the newcomers to the village for the time in the street, 'They look at you as if you're going to mug them.'

Occasionally you would get a refreshing acceptance that not everything was better years ago. One evening in the pub, the subject of Dunkirk came up, and the remembrance that for a while little more than the Home Guard stood between us and the Germans. 'I tell you what we did have though,' said Pete, pausing but not blinking, to make sure you were listening, 'fighting spirit.' Johnny, who lived through it, gave a dismissive, 'Nah, we wouldn't have stood a chance.'

My initial instinct when I heard these pessimistic prognoses was that people were just wrong. But, as I often found, just because something is repeated in the *Daily Mail* it doesn't necessarily mean it's false. I usually discovered that there was at least a large dollop of truth in most stories of decline. For instance, the UK murder rate has indeed more than doubled since 1967, from 350 to more than 800. What's more, the rise is almost exclusively in men of working age living in the poorest parts of the country, and were sudden acts of violence, rather than carefully planned. But the point is that this rise in the murder rate has not transformed the country. 'More than doubled' sounds alarming, but 800 murders a year is still pretty low – and in any case there are around twice as many murders per head of population in Scotland as there are in England and Wales. There's change, but it's not radical. The mistake people make is usually not that they are wrong to identify changes that have happened, but to see them as being fundamental when really they're not.

Pubs may have changed, but for all the talk of binge drinking, if anything we used to be even worse. The old steelworks actually used to give their employees beer tokens, which they would use during twenty-minute breaks. Eight pints a night every night was normal for miners. And it goes back even longer than that. One reason why the English lost the Battle of Hastings in 1066 was because they spent the night before getting tanked up while the French prayed for victory. They didn't need any divine intervention when the English were set on mortal inebriation.

The trouble is not that people remember incorrectly, but selectively. Past horrors are excused while present ones are lamented. For instance, one former miner who drank eight or nine pints every day, more than many so-called binge drinkers do now, insisted that the important difference is that they didn't used to drink with the explicit intention of getting caned. Although one in four of us are now regular binge drinkers, when you consider the definition of binge drinking is the equivalent of four pints, that sounds par or below par for the historical course to me. When pressed, people who insist things have got worse tend to admit, as Andy did between puffs on his panatella, that the change they don't like is that 'the women are getting as pissed as the men'. In the last ten years, the gender split among pub users has shifted from 64% men and 36% women to 58% men and 42% women, continuing a trend that marks a real change from the days when pubs were virtually all-male domains.

Even if any increase in drunkenness is lamentable, at least the greater equality could well be seen as a good thing. But the ways in which life has got better or remains largely the same just don't receive the same attention as the ways in which they have got worse. The most striking example of this is the so-called rise of yob culture, when the stories you hear of how the pubs used to be suggests that, if anything, young thugs have gone soft. Ye Olde King Henry is not olde at all, since it only changed its name from The Ball a year ago, a change which many local people refuse to register in their conversations. One major reason for the renaming was its reputation. If you wanted a fight, that's where you'd go. If you didn't want one, you'd get one anyway. Bramley boys would routinely clash with Maltby lads. This went on for years and it is only recently that Bramley has ceased to have a pub that specializes in gratuitous violence. Of course, there's still the odd bit of trouble, but it is not nearly as common. At The Masons, for example, there's some aggressive posturing by posers with big pecs who like to shove you out of the way to impress, but rarely are many fists thrown. It's a story I've heard time and again from people who remember post-war England. Yet somehow this kind of violence is deemed to be tolerable while contemporary counterparts are not. It's seen as ritualistic and you knew where you'd find it. Today, however, people say the violence is so random, even though statistics suggest that if you avoid groups of drunk young men, you're generally safe, which is the way it has always been. As Kate Fox points out in her *Watching the English*, in this country, but not elsewhere, young men plus alcohol has always equalled violence.

If there's been one indisputable improvement, it's been in attitudes to drink-driving. Reg, for instance, never drinks and drives. 'It's not worth it,' he told me gravely, weighing up the cost. 'It's too precious a thing to lose – your licence.'

The greatest ambivalence about change, however, concerns the closures of the pits and steelworks. This is echoed around the country, where large industries used to dominate and almost all working-class men would work in them. In my birth town of Dover the docks provided the same function, and although they remain a major employer, they are no longer as all-important for the town as they once were. How much this kind of decline is to be lamented, however, is not a question many are able to give a clear answer to.

At Rotherham's Clifton Park Museum there is an interactive display about the miners' strike. It runs a poll of visitors to the museum, which shows 57% either took part in the miners' strike or have family who took part in it, 65% thought the miners were justified in breaking the law, 73% thought the media did not report the strike fairly, and 71% do not think it is a good thing that the pits closed.

However, it seemed to me that the strong loyalties the bitter dispute reinforced have left many people conflicted in their feelings about the decline of the industry. One striking miner, Peter Pleasants, offered an interesting and telling quote in the exhibit: 'I'd do it again. I'd stand up for my rights but I wouldn't work at that pit again . . . When we did close the pits, I were made redundant; it opened up other things for me, so it were a blessing in disguise really.'

This echoed what I heard from everyone I met who had

worked in coal and, to a lesser extent, steel. On the one hand, they were loyal to their colleagues and the industries, but now they look back and are glad things have moved on. Neil was even more forthright: 'Those idiots during the strike who were saying we've got to save these jobs for our kids – it were horrible work,' he complained, beads of indignant sweat forming on his over-heating pate. 'My dad said to me, "if there's a war, you can choose between the pits or the front. Otherwise, never go down a pit."'

Others agreed. Reg, for example, described the closure of the steelworks as the best thing that ever happened to him, in a tone of voice that suggested it was the worst, although of course he never voted for Thatcher and was against the closures at the time. He remembers the 1966 Silverwood pit disaster in which he pulled the first miner out, a man who lost both his feet and died ten days later. Before Reg's steelworks made him redundant, he'd never had money. Afterwards he never looked back. He got £16,000 and discovered that when you get money, you tend to get more. Since then he'd always had new cars, never keeping one long enough to need to put it through an MOT. And had he stayed at the steelworks a bit longer, he would also have done well, getting a bigger pension and better pay. What at the time looked like the breaking of the working classes was for many the making of them.

Andy feels much the same. He's glad the old heavy industries have gone and that all the ex-miners he speaks to agree – although none of them voted Tory then or vote Tory now. Yet Andy says Thatcher was right to close them down, talking about how much cleaner the area is as one benefit. And as he points out, 'There was no ballot, but you would stand by tha work mates. Tha would never cross a picket line. I tell thee, if there had been a ballot, there never would have been a strike.'

Of course, many did not do well out of the closures. Many in Maltby in particular never got another job, and there are now

people being born who are the third generation to live on benefits. But there was another price everyone paid, whether they
bounced back or not. People miss the camaraderie and closeness
that comes with working en masse with people from your area.
Andy has some fond memories of pranks they used to play on
each other. There would always be some rotten apples who would
steal your drink or your 'snap' – the meal taken down the mines,
usually some kind of sandwich. One guy knew his was being
nicked so instead of putting his usual beef in his sandwich he put
a dead mouse. Another pissed in his water bottle for the same
reason. It was common to bury your tools to keep them safe, but
if some people saw you do that they would dig them up and shit
on them, so when you went to get them . . . Like stories of
public school rugby team japes, the details are pretty gruesome,
but it's how many men bond.

It is this decline of a closely knit working and local community which people most bemoan. But even here, the decline,
though real, is overstated, not least because the kind of people
who usually write about these things come from the most mobile
sectors of society and live in the most anonymous places, like
London. I've lived in three English cities since university and I've
only got to know a few of my neighbours, and even then not very
well. But then where was I living? In London, Manchester and
Bristol, in areas of those cities with large transient populations.
When I recently went back to Manchester, the only person I
bumped into whom I knew was a *Big Issue* seller.

Moving to Bramley, however, things were completely different. I won't say that I became best friends with my neighbours,
but I certainly knew their names and those of their children and
pets, and we could also rely on each other as neighbours are supposed to. The ever-cheerful Sue was around the most, both a
homeworker and a home-maker. Despite seeming to have a million things to do, she still offered to do my washing, gave me six

mugs when I went round to borrow one and was always obliging with milk and sugar. Sue could see the house she was born in from her front door, while my neighbour on the other side, Dave, wanted to move back to where he grew up – a ten-minute walk up the road. Neighbourliness still exists at least in part because people simply don't move as much as urban professionals think they do. Andy is one of ten siblings, and the one who lives furthest away still has a Sheffield postcode. In fact, it is said that two-thirds of Britons live within five miles of where they were born.

Locality remains extremely important to people. Local commercial radio attracts 25 million listeners a week, each listening for an average of 14 hours. In contrast, the most popular national station, Radio 2, has a weekly reach of 13 million, with each listener tuning in for an average of 13.1 hours. BBC network radio as a whole has an audience share slightly smaller than that of BBC and commercial local radio. (The most popular BBC local radio station in England is Radio Norfolk.) Everywhere you go, the most listened to station in any given area is almost always a local one. Likewise, whereas around 60–70% of us read a national daily paper, depending on which study you believe, about 80–84% read a local or regional one. Wolverhampton's *Express & Star* sells just under 180,000 copies, a very similar number to that sold across the whole country by the *Independent* before it went tabloid.

The parochialism of mainstream English culture, as a strong attachment to local community is disparagingly called, is also reflected in the nation's leading papers' lack of interest in foreign stories. In October, there was a particularly egregious example. For ten nights riots had raged all over France. The only mention this got in the most popular Sunday tabloids concerned the threat to British holidaymakers. 'Brits in France told "take care",' warned the *News of the World*, while the *Mail on Sunday* said, 'FO warns British holidaymakers as Paris riots spread.' Likewise, on the day after Iraq's first full general election the *Sun* had one short story about it on page 2, then on page 33, the views of one Iraqi who voted in Wembley. And on Baghdad's bloodiest day of the occupation to date, in which 152 died, the article on page 27 was the first and only foreign story in the *Mail on Sunday*.

Despite the enduring appeal of parochialism, it's certainly true that community ties have been weakened. Sue used to know everyone who walked past her front door. Now, with all the newcomers to the recently built estates, many of whom spend almost all their time either at work or at home, the majority pass by unrecognized. As the car has come to dominate us, so local shops are also less important. Before I came, I had the romantic view that the newsagent, the post office manager, the butcher, the baker and candlestick-maker would all be linchpins of the local community. But the closest I came to this were the women who worked at the Spar.

Although we may regret the decline of community cohesion, the major force driving it is something we almost all see as a good thing: education. Take a pair of retired couples I met at The Transport Club. The two women were friends as girls and always said they should marry two boys who were friends and live near each other. That is exactly what they did, and their husbands have been mates since they were at primary school. Until recently they lived just eight doors apart, and one couple only moved because the wife became disabled and they had to go into a bungalow.

It's a lovely story but it is also a tale of four people who had no realistic opportunities to go very far anyway. How very different it is with their children. One went to Cambridge from a comprehensive that sent very few children there. Now he is a city financier in London, though 'he hasn't forgotten his roots'. Another also went to university and now lives in the south. A third did a Ph.D. in biological sciences and works in The Hague. Whereas the four of them never strayed more than a few miles from where they were born, their three children are now far away. If we really wanted to preserve traditional communities it is clear what we should do: stop people getting degrees.

This is not a flippant point. The question of how to make a happier country has risen up the political agenda, with people citing various studies which all seem to show we were happier – or at least no less happy – when we had less. One such report that came out while I was in S66, by a team of psychologists led by Prof. Mansel Aylward, claimed with incredible precision that those living in the 1930s were around 10% happier than those living in 2005. The reason: 'Better family and community networks.' Aylward said, 'The most important ingredients for happiness are family relationships, family networks and a camaraderie which bring a sense of community and belonging.' 'Community and friends' is also one of the 'big seven factors affecting happiness' listed by Richard Layard in his influential book on happiness.

If we are to make public policy accordingly, then keeping the working classes in their historic place would be the obvious answer. Why then is this clearly absurd? One reason, I would suggest, is that happiness is not everything. Many of us would choose more education and a wider experience beyond our own home town even if we could see that it was unlikely to make us happier. A simpler, happy life may seem attractive, but in practice, people who have widened their horizons often find it very hard to go back to narrower ones. Close-knit communities may be a kind of paradise, but for many who have eaten from the tree of knowledge, there's no going back to Eden.

I once heard a more extreme version of this from a former Hungarian dissident. Unlike many of his peers, he believed that the material quality of life in many former Soviet countries is worse now for more people than it is better. What's more, if you ask people, many would say that they would rather see the Soviets back. But, he said, this is dishonest. As a matter of fact, no one would tolerate a return to central state totalitarianism for one minute. Their political freedom hasn't made them richer or happier, but they wouldn't trade it, because it enables them to live more fully as human individuals.

In England, of course, people have got materially better off, and that too has almost certainly undermined communal life. For instance, less than twenty years ago I used to go to the laundrette at Kentish Town municipal baths. It was a real old-fashioned one, with presses and rollers everyone could use. If you went there and pulled out a sheet, someone (invariably an older woman) would automatically come and take the other end to help you fold it. So I arrived in S66 thinking that the laundrette would be one focus of local life.

The first clue that I was wrong was that their nearest laundrette was miles away: I couldn't find a single one in S66. Washing machine ownership is now nearly universal at 93%, and given it costs at least £4 for a small wash and dry, it's more expensive *not* to have your own machine. Laundrettes where people do their regular washes are in mainly urban areas serving single people and students. That's why there are three within walking distance of my home in Bristol, even though it is not a poor area. At the Stag laundrette in Brecks, by contrast, the main business these days is service washes for people who can't be bothered to do their own washing at home, not those who can't afford to. There's also a big trade in dry cleaning and duvets.

Affluence and an increased material quality of life have thus robbed us of one more communal activity. When people get money, they buy privacy and independence. They have their own cars, more comfortable homes with all mod cons, and so stay at home more, depriving themselves of the social contact that they need. That's another reason why the regulars down The Travellers are a dying breed: many people today are what they call 'tinnies' – people who drink their beer from cans in front of the telly. In other homes, the equivalent might be the couples who open a bottle of wine when they come home from work and never venture out again. Increased opportunity has actually made us materially better off, but not necessarily happier.

Nevertheless, if you have experienced a life with more options, choices and opportunities for personal expression, it can be hard to go back to one where those freedoms are restricted. The fact that many nevertheless do shows just how appealing ties of community are. I certainly know of several people who have either gone to university or worked in one of the big cities, but who have returned to where they grew up around the time they started a family. But there are many others who would not go back, despite the obvious advantages. Lamenting the lost past is therefore understandable but pointless. Much is as it always was, and while that which we have lost is valuable, it's a price we're willing to pay. Does that mean that the life most people have now is better than the one of their parents and grandparents, or have we made a bad bargain? It's a question I won't be ready to answer until later.

Perhaps the greatest symbol of the centrality of working-class culture to English life is football. Jean-Paul Sartre once claimed that 'Three o'clock is always too late or too early for anything you want to do.' For many Englishmen, however, 3 p.m. on Saturday is the most sacred time of the week. As a full-page advert by league sponsors Coke the week before the season started put it, 'Life resumes, Saturday 3 p.m.' The public school sports of cricket and rugby and athletics may capture the nation's imagination from time to time, but it is football that has become the working-class game and the country's most popular sport by a long shot.

But why? Although it certainly can be a beautiful game, people do not follow teams like Rotherham United for aesthetic reasons.

I went to Rotherham's first game of the new season against Walsall. There is always a buzz at the start of the footballing year, as people allow themselves to imagine things will be better this time. But there is an element of masochism in the diehard fan. Last year, Rotherham's followers endured a season without a single home win, yet they still sing 'I'm Rotherham till I die' to the tune of 'I'm H-A-P-P-Y'. Little do they know the new season will be just as traumatic, with threats of liquidation and a 17-match run without a win.

It is a gruesome match. The Millers, as Rotherham are known, fall behind to a soft goal in the third minute and play terribly for the first 20 or so. The second part of the first half picks up, and one fan near me even says out loud, 'We're playing good football!' as though it were the last thing you'd expect to see here. The strong spell culminates in a Martin Butler headed equalizer on 42 minutes. But the second half is very uneven, with neither side doing that well. The fans' loyalty doesn't prevent them from laying into their own players throughout for their failure to 'kick it!' or 'kick 'im'. They don't heed the encouragement. In the third minute of injury time, goalkeeper Gary Montgomery fumbles a hopeful lob from Jorge Leitao and that's it. At the end the guy next to me says, 'Another year, new team, new manager, same old story.' Aye, but he'll be back.

Of course, it is the emotional engagement with the team that makes it so gripping and inspires this loyalty. And to really feel that you need a strong sense of tribal loyalty and attachment to place. That's why many graduate followers of the game who adopt teams in adult life often seem either a little apologetic or to be trying too hard. They want to belong, they really do, but they don't, and frankly find all the belonging business a bit embarrassing anyway.

There is no such squeamishness among the genuinely home-grown fans. The whole set-up is that of a small, insular, parochial community, close-knit but hostile to outsiders. When Walsall's keeper goes down injured the home crowd cheers. When the medic comes on they jokingly sing a siren: 'Nee-nar, nee-nar!' When he gets up they boo. They cruelly chant, 'Merson is a smack-head' because Paul Merson, the Walsall manager, is a recovered drug addict. The referee's performance is, of course, judged in nakedly partisan terms. No foul by a Miller is so blatant that the ref who spots it isn't rewarded with calls of 'You don't know what you're doing' or, more bluntly, but beside the point, 'You fat bastard'. One fan shouts to a Miller who makes a mistake, 'Go back to where you came from.' I'm not sure if it was because he was a new signing or black, but the sentiment that motivated the cry is surely born from the same instinct to divide the world into us and them. You don't sense real hatred, but the obvious insider–outsider dynamic is at work, which is exactly the same one that allows people to bond to their local communities and nations. This undoubtedly has a nasty side. After 7/7, there were reports of Hull fans chanting at their London-based QPR counterparts, 'You're just a town full of bombers' and 'Not enough Londoners dead'.

The local working-class culture permeates every aspect of the afternoon. Half-time is full of all the clubland favourites. You have your '50-50' raffle; a kind of just-for-fun pub quiz, where they play the top five from this 'year in history' and you have to guess which it is; and they announce the death of a long-time fan and read out some birthdays. There was also a pre-season scandal: it seemed for a while that the fans' favourite Pukka Pies were not going to be available this year. Thankfully, that catastrophe was averted.

This is just as true of corporate hospitality suites up and down the country as in the public stands. Later that season I had the chance to see Wigan play, as the guest of a working-class entre-preneur who had done so well he has a table in the suite for every game. The package included the opportunity to have a flutter, take part in a quiz and a raffle. Even the host sounded like a tra-ditional clubland comedian, with his politically incorrect jokes based around regional and sexual stereotypes. 'Liverpool has been named city of culture which should create a million new jobs,' he said. 'Scousers are shitting themselves.' Huge laughs, even – *espe-cially* – from the Liverpudlian he's ribbing. '"City of culture" means people will wake up and find the wheels of their cars sit-ting on piles of books,' he continues. As for his wife, 'She can spot a stray hair in the dark at four in the morning but can't see the garage door.' People love it, many gags are funny, and no one seems to take offence.

The reflection of mainstream working-class life even goes as far as the ethnic mix. At Wigan, a friend of my brother is the only black person in the room. He's such a novelty that someone even asks him if he's related to Edgar Davids, the dreadlocked Dutch player who scores for Tottenham, the visiting team. It's meant to be a good-natured joke, but its target is fed up of being a novelty most places outside London. At Rotherham, there seem to be more black people on the pitch than in the crowd. I don't see anyone from an ethnic minority in the stands. I'm not sure that I'd want to come to this very Anglo-Saxon place if my face wasn't as pasty as everyone else's.

Football is such a central part of national life that it trumps all else. For instance, the hard-drinking, philandering, wife-beating George Best represented all that the *Mail on Sunday* stands against. But he was a football giant so when he died the paper joined in the wide mourning for his passing, on pages 1, 2, 3, 4 and 5. The working man's game is the national game because the nation remains working class in outlook.

However, it is ridiculous to think that means every working

man is obsessed by the sport; none of the locals I knew in The Travellers were that bothered about football. Pete and Andy preferred ice hockey. Local loyalties need to stretch further for this, since the professional league is small with few clubs nationwide. So it was to the Hallam FM Arena – or the 'House of Steel' as it becomes on hockey nights – that I went to see the Sheffield Steelers.

Ice hockey sells itself as a family sport. You can bring the kids because there's no swearing. The announcer will actually sometimes call on people heard swearing in specific rows to stop it. He also refers to the team as 'your family' and an ex-player and coach who are returning with the Nottingham team are described as 'ex-family members'. Mind you, they are still roundly booed before they get their more polite and warm applause. The announcer even tells off the booers, reminding them that the former coach brought the club ten trophies. And the referee is as despised as he is in football, only at ice hockey they heckle him by name.

But the family still likes a good punch-up. Ice hockey must be the only sport where there are specific penalties for fighting. There was one in the third period in my first game, when a good right hook resulted in blood on the ice that had to be scraped off. As the fight gets going Gary Glitter's 'Leader of the Gang' is pumped out over the PA, the part where the crescendo of 'Come on, Come on!' builds. The Sheffield player who lashed out is applauded by the crowd as he makes his way to the sin bin. And there is always a cheer when an opposition player gets well and truly clobbered. There seems to be a trade-off with ice hockey: you stop swearing and fighting in the crowd and we'll get all the aggression out for you on the ice.

The strange thing about presenting the club as a family is that there is very little continuity between seasons. Players come and go remarkably quickly, and most only have one-year contracts. In one way, though, this is a perfect metaphor for real families. The idea of family and the need to belong to one has endured, even while what actually constitutes a family has become more complicated and flexible. The ice-skating family is thus a very modern one. Members change, but at any one point it is a valued focus where people come together.

Indeed, in some ways the apparent decline in the family is actually a testament to the triumph of family values. For the post-war generation, though in many ways family mattered to the working class, in other ways, which we would now consider the most important, it didn't at all. Children were endured more than enjoyed, in part because bringing up big families was hard work and there was little time to play. Kids were also sent out to work as soon as possible, not supported through higher education well into their twenties. Husbands and wives had their own roles, and in married life, the man would make all the important decisions, including sometimes how his wife voted (or so she let him think). Now, we demand more, from our parents and spouses. So we tolerate less. We divorce because family is too important for it to be second best. The triumph of modern family values has meant the dismantling of many families that don't live up to our heightened expectations.

That's why Tory politicians like Alan Clark who advocate traditional family values and then have affairs are not hypocrites. It's just that their old-fashioned family values are based on the keeping together of the unit above all else, just as the *Sun*'s agony aunt suggested. A family matters more than an infidelity; whereas now the idea is that a family is destroyed by an infidelity. Cohesion and continuity (conservative values) matter less now than getting your rightful share of good family life.

So, again, there are changes in how we live and what we think, but the undercurrents still pull in the same directions. And the hockey provided another example of how things have not altered as much as people often suggest. In his book *The English*, Jeremy Paxman confidently wrote, 'No one stands for "God save the Queen" any more.' He should visit the House of Steel, where this is exactly what everyone does before a match.

The traditional linchpins of English working-class life are all still in place, even though they have modified. Families have changed, but they are still central. Communities have weakened, but our attachment to locality remains much stronger than many accounts of decline suggest. Patriotism too counts, though we may now feel more English and less British than we used to. Even the ways we enjoy ourselves continue to follow a template set down in the working men's clubs. Things aren't entirely what they used to be, but stability, community and continuity still count, and there is little about the English mainstream today which can't trace its roots back to the working-class majority of the past.

Social commentators often make the mistake of looking at trends and then over-extrapolating from them. It is true that we are becoming more individualistic and more middle class, but the direction we are heading in should not be confused with the place we are now at. We remain a people with a predominantly working-class culture, and this provides the social background necessary for understanding the English philosophy. Once you see this, the rest makes a great deal more sense.

2

Culture Shocks

Local shops for local people

'Paki.' I can't honestly remember the last time I had heard that word outside of a news exposé of the far right or a 'hard-hitting' drama about racism. That was until my first proper conversation in Everytown, when it was dropped into a sentence as though it were just another adjective, like tall or Italian. Clearly I did not know England very well at all, because I hadn't stumbled across the village racist – I had simply discovered how many people normally speak.

It was during my first conversation with Reg, who would demonstrate the famous Yorkshire bluntness. He was talking about what amenities there were in the village, when he mentioned the 'Paki shop'. The effect was magnified by the fact that he said it so casually. It was not part of some racist diatribe, but was simply a matter-of-fact description of the ethnic origins of the shop's proprietor. Taboos are broken most powerfully by those who have no sense there is any taboo to break.

Over the coming weeks, it became clear that Reg was no anomaly. Almost everyone used the word 'Paki', yet of everyone I got to know, only Neil – happy to be described as somewhere to the right of Attila the Hun – would merit the charge of being truly racist, and even then he could mount a plausible defence that he was no such thing. Nor was use of the word confined to the older, male drinkers I mixed with. Customers chatting in Rotherham's cultural oasis, Philip Howard Books, came out with the word. On the round walk, the 16-year-old daughter of a successful small businessman shared with us a joke video-clip she had downloaded onto her phone. It showed George W. Bush, in a broad Yorkshire accent, saying 'I hate Pakis.' 'Not very politically correct!' laughed her dad approvingly. Even though the joke was presumably on Bush and was not an endorsement of the sentiment, the acceptability of the language was still surprising.

Although Reg's use of the word made me feel uncomfortable, there was a kind of innocence in his use of it that made me react less strongly than I would have imagined. There was no edge to what he was saying: to him it was just a description. Although I never found myself using or wanting to use it myself, it didn't take long before I became able to hear it without assuming the speaker was racist, and I don't believe this was simply a matter of habituation and tolerance for the intolerable. Language does matter and 'Paki' belongs to history, along with 'nigger' and 'coon'. (In Rotherham, at least there is some geographical accuracy in the use of the term, since Pakistan is indeed where most of the town's Asians can trace their ancestors.) But understanding why some such words are still commonly used without rushing to conclude the English mind is essentially racist is a vital part of understanding the reality of multicultural England and how we should move forward.

The urgency of the issue was made clear when, a week after I moved to S66, four Muslim suicide bombers struck in central London, killing 52 people and injuring over 700. In theory, the response to the outrage would provide a clear test of how people of different religions and ethnic origins view each other in England. However, in practice, from the very start it was very difficult to assess accurately just how the country was responding. The incident demonstrated the truth that we tend to see what we want to see, or what our preconceptions tell us we should see. And in times of trouble, what we want to see are the mythical qualities that make our country great.

The most potent of our national myths is that of defiant resilience: the spirit of the Blitz. This is so central to our self-image that it was no surprise to see the BBC's Great Britons poll in 2002 turn out Winston Churchill as the winner. The 7/7 bombings provided plenty of opportunities for people to see the bulldog spirit in action. Londoners did remain extraordinarily calm after the attacks. The next day the Italian daily *Corriere della Sera* said, 'In all the confusion, there was no panic.' Italian national television news made the same point, contrasting London with New York and Madrid. However, what this calm meant was never questioned by the English: of course it indicated toughness and defiance of the terrorists. No one I read suggested that, actually, all that had happened was that London's great vice had been transformed into a virtue by a dramatic change of context. The old jibe about the capital was that you could drop dead and people would just carry on with their business, stepping over the corpse if necessary. Now 52 people had died, and the city was carrying on with its business, but now instead of being callous it was being courageous. As the *Sun*'s front page on Friday cried: OUR SPIRIT WILL NEVER BE BROKEN while its leader the next day saluted: TRUE BRIT GRIT.

Of course, the truth is that the English in general and Londoners in particular are neither great heroes nor indifferent. Londoner Martin Jay provided a rare voice of dissent when he told BBC News Online, 'I have to laugh at the suggestion that Londoners are sending out a defiant message to the terrorists by going to work. I know I'm not. For me it's simply a case of go to work or be out of a job.'

The desire to interpret their reaction as embodying the spirit of the Blitz defied the evidence that was before our eyes. Weeks after the blast, tube travel was still down 15% on weekdays and 25% on weekends. In August *Metro*, the free newspaper for commuters, was reporting a poll that suggested 'Black cabs are taking commuters to and from work in record numbers as Londoners ditch public transport for fear of bombs.' Optimism about prospects over the coming months among cabbies had risen from 2% in April to 97%. It's not difficult to see what had changed.

There was a 77% drop in the number of people in the Central London Congestion Charging Zone on the day of the bombings, a figure which steadied at 25% in the days that followed. The *New Zealand Herald* reported another fact that the British media didn't want to highlight, that 'Shops in central London were reporting sales 50% down over the weekend.' You might think that this did not reflect fear but a noble sense that now was not an appropriate time to grab a bargain. But the same weekend that sales in London's shops were 50% down, and only two days after the attacks, the *Daily Mail* was confident people were ready to see '2 for 1 luxury Caribbean Holidays' and '3 for 1 UK hotel breaks' splashed over its front page, which did not generate any adverse reaction from people claiming it was in bad taste.

The obvious explanation is that people were scared. Indeed, 21% admitted that they would change 'plans or normal routines when it comes to things like travel, holidays or a trip to central London as a result of Thursday's terrorist attack'. If this many people admitted that they had been cowed, you can be sure many more will have been. Similarly, the *Mirror* chose to highlight the fact that 65% 'showed that the terror attacks will not stop them travelling to London', glossing over the 35% that didn't. Reg was one of those who did carry on as usual. He had actually chosen 7 July as the day to make a rare visit to London to see a friend. His train would have taken him to King's Cross, where one of the bombs went off, but it didn't even depart. Still, he went back the next week, undeterred. In contrast, the person who surprised me most was a veteran of Bomber Command who flew a full tour of thirty sorties during the Second World War, something most people didn't survive. Yet he refused to travel through London in the aftermath of 7/7, saying that it wasn't worth the risk. Despite the mythologizing, the English of all ages were no braver or more defiant than anyone else would be. We simply confused our typical understated surface reactions for something deeper.

Another example of how we saw what we wanted to see was manifest in the desire among opinion formers to portray the general reaction to 7/7 in the most uplifting terms possible, even while the general population was feeling deeply pessimistic and angry. One writer I spoke to said she felt heartened that there had been no knee-jerk demand for justice and retribution. Well, maybe not in literary London where she lived, but around the country as a whole, this is just what was called for. WE'LL HUNT DOWN THESE EVIL KILLERS screamed the *Daily Mail*. As ever, the readers were even less squeamish than the editors. 'If necessary, the government should suspend its links with human rights provisions as these people do not deserve to be treated with kid gloves,' wrote Mr Foster of Sunderland to the *Mail*. 'It is time to go on the offensive and bring back hanging for terrorism,' added Mr Charles of Sheffield. A poll in the same paper showed 60% agreed with the capital sentence, if not the precise method. 'Human rights do not apply to the monsters responsible for this outrage,' wrote Ms Curtis of Truro to the *Sun*. I asked the London literary writer if she had read the tabloids, spoken to people outside of London and seen the polls. She said she had, but was still convinced that the reaction had been measured and unvengeful, and anyway, you can't trust polls. I despaired that it was possible for two people to see the same world.

Proof for me that we were mythologizing our reaction to the attacks came a week after the explosions when there was a national minute's silence for the victims of the attack. The *Sun* was imploring its readers to 'Make a stand today' and 'Defy terrorists at noon'. To see how the silence was observed, I went to Wickersley, where two rows of shops line either side of a dual carriageway. I sat myself on a low wall near the bus stop so I could see as much as possible. To my left was the main road, in front of me the car park, and on my right a couple of dozen shops. I checked my watch at a few minutes before midday but then didn't look at it again. I just wanted to see if the place did 'fall silent' as newspaper reports would no doubt claim it had. I waited. I kept thinking that midday had not yet come. At no point did the number of people walking in and out of shops visibly alter. At no time did the volume of traffic either pulling in or pulling away go down. The stream of traffic on the Bawtry Road never reduced. At most, there was one person who got into their car and didn't drive straight off: perhaps they were sitting in silence for sixty seconds. If this was typical of the country, then it did not fall silent as one.

Of course, had I been in one of the shops, perhaps I would have witnessed an impeccably observed silence, as the woman in the Co-op reported there had been. Most people if they find themselves somewhere that a silence is being observed will join in. But not many will do so independently. This doesn't surprise, shock or disappoint me, since I've often missed silences because I've been at home, or just forgotten. It simply exposes the myth that the nation was so united in grief that we were all determined to show our solidarity against the terrorists whatever.

As was often the case, some would try to dismiss my experience as being a 'Yorkshire thing'. But anecdotal evidence suggests otherwise. When I walked around the floral tributes to 7/7 in London a few weeks later, I saw one wreath from 'the people of County Durham' and no one I spoke to in Rotherham was anything less than outraged and sympathetic to the victims. I also had conflicting reports about what happened only a mile or so from one of the blasts on Islington's Upper Street – which is not surprising because it is a long road. One witness reported a universal observance whereas another found, as I did, that on the streets there was no visible response.

Our mythologizing of the reaction to 7/7 doesn't reveal a great deal about our national philosophy, but it does expose an enormous difficulty in getting to grips with it. As I found time and again when talking to people about what I was doing, we have very fixed ideas about who we are and what we think. The English mind is something we are all experts on, and people are very resistant to changing their opinions, even in the face of good arguments and sound evidence. My experiences in S66 did, however, change my views on how we need to respond to 'the challenges of multicultural Britain' (as liberals who want to discuss the topic in anything other than wholly positive terms are obliged to describe them). Reaction to 7/7 simply convinced me it would be an even tougher job than I'd imagined to get anyone to change theirs.

Being in Rotherham rather than London certainly helped me to get a firm grip on the realities of multiculturalism. Rotherham is much more typical of the country as a whole, even though the bare statistics might suggest otherwise. The town's ethnic minority population is only 3.1%, compared to around 8% of the UK. But averages mislead, because ethnic minorities are concentrated in certain areas: 47% of all Britain's ethnic minorities live in London. So the experiences of a Rotherham resident are typical of their compatriots: few people from ethnic minorities live among the white majority, though there will be some concentrations relatively close by, as there are in certain areas of central Rotherham. The question of how we can all live together is therefore being addressed from a realistic starting point in which there is little actual living together anyway.

It may seem platitudinous to say that, if we are to answer this question, we need greater understanding. Everyone would agree with that. But among opinion formers and commentators, there is often an understandable, though flawed, asymmetry in this understanding. They often see the best in ethnic minorities and foreign cultures but are quick to condemn majorities in the native culture. While attempts are made to sympathetically understand minority practices which seem, for example, to oppress women or be cruel, white Britons who say 'Paki' are condemned out of hand, and all their liberal good intentions about trying to understand those who don't think and speak as they do go out of the window. That's why in trying to take seriously the concerns of the white Britons who use these words and argue that the majority of them are not prejudiced, I know I risk being accused of being an apologist for racism.

It should be obvious that whether or not someone uses an offensive word does not in itself reveal the beliefs and intentions of the speaker. A colleague of Councillor Shaukat Ali, head of the Rotherham Multi Agency Approach to Racial Incidents (MAARI), told me that many young Asians in the town would talk about 'Paki' shops, in much the same way as many black people have reclaimed the word 'nigger', or homosexuals 'queer'. Obviously there is a difference between a white Briton and an Asian Briton using the word 'Paki', but that difference is not a straightforward one. There is no contradiction in asserting that the words someone uses are racist (because they cause offence), but the person is not (because they mean none). Words do matter, and we should drop certain terms which are offensive. But there is often a stress placed on language by educated liberals which it does not deserve. It would be a mistake to jump to conclusions about what the English philosophy is on the basis of unfair assumptions about the vocabulary in which it is expressed.

The same potential to falsely ascribe prejudice emerges when one hears the kind of jokes that circulated after 7/7. The Slovenian philosopher Slavoj Žižek provided a warning about misinterpreting what jokes mean when he talked about how the jokes based on supposed national characteristics of Slovenes, Croats, Bosnians and Montenegrins flourished when Yugoslavia was one country, and disappeared when the tensions leading to civil war started in the early eighties. Mocking humour can be a sign of healthy coexistence as well as mutual distrust.

What are we to make of these jokes, told by a teacher in further education to a small group of people she knew? The first was about a Muslim trying out a backpack in a shop, asking 'Does my bomb look big in this?' Another was of someone buying an inflatable woman at a sex shop and being offered Muslim or Jewish versions. The difference was that the Muslim doll blew itself up. On these occasions, I detected no hint of race hatred. Both jokes were excuses for some old-fashioned word play. They were certainly in bad taste, but there is a certain frisson you get from bad-taste jokes which means people love to tell them only on appropriate occasions, precisely because they would offend on inappropriate ones. Context is all, and I got the impression the teller here would be horrified if the jokes were repeated in front of Muslims she did not have good reason to think would find the jokes funny (and I'm sure there are situations in which at least some would).

However, someone else on another occasion also told a joke about a chemist who accidentally gave a Muslim customer arsenic instead of aspirin. Realizing his mistake he ran after the customer and explained his error. 'What's the difference?' asked the Muslim. 'Three quid,' replied the chemist. Here the joke seems to depend on your finding the idea of valuing a few quid over the life of a Muslim funny, and that's what makes it objectionable. Jokes can be in bad taste, racist or both, but the two types are not the same.

So in order to understand mainstream English thinking about multiculturalism, we have to avoid drawing simplistic conclusions from the way people speak. What the frequent mention of 'Pakis' indicated to me was not that people hated all British Asians, but that there was so little mixing between the two groups that a term which would be offensive in mixed company could be frequently used without anyone minding. In that sense it's quite like the use of the Hindi word 'goreh' among British Asians to mean white people. Many argue that 'goreh' is not at all derogatory, since it literally just means 'white'. But then 'Paki' is literally just an abbreviation for 'Pakistani', so that in itself proves nothing. The point is, in what contexts are these words used? Both 'Paki' and 'goreh' are 'our' words for 'them', only used among 'us'. It's certainly true that if you break this rule and use either word in mixed company, the effects are different, but that's at least in part to do with the fact that most white people don't know what 'goreh' means and it does not have a history of abusive misuse as 'Paki' does. In an England in which whites and Asians mixed freely, I don't think we'd hear either word very much at all.

The use of 'Paki' is therefore not primarily a symptom of race hatred but of a divided nation. The racial divide used to be about black and white, but now it is mainly between British Asians and the rest. Black and white youths who once fought each other now often fight together against Asians. When people talk with concern about British Asians, usually they are thinking specifically of Muslims, who make up around 3% of the population, rather than Hindus or Sikhs. Although not always careful to make these distinctions, in conversation I found that people were very definitely of the mind that Islam posed a particular problem.

However, if that is where the main cultural divide lies, immigration and the growth of the so-called 'non-indigenous' population is certainly an issue too. Many think that the ethnic minority population as a whole has got too large and threatens the cohesion of the country. It is not just accidental that Muslims are the focus of many of the debates, but people's concerns are wider than those concerning a clash between Islam and Christianity.

Given his reputation, it was no surprise that Neil was the first to give his frank assessment of what the problem, as he saw it, was. His blood pressure rising, he told me that his wife quit her job at the benefit office because she was 'fed up with the Pakis claiming more in benefits than she was earning'. Pete backed him up, looking me straight in the eye and telling me that they get so much help filling in the forms they claim benefits we don't even know exist. Someone complained that there weren't enough jobs even for 'us' and that there would be more of 'them' than 'us' before we know it. Johnny, more of an old cynic than a firebrand, chipped in with a joke: apparently an old working men's club was due to be turned into a mosque, but they couldn't go ahead because it's not facing Mecca. The joke was that it should really be facing the dole office. 'Mustafa Giro!' quipped Pete and they all had a laugh. 'Mustafa Giro!'

You can perhaps see now why I have taken so many pains to caution against jumping to conclusions. On my sixth day in Everytown, writing in my journal about this conversation, I put: 'Racism. I'm afraid it's rife.' To say that I was not used to hearing such opinions aired so freely is an understatement. And although they weren't playing up, there was some awareness that these views might appear shocking to a journalist who had written for the *Guardian*. But there was something about the lack of malice in their tone which made me doubt the confident accusation of racism I had put in my diary. Prejudice is everywhere, so why do we label some as bigots and excuse others? Think how in recent years 'chavs' have been fair game among the more affluent: poor, uneducated members of the white working class are mocked and laughed at in the mainstream media and given a name every bit as derogatory as 'Paki' or 'towel-head'. Nor will otherwise impeccable liberals tend to accuse you of being prejudiced if you talk about American Republicans as stupid, bigoted imperialists, thus condemning around half the population of the USA. And as Neil said, it is not as though Asians are totally unprejudiced themselves. He told the story of an Asian at his place of work who wouldn't talk to another, saying he was a bad man. The reason was that he was Yemeni, and there was some kind of regional rivalry. If any hint of prejudice is to be condemned, then there are few, if any, without sin entitled to throw the first stone.

I'm certainly not saying there is no racism in Everytown. Neil tellingly concluded his story about the Yemeni by saying, 'They hate each other as much as we hate them', frighteningly implying that 'we' do in fact hate 'them'. But Neil was the exception, and people would often comment that his views were far too extreme. For the most part, even the conversation above can be understood to reflect a mixture of fact, understandable concern, and simple misinformation.

Neil's wife, for instance, probably did often give out more in benefits than she was earning. An out-of-work family with several children could easily receive more in benefits than someone would earn for 35 hours on close to the minimum wage. And because in Rotherham Asian families tend to be larger and poorer than average, she would see more such payments going to them than white families. Of course, that does not mean that they were getting the money because they were Asians, but you can nevertheless understand why it might be galling to see people in a particular segment of society take more in handouts than you earned, and to resent them for it.

Similarly, it is true that many local authorities do provide help for people to fill out forms if English is not their first language, and this might actually result in them making more claims than those who simply fill them in themselves. Again, this is not a deliberate pro-Asian bias, but if the effect is that one racial group get more attention than others, you can understand why others feel aggrieved. That's why 'Mustafa Giro!' may sound terrible, but it is not essentially a racist joke. They mock all they perceive to take benefits without trying to work, regardless of race, creed or colour: many of the local white people who go to the working men's club, for example, are called 'dole wallahs'.

Add to that some misinformation, such as the idea that the ethnic minority population will soon become the majority, when in fact it still only stands at 8%, and you can see how the kind of conversation which would shock a liberal urban dweller is actually motivated by factors other than naked racism. To say that a viewpoint is understandable, however, is not the same as saying that it is right. All I have tried to show so far is that we are dealing with a point of view that can and should be engaged with, and not just dismissed as a set of paranoid, racist fears.

We need to go further, however. To say that people base their opinions on many things that are in fact true and that they are not usually prejudiced tells us about some facts. But if we are to really understand the English philosophy, we need to know the values that, together with these facts, produce the folk political philosophy. You can find clues to what these values are by reading the *Mail* and the *Sun*. During my stay in S66 I read only these papers and their Sunday equivalents regularly. The reason for this was that these are far and away the most popular newspapers in the country, and as such reflect the reality of mainstream English opinion more accurately than others. The *Sun* sells over three million copies each day, while the *Daily Mail* alone sells in excess of two million – more than *The Times*, *Telegraph*, *Guardian* and *Independent* combined. The tabloid press does have the power to shape opinion, but this power is not limitless. The papers that do best are those which reflect the basic values their readers already have. If they fail to strike a chord, they just won't sell. That's why, although imperfect, they are more reliable barometers of national opinion than many would like to think.

The *Mail* expressed the dominant view of multiculturalism in an editorial on 17 July: '[The] malign impact of multiculturalism and political correctness has for years seen Britain segregated into inward-looking communities that eschew British values while the forces of law and order walk on eggshells, desperate not to offend.' Put more positively, and in pub terms, it's that people 'don't mind who lives here, whether they're black, white or green, as long as they follow our way of life'. Interestingly, although we're not a particularly religious country, most people do think that our values are in some important way Christian ones. A BBC poll reported that 61% believe that 'our laws should respect and be influenced by UK religious values', with even 49% of those with no religion agreeing.

Antipathy towards British Asians in particular is thus based largely on the perception that they do not wish to adopt the 'British way of life' or that their numbers are getting so large that the English way is being diluted too much by their mere presence. This is manifested in such factors as their alleged taking of more than their fair share of public money and resources, through living in self-segregating communities, and at an extreme – and virtually everyone I talked to accepted it was only a small minority – by actually waging war on England and what it stands for. The generally accepted solution is simple: live like the English or get out. Again, it should not be presumed that this is racism in disguise. The mainstream wants to expel from society, through forced emigration or incarceration, all sorts of people who refuse to conform, and the fact that the majority of those they currently want out have different coloured skins is a historical accident.

This argument may be flawed but it is based on several truths that we would be foolish to ignore. The first is that it is true that many minorities do not fully integrate into mainstream English life. This is plain fact. Ethnic minority populations do concentrate in particular areas. The impeccably liberal *Guardian* proved as much with its maps of multicultural Britain and London, in which it highlighted where the different ethnic populations lived. Although mixed race marriages are on the rise, they still comprise only 2% of all marriages. Only 6% of British Indians, 4% of Pakistanis and 3% of Bangladeshis have married a non-Asian. In contrast, 29% of black Caribbean men and 48% of other black men have married non-black women. For the most part, people mix and marry with people mainly of their own cultural background, as determined by a combination of country, family origin or religion. This is the same the world over. For instance, while in Spain I saw a newspaper report on a study which showed 75% of immigrants there did not have a Spanish friend.

The key point, however, is that every sector of society does this. It's no use pointing the finger at ethnic minorities. England is a patchwork of almost hermetically sealed sub-worlds, in which class as much as race is a crucial factor. This was something I felt very acutely moving from one to another. Many professional urbanites regarded my move to Rotherham as though I was going to Outer Mongolia. More than one joked about sending me food parcels, as though it would be impossible to get such staples as balsamic vinegar and buffalo mozzarella in Rotherham, and that life without such things would be intolerable, both of which are ludicrous suggestions. (As it turns out, Morrisons stocked plenty of exotic foodstuffs such as octopus and excellent regional sheep's milk cheese.) They were joking, of course, but the joke depended on the real sense that my journey of a mere 175 miles across my own country would take me into another world. Another was horrified to discover that all the local cafés were closed by 4.30, because most mothers like to have a coffee and cake with their kids after they have picked them up from school. This simply exposed how ignorant those who live in the world of yummy mummies are about how the rest of the country lives. For one thing, around here, cake after 4.30 would be far too close to your tea time (which is your evening meal, not tea and cake).

We all like to feel that we're open-minded people who can be friends with anyone, and we also can probably come up with a few examples of friends who do not match our demographic profile to prove our lack of insularity. We might even be able to pull out that great English get-out-of-alleged-snobbery-free card: a working-class background. But if we are honest, the vast majority live, work and socialize overwhelmingly with people of a similar social type. Demographic maps prove the point. The obsession with school catchment areas, for instance, has the effect of social segregation, as parents of a certain class and their children cluster in enclaves of their own kind.

In any town people know what it means to live in certain areas. When Pete, for instance, was reminded that his family came from the Valley Road, he said, 'Ah, but the posh side, mind', the joke being there is no posh side. In somewhere like London, just as there are Bangladeshis in Brick Lane and Orthodox Jews in Stamford Hill, so there are literary clusters in Hampstead, media folk in Brixton, old money in South Kensington and so on. The desire to live amongst people you perceive to be like yourself is pretty much a human universal.

Demanding that ethnic minorities mix in is thus both hopeless and hypocritical. There is even some evidence that Muslims are more keen to fit in than many white people are to have them. A BBC poll, for instance, showed 90% of Muslims thought immigrants should learn English, against 82% of the population as a whole. But the opportunities to mix are limited because many areas remain deeply inhospitable to 'outsiders'. Rawmarsh and Dalton, for example, are areas in which there is too much racism for Muslims to seriously consider living there. Communities are kept together both by factors pulling them in and factors keeping them out of others.

The point about multiculturalism and integration is therefore a red herring. All sorts of social groups don't mix very much, yet we don't chastise them for it. The trouble is not caused by not mixing, but refusing to do so in ways which seem to threaten other groups. As long as staying apart isn't threatening, it is not only accepted, it is actually what people want. Take the phenomenon of white flight. While on holiday in Mallorca (more of which later) I met a couple who grew up in Muswell Hill, but moved away in the sixties. Why? 'It had changed, with the people moving in,' explained the wife, sheepishly. And who were these people? 'Asians, mainly.' She was clearly uncomfortable spelling it out, because she knew it sounded prejudiced. (This is one reason why it's very hard to get a real sense of what people think: they will often tone down their real views.) But by that time I had ceased to assume that people who said such things were all closet racists. White flight is too often seen as driven by a prejudiced dislike of newcomers, when the simple matter – in this case at least – was that they had grown up in an area with one type of character, and that character had changed. All they wanted was to carry on living somewhere that was more like what they were used to. That's not racist or deplorable, and nor is it an argument against immigration. The fact is that areas change their characters all of the time. But when they do, we should not be surprised if people move on. It is no more a sign of prejudice than it would be for someone to move because a previously small village had expanded too much for their tastes, or because a once family-orientated area had become much more of a student one. What it does show, however, is that mixing is not a top priority for the white majority, so neither should it be made an obligation of ethnic minorities.

The political problem is that many people who are justifiably keen to promote the idea of multiculturalism of various kinds have failed to spot the difference between the ideal and the reality. The ideal is for people to all live and mix together, regardless of creed, colour or social class. But the reality is that even people who enjoy the variety of a multicultural society still, on the whole, mix far more in some circles than others. And the people they are mixing with are generally the most liberal and Westernized of the ethnic minorities anyway. Even more don't really want to mix, even though they have nothing in particular against those they keep themselves apart from.

What we need to realize is that on the whole, this works. England is a country where people of all races can get along, not because we're all such a culturally promiscuous bunch that we don't care whether our local butcher sells Cumberland sausages or halal chicken legs, but because we don't mind what others do, as long as they don't bother us with it. That's why multiculturalism has recently become such a hot issue: people are feeling bothered by what they perceive British Muslims to be doing. But why are Muslims a particular source of concern? Britain's Chinese community, for instance, rarely attracts any antipathy, despite the fact that the Chinatowns of London and Manchester are bold, public statements of a refusal to become Anglicized. The crucial factor is that the Chinese difference does not appear to threaten the English 'normality', partly because their numbers are smaller and partly because there is no talk of a clash of civilizations between Confucianism and the West. In contrast, there is a sense many people have that British Muslims are not fully prepared to accept and support British laws and norms; and that their own way of life was under threat from the rise of Islam in this country.

On both these matters I did disagree with my new-found drinking companions. My feeling was that the extent to which Muslims dissent from the fundamentals of British democracy is overstated, and that the threat of an Islamification of British culture is grossly exaggerated. After all, the Muslim population is still less than 3%. As Amartya Sen has recently emphasized, it's also far too simplistic and politically dangerous to think of a monolithic 'Muslim community' anyway. Even if there are real problems, to deal with them as though they were integral to Islam is foolish. What is more, to focus on the small threat to the English way of life seems like a case of warped priorities when ethnic minorities still face unacceptable levels of discrimination. Five days after the 7/7 bombings, for example, you had to wait until page 34 of the *Daily Mail* before you read about the worst example yet of the anti-Muslim backlash: a gang of black and white youths had attacked an Asian man who later died.

Metro also had a postbag full of fear reflected by anyone who looked Asian. 'I have not been allowed outside of the house since the bombings. My family are scared,' wrote Ms Khan of London. Laila, a white, British-born convert to Islam from Cardiff, said, 'My friend was spat at on a train last week.' A self-identifying British Muslim from Scotland said, 'I have been avoiding public transport – I am sick of the abuse.'

Rotherham's Multi Agency Approach to Racial Incidents recorded 30 racial incidents in the town the weekend after the bombings, compared to 282 for the whole of 2004. Yet this is something even the head of the agency, Shaukat Ali, thought prudent to play down. He told the *Rotherham Advertiser*, 'Whilst it is sad these incidents have happened, it is important that we do not concentrate on them because the real message to come from this is that communities are coming together and showing real solidarity and unity.' But although we may have needed the myth of unity and solidarity to help us get through the short-term reaction, I think we need to expose the myth if we are to succeed in the long term.

We have to be honest because we need to understand what fuels the resentments in order to stop them leading to racial incidents. Ali told me of a few terrible examples of this in the aftermath of 7/7. One taxi driver had a customer who lit up, despite the no-smoking signs. 'Would you mind not smoking?' he said. 'What about all the smoking you've been doing in London with your bombs?' said the (drunk) man. The driver couldn't retaliate and was just relieved when the guy left the taxi without further incident. Another young British Asian man had been working in Morrisons for three years, and a white customer said, 'I don't want to be served by you – you're Paki killers.' The worker called the manager who took the person's shopping back and told them to leave because they didn't want their custom.

This side of the story is still not heard enough. However, if we are to create a more harmonious society, we need to understand the causes of racial tension, and to do that properly we need to understand that illegitimate prejudice can grow out of legitimate concerns, if they are not addressed. And I do not think that the fears a lot of people have about the rise and threat of Islam are total delusions, even though they have become exaggerated and distorted. Various surveys and opinion polls have convinced me that the view that there is simply no tension at all between the Islamic values which people actually hold and those of secular liberal democracy is wishful thinking. For instance, 'muscular liberal' David Goodhart wrote after 7/7 pointing out that an ICM poll for the *Guardian* a year earlier had shown that 13% of British Muslims thought the 9/11 attacks were justified 'and according to other polls as many as 25% do not identify with Britain in any way'. A year after the atrocities, a *Times* poll showed that 13% of British Muslims still considered the London bombers to be martyrs.

Despite the talk of the media encouraging Islamophobia, if anything I found the *Sun*, in particular, keen to underplay any tensions between Islam and 'Western democratic values'. Reporting a poll of British Muslims published three weeks after the 7/7 bombings, it chose to highlight the fact that 91% said that suicide bombs are anti-Islam and that 52% disagree with the statement that 'Islam is incompatible with the values of British democracy'. A different editor could have picked up on the fact that 9% were not prepared to agree that suicide bombs are anti-Islam, and 2% thought they actually are Islamic; and a staggering 41% agreed that 'Islam is incompatible with the values of British democracy'. And 7% also said that they 'personally know a Muslim whose religious views you would call extreme or radical' . . . 'and a majority of those confess they would not tell the cops'.

I sometimes found myself arguing with people who portrayed Islam as either 'unBritish' or plain murderous by pointing out that according to many experts 'true Islam' is fully compatible with liberal democracy. For example, Johnny said, 'I can't approve of a religion whose sacred text says that suicide bombers will go to heaven, Justin.' When I pointed out that most Muslims didn't believe the Koran says that, he agreed yet didn't change his mind. His response was not contradictory. The fact that the Koran actually prohibits suicide bombings is neither here nor there if a small but sizeable minority of Muslims thinks it does, which various polls suggest is the case. Survey after survey has reinforced the finding of a poll that showed that 6% of British Muslims thought that the London attacks were justified, while a full 32% agreed that 'Western society is decadent and immoral and that Muslims should seek to bring it to an end.' This is not a scholarly debate but one about opinions held on the ground, and at that level there are clearly some conflicts between the values of many Muslims and those of liberal democracy. It is therefore not unreasonable that, where there are such conflicts, people look to defend the latter over the former. Nor is this a reactionary move. Consider, for instance, the Pew Global Attitudes survey, which showed that 44% of British Muslims were very or somewhat worried by 'Muslim women taking on modern roles in society'. Surely it is the progressive left which should be primarily concerned about this, not the nationalist right.

As to the worry about 'Muslims taking over', many do feel something like this concern. At one pub quiz in nearby Firbeck, a team of students had totted up their scores incorrectly. The quizmaster joked, 'Who's going to be running the country in twenty years?' One wag volunteered, 'Pakistanis!' It got more 'oooos' than laughs, but the fact that he could say it in public shows that it's hardly a heretical viewpoint. While 54% think that 'parts of this country don't feel like Britain any more because of immigration', only 12% (still one in eight) think that this is true of their own area. Although on a national scale the fear of minorities becoming majorities is clearly absurd, we should be able to see why people might worry about large immigrant influxes and ethnic minority populations at a local level. The chief executive of Slough Borough Council also warned in 2006 that the unprecedented influx of mainly East European immigrants was putting council services under intolerable pressure. (This also suggests that while Muslims are the focus of most attention in the multiculturalism debate, that is just circumstantial and Islamophobia is not the root cause of this.) Johnny once claimed that by 2010, in London, ethnic minorities will be in the majority. He was wrong, but he could have pointed out that in two London boroughs, Brent and Newham, ethnic 'minorities' are in fact majorities. So, while across England as a whole the idea of the white majority becoming a minority is sheer alarmism, in specific areas it is the plain truth. Again, you don't have to be racist or Islamophobic to want where you live to retain its current character, and if you see some parts of your town turning into monocultural ghettos, your fear that your area may be next is not entirely unjustified. In much the same way, I would not like to live in an area where there was a strong visible presence of evangelical Christians, and unless you're one of them, I would find it hard to believe if you claimed it would make no difference to you. If no one cared who their neighbours were, all areas would have more or less the same kind of mix of residents, which they quite evidently do not.

Well-intentioned promotion of multiculturalism can actually exacerbate this feeling of being under threat. When people are informed by local and national governments that they ought to embrace minority cultures more than they do, they feel they are being told that their own way of life simply isn't good enough. 'You need to change' is the implied message, and if they are honest, this is precisely what many promoters of multiculturalism think. But again, just consider the flagrant double standard of this. Insisting that minority culture open up more to the majority one is seen as intolerant bullying; to insist that the majority cultures open up more to minority ones is seen as enlightened and liberal. The truth is that human nature is not that different, and that the desire to embrace the other is equally weak in most cultures, minority or majority.

This is all clearly bad news for optimistic multiculturalists, and some will think that it suggests a bleak view of human nature. On this view, the best we can hope for is what has got us this far, with relatively little tension between communities: mutual tolerance. Toleration has become a dirty word in the multiculturalism debate. It is judged to be not good enough. People don't want to be tolerated, they want to be fully respected and acknowledged. Toleration implies putting up with something you don't much like, not embracing difference. But it is not just utopian to suggest that we should all not just tolerate but love all other ways of life, it's intellectually and morally unsustainable. I, for example, am an unrepentant atheist. That means I can indeed respect and learn from many varieties of religious belief, but I can no more than tolerate the kind of religious fundamentalism that sees atheists, homosexuals and unmarried couples as wicked, and only in so far as it does not threaten the kind of secular, liberal values I believe our political system rests on. This is not because atheists are particularly intolerant: devout Roman Catholics also can do no more than put up with many others in society who offend against the deepest values of their religion, such as abortionists or polytheistic Hindus. To ask everyone to embrace everyone else is clearly absurd. Toleration is the best we can do, and what's more, it works.

Toleration does not imply any kind of lack of human warmth on the personal level. To say I merely tolerate, say, Scientologists, does not mean that I refuse to deal with any of them in a friendly, civil way. A country in which we tolerate one another should be one in which we deal with each other in a fair, open and friendly manner. And that's precisely what the white people who expressed their concerns to me about Islam do. Their interactions with Asians are not begrudging or rude but as friendly and civil as they are with anyone else. Nor is there any contradiction between merely tolerating a religion and being a friend with someone who belongs to it. People with incompatible ideals about how society should be run can often get along very well on a personal level.

One of the main complaints about this view is that it does not give us the shared values we need to glue society together. Live and let live can't work if we're all living differently. The answer to this is simple: the shared values we all need to sign up to are actually pretty minimal and civic, rather than religious- or culture-specific. As long as we all have respect for the rule of law, the democratic process and the basic rights agreed to by most liberal democracies, from the point of view of maintaining civic society it doesn't matter one jot if in our private lives we love Jesus or worship Satan.

Liberal Democrat Vince Cable argued for something similar at a Fabian seminar on Britishness in June 2006. But although he received some support, most present thought this wouldn't work, arguing that we need an emotional attachment to national identity. These critics had made a mistake. The English differ in how strongly they feel English, with many preferring to see themselves as British. (It's interesting in this regard that many are comfortable with hyphenated designations such as British-Asian but not English-Asian.) But whatever identity people feel, it should be obvious that what it means to feel British or English varies considerably. The urban poor do not feel their Englishness in the same way as fox-hunting country-dwellers. This simple fact is missed by many who wring their hands over the question of national identity. Their confusion is actually pretty simple: they mistake the need for everyone to feel as though they belong to their country with the need for everyone to feel the *same* kind of attachment to their country. While the former is politically essential, the latter is psychologically impossible. If we try to impose a singular sense of what it means to be English, we can only make those who have a different sense of their Englishness feel more alienated from their country. The alternative is thus to allow everyone to feel that this is their country, but in their own way. The white majority of Rotherham need to feel that the country they know and love is theirs, even if it is a country that British Asians or professional Londoners have no sense of whatsoever.

Toleration is key to achieving this, and toleration is England's dominant philosophical concept for maintaining a harmonious society. Let us all be English in whatever way we choose, and as long as your Englishness doesn't threaten mine, it doesn't matter if it's different, so long as we agree to live and let live. If that sounds too modest then it's time we got real. As I have argued, this is not and never has been culturally one country. When I moved from Bristol BS8 to Bramley S66, I moved from one world to another, in the same country. Political philosophers can talk all they like about pluralism, stoic cosmopolitanism or multiculturalism, but these can provide no more than distant objectives we can edge towards. National psyches do not change overnight, and unless we go with the grain of widely held beliefs, we will not only fail, we will provoke feelings of fear and increase tension.

To reduce this tension we have to promote a sense that everyone is being treated equally under the same rules. That is what provides the reassurance necessary for everyone to live differently in the same country by sharing the same set of minimal civic values. It sounds like a perfectly traditional liberal stance, but it does have a tough edge. It impacts, for instance, on how local authorities help those who do not speak English. This is a real issue of social justice, because if nothing is done, people are deprived of their entitlements. But if they provide services in 'community languages' or with translator assistance, it only seems to reinforce the 'us and them' mentality, and the sense among the majority that people are being given preferential treatment. You fully respect minorities as equal citizens when you treat them the same as all other citizens, not as special cases. So it is far better to focus much more on helping people to access services in the normal way by providing English-language lessons for non-English speakers. This is a popular measure among the white majority and ethnic minorities, since it helps tackle the roots of segregation, rather than managing and sustaining it once it has flowered. Ultimately, it helps everyone to feel that they are part of the same country.

Toleration, coupled with respect and openness, does in the long run lead to greater integration of communities. But as Neil pointed out, it can take a very long time. 'Yes, the Jews are more integrated,' he said, showing a thoughtfulness and knowledge that his more strident opinions often occluded, 'but we're going back to 1190 when the Jews were massacred in York – it's taken nearly a thousand years.' It needn't take quite that long to make England's Asians feel at home. Although anti-black racism is still a reality, it seems to me that we have already come a long way from the sixties and seventies.

Toleration is an underrated virtue. The most racist person I met in S66 was in some ways frighteningly close in his opinions to those of the majority. His grievances against Asians were based on perceptions of British Muslims that are widely shared, only more extreme. He now refuses to get into a taxi if the driver is Asian, or eat from an Asian restaurant or takeaway. And he also said that if he knew he was dying, he'd walk into the nearest mosque and blow himself up. He was the mirror image of a small number of British Muslims, whose grievances against England are also widely shared, only taken to more of an extreme. People like this are never going to embrace other cultures. Obviously there is something in them that despises difference so much that they see the worst in others. And although these extremists are rare, I would suspect that the majority are also unlikely to ever truly love the other. Getting such people to tolerate others is the only realistic way we have of making sure they don't express outright hostility.

Thinking these issues through helped me to see the English philosophy coming together. The importance of tolerance and the unwillingness to see the mainstream way of life changed too radically clearly fits in with the traditional working-class culture which values continuity, community, stability and a sense of belonging. Attitudes to multiculturalism are intimately linked with the prevailing wisdom about how we should live in general, and the dominant political philosophy of the English people.

3

Illiberal Democrats

My neighbour gets a new flag at last

I read many accounts of the English and British while research-
ing this book, but I found that the most accurate portraits of
the national psyche came from comedians. Whole scenes leaped
straight out of sitcoms in front of my very eyes. *The League of
Gentlemen*'s catchphrase 'This is a local shop for local people'
echoed in the billboard above a shop proclaiming 'Local jobs,
Local people' and a car dealer's advert proclaiming 'Local people,
with family values'. I saw Peter Kay's doorman Max in the people
recommending places to eat who counted out on their fingers all
the various items put on your plate: 'You've got your meat – beef,
chicken, pork; potatoes – roast or boiled; Yorkshire puddings . . .'
Like John Shuttleworth, the ideal place for many to take a stroll
was around a reservoir. They may not have actually read the levels
as he did, but they would have been noticed.

One East Anglian character who would pop up with alarming regularity was Alan Partridge, the perfect embodiment of
England's illiberal political outlook. Partridge came to mind when
I was reading in the *Sun* about Essex's new 'get tough' chief con-
stable who 'ordered his officers to make 600 extra arrests in his
first week – and they beat the target by 200'. Eleven letters were
printed backing him, although one warned gloomily that 'The
CPS and the magistrates will find numerous excuses to keep the
crooks arrested out of jail.' Why, I wondered, wasn't anyone concerned about a police chief simply ordering an arbitrary increase
in arrests? The answer, as Alan Partridge once said, is 'Well, with
the greatest respect, the police are hardly likely to arrest him if
he's innocent, are they?'

Thus speaks the authentic voice of illiberal England. This
may be the home of liberty, 'mother of the free', but what freedom means to the English is not what the disparagingly called

'civil liberties brigade' think it is. The freedom people want is 'our' freedom to carry on with our lives as easily as possible, not some kind of universal right which allows others to do things we don't like. That means the 'we' which is the English mainstream has no problem with illiberal measures that infringe the liberties of 'them' for our sake.

This is certainly the view echoed down to The Travellers, where the regulars saw no reason why terror suspects should not be deported to countries with the death penalty. 'Let them deal with their own,' said Andy, in his typically nonchalant manner, reflecting the feeling that rights are as much subject to national borders as welfare eligibility. The main concern is not what happens elsewhere, but that the riff-raff are kept out. 'This country is becoming a haven for terrorists,' insisted Neil with characteristic conviction, even if that haven is Her Majesty's prison. Nor does anyone like the fact that the authorities 'know who these people are' yet can't take them out or bang 'em up. Appeals to the rule of law or due process cut no ice: the rule-book only applies to those who play by the rules, although, for reasons I'll come to, the rule-book isn't quite the right metaphor.

A *Telegraph* poll into what defines Britishness provides some pointers to understanding this. (Remember that since the English make up nearly 85% of the British, such surveys are largely about England.) People were asked to say which of a list of phrases or words is 'very important to them in defining Britain and what it is to be British'. The top answer (61%) was 'British people's right to say what they think'. The second answer reiterated the myth of the bulldog: 'Britain's defiance of Nazi Germany in 1940' (59%). The third is perhaps the most interesting: 'British people's sense of fairness and fair play' (54%). This links with 'their tolerance of other people and other people's ideas' (41%).

In the light of people's expressed beliefs on specific issues, it is easy to disparage these results as complete self-delusions. The idea that the English value fair play, for instance, is severely challenged by the total disregard for due process when it comes to dealing with people merely suspected of being terrorists or criminals. After 7/7, for instance, the *Sun*'s letters page was full of letters from the likes of Mr Evans of Swansea, who wrote that 'political correctness must now be rescinded. Terrorists who bleat about their human rights upon capture must be ignored.' 'To hell with the human rights brigade,' said Mr Robinson of Burnley. 'What about our human rights?' asked Ms Haley of Frampton Cotterell. The *Sun* itself backed this line. 'Hand-wringing judges must stop putting the human rights of terror suspects before OUR human rights,' it wrote in one leader. 'Do whatever it takes,' it implored in another, 'and do it now. Ignore the whining civil liberties brigade. We can worry about the erosion of minor personal freedoms once Britain has been made safe to enjoy them.' 'Minor' rather begs the question.

While a disregard for the rights of terror suspects might be understandable after an attack that killed 52 people, a lot of people are not even that concerned with the rights of ethnic minorities. And 30% thought that 'given the threat to Britain from terrorism' we should be 'less concerned about ensuring the rights of ethnic minorities are protected'. That's nearly one in three people prepared to grant different rights to members of the population on racial grounds. And 37% also wanted to 'stop all asylum into the UK'. Interestingly, among Muslims the figure was almost identical, which should remind us that white English people have no monopoly on being illiberal.

Such illiberalism should not surprise us. The liberal left has always been embarrassed by how much it disagrees with the views of the working men and women it claims to support. As George Orwell wrote, 'It must be remembered that a working man, so long as he remains a genuine working man, is seldom or never a Socialist in the complete, logically consistent sense.' The working man simply (and understandably) wants to defend his interests against those outsiders who threaten him. It is therefore to be expected that the rights of 'us' count more than those of 'them'.

This division into the 'them' whose rights are suspended and the 'us' whose rights are protected is essential to making this line of argument sustainable. In order to sincerely believe that human rights need not be applied to certain sectors of society, you have to be certain that you do not belong to such groups, for no one will argue that their own human rights need not be respected. To do this might seem to require an amazing faith in the police and security forces to identify suspects accurately. In fact, all it requires is that you believe, if mistakes are made, it will not be ordinary, decent, law-abiding white English people like you who will suffer.

And on that score you'd be right – usually. The *Sun*, for instance, was livid that the Islamic philosopher Tariq Ramadan was being allowed into the UK to speak. 'Just five days since 7/7,' it screamed, 'and the flagrant abuse of Britain's freedom-of-speech laws is laid bare yet again.' The trouble is that although Ramadan was denied a visa to the USA from 2004 until the time of writing, I've heard him speak and there is simply no credible way to say that he is an extremist. *Prospect* magazine even hailed him as the man who could reconcile Islam and Europe. But he's a Muslim and foreign. (He's actually from that well-known terrorist safe haven, Switzerland.)

The *Sun*'s own columnist Richard Littlejohn, in contrast, is a white British male, and need have no fear that his right to free speech is likely to be curtailed, even though he is much more of an extremist than Ramadan. After 7/7 Littlejohn wrote a column moaning about how the allegedly politically correct BBC failed to tell things as they really were. To make his point, he imagined how such a PC BBC would have reported during the Second World War. 'The Prime Minister, Winston Churchill, said those responsible were a tiny minority of criminals whose views did not represent the mainstream Nazi community, which is overwhelmingly peace-loving and law-abiding.' He's clearly mocking the (true) line taken that the suicide bombers are a tiny minority of criminals who do not represent the Muslim community, implying is that this is PC nonsense, and the majority of Muslims are no more peace-loving than the majority of Nazis. Whether the implication was careless or intentional, it is still poisonous.

But, of course, Littlejohn's freedom of speech must not be questioned, whereas Ramadan's can and should be taken away from him. Is this gross hypocrisy? Look back at that *Telegraph* poll: what people supported was '*British* people's right to say what they think'. There is no double standard because all people ever wanted to do was defend 'our' freedom, not that of other people. As another poll showed, 52% want to 'limit freedom of speech to prevent the spread of radical Islamist views'. 'Our' rights take priority, not those of others. As Mr Burke of Langley wrote to the *Sun*, complaining of the inability to deport the admittedly nasty Muslim cleric Omar Bakri, 'Send them back to Syria or wherever. We shouldn't worry if they are executed when they return there as they don't worry about what happens to us.'

The politics of the *Sun*- and *Mail*-reading mainstream only appears to be totally incoherent if you assume a traditional liberal framework of universal rights and values which applies to everyone. This is often taken as a given, and anyone who thinks otherwise is condemned as some kind of moral monster. Article 2 of the Universal Declaration of Human Rights, which institutionalized this framework, reads, 'Everyone is entitled to all the rights and freedoms set forth in this Declaration, without distinction of any kind, such as race, colour, sex, language, religion, political or other opinion, national or social origin, property, birth or other status. Furthermore, no distinction shall be made on the basis of the political, jurisdictional or international status of the country or territory to which a person belongs, whether it be independent, trust, non–self-governing or under any other limitation of sovereignty.'

The Declaration is liberalism's tablet of stone, and to question it is unthinkable. Yet the truth is that many English people simply do not accept the fundamental principle of inalienable human rights, or at least if they do, they accept so few of them as genuinely universal they may as well not exist. Proof of this comes in the form of resistance to the Human Rights Act, which did no more than enshrine the European Convention of Human Rights into UK law. The rights upheld by the convention are much like those found in the Universal Declaration of Human Rights. Yet it has been opposed virulently by the voice of the masses, the *Sun* and the *Mail*, as well as by the Conservative Party.

It is too easy to dismiss opposition to the idea of universal, inalienable rights as ill thought through and incoherent. Yet there is an intellectually coherent way of understanding this opposition – the English are not classical liberals, but communitarians.

Communitarianism's most famous slogan was borrowed by New Labour in its early days: 'No rights without responsibilities.' This equation at a stroke contradicts the fundamental premise of the European and UN declarations of rights, in that it makes rights conditional, not absolute: if you don't fulfil your responsibilities, you lose your rights. That sounds very much like some of the *Sun* readers' letters: 'We shouldn't worry if they are executed when they return there as they don't worry about what happens to us', and 'Terrorists who bleat about their human rights upon capture must be ignored.' Sober academic theories find a strong echo in such populist cries of outrage. But while the former are given full respect, the latter are often dismissed as ignorant rants.

Another strong strand in communitarian thinking has been the importance of history and tradition in shaping values. In place of the universal human nature which has formed the core of the post-Enlightenment conception of political morality, communitarianism emphasizes the particularities of time and place that make individuals raised in distinct cultures different. There may well be values which are shared between someone raised in an American Amish community and someone else brought up in Catholic Ireland, but there will also be important differences, differences which make imposing a one-size-fits-all value system on both impossible.

Of course, I am not suggesting that the English philosophy corresponds exactly to the detailed political philosophies of communitarians like the American sociologist and public intellectual Amitai Etzioni. But what I am suggesting is that it is essentially communitarian in character. The rights and liberties held so dear by mainstream England are not abstract rights and liberties that apply to all; rather they are specific to its history and traditions, and they do not apply to those who reject that history and those traditions. To be granted those rights, you must be a full member of the community which grants them. That is a deeply illiberal position, but it is not an unprincipled or incoherent one.

It also helps further explain attitudes towards multiculturalism which I discussed in the last chapter: if values and rules are specific to the culture out of which they arise, then different values can in the short term be no more than tolerated, and only as long as they do not fundamentally conflict. Over time, of course, cultures can absorb and evolve in response to exposure to difference, but this can only happen gradually and organically, or else it becomes a change forced from without and not an evolution from within.

Whether or not liberalism is superior to this kind of communitarianism, unless we recognize the fact that England is not liberal, we will be going against the grain of popular thinking every time we try to implement popular policies that rest on the assumption that it is.

But how does this view fit in with the supposed English virtues of fairness and fair play? Actually, it fits in very well once you understand what fairness in this sense means. A sense of fairness might be thought to imply the requirement that everyone plays by the same rules and no one cheats. And this is indeed what many people will tell you. But as a matter of fact, the English sense of fair play has little time for rules. Indeed, to be too hung up on the rules makes you look a bit too much like the kind of German who won't cross a deserted street until the green man flashes. Sticking to the rules is authoritarian nonsense; playing fair is something else.

One small incident illustrated the aspect of life in which our relative disregard for the rules is most prevalent. Towards the second half of my stay I appeared on *Richard and Judy*. Until then, I had only popped up in the likes of the *Guardian* or on Radio 4, so my somewhat slender 'national media profile' went unnoticed. When you're in a demographically typical area, it's not being on Radio 4 with Melvyn Bragg which gets you noticed, it's chatting on the couch with Madeley and Finnigan.

People's first question was generally a rather baffled, 'How did you get on that then?' But it didn't take long before the question turned to whether I got paid to appear and if so, how much. The one respect in which Yorkshire folk are totally different from the rest of the country is in their bluntness about matters of money. What was most interesting was not how much I got, however, but how I got it: I was handed a brown envelope stuffed with used banknotes. To which everyone replied, 'You won't have to declare it then.'

Yes, the land of people who play by the rules is also the land of people who will never pay the authorities any more than they are forced to, whatever the rules say. I came across this time and time again, and it cuts across all social classes and even political convictions. I know middle-class left-wing professionals who are officially disappointed that New Labour isn't really socialist, yet they still open tax-free ISAs and the like in their children's names in order to avoid giving money to the Exchequer. The accountant for *The Philosophers' Magazine*, which we run as a partnership, was frankly baffled when we told her that we just weren't interested in setting up our corporate structure in such a way as to make us pay less tax: such a thing was unheard of. In S66, they would also think you were mad if you paid taxes you weren't forced to. Lifelong Labour voter Pete, for example, had taken early retirement and said, 'I wouldn't even consider taking a job now unless it were cash in hand. I've paid more than my fair share of tax in my time. More than my fair share.'

Like many aspects of English behaviour, what at first sight looks like blatant hypocrisy turns out on closer examination to be something far subtler. Playing fair does not mean playing by the rules, it means each person getting their due. And once you accept that, the door opens to all sorts of plausible self-serving justifications that can convince you cheating is the best way to achieve this. Avoiding taxes is easily justified if you believe that, as a decent hard-working person, you have already paid your fair whack and that it's the spongers at one end and the rich at the other who are freeloading off the common man. What's more, you wouldn't be entirely wrong. Many people do cheat the system as a matter of routine, so if you stick entirely to the rules all the time, you're being a mug. And that's not fair.

The trouble is that this justification is just too flexible. I know of one person who borrowed a relative's disabled person's railcard, on the grounds that they were unemployed so couldn't actually afford the absurdly high fares. It sounds fair from the point of view of the fare dodger, but it would clearly not be an equitable system if we all unilaterally adopted the policy of simply paying what we thought we could afford.

Perhaps the most convincing piece of evidence that we almost all cheat if we can came when I changed trains at Doncaster once for the branch line to Rotherham. Usually there is a guard on this train who will take your fare, but on this occasion, by the time I alighted, no one had come around. Furthermore, there is no ticket barrier at Rotherham, so I could easily have just walked out. Instead, I went to the ticket office and explained that I hadn't been able to pay my fare and would now like to. Unless you're very unusual, your reaction reading this will be the same as the ticket clerk's: blank incomprehension. I don't think he had ever come across this situation before, and he simply told me to go away and not worry about it, as though I was mad to suggest doing otherwise.

However, it would be wrong to think that the English are fundamentally dishonest. It's just that their first reaction when the chance to cheat comes up is: do it. Evolutionary psychologists would suggest this is a universal human trait, since the most successful survival strategy is one on which we cooperate most of the time but cheat when there is very little chance of getting caught. That's why fair cooperation is actually the norm, and while we are quick to see chances to cheat, we don't always take them up.

There was a clear example of this at the pub quiz one night. The Travellers' quiz was a somewhat half-hearted affair. In most pub quizzes, there would be a quizmaster reading out the questions over a PA system, while the teams filled in their answers. There would be musical and picture rounds, and at half-time the pub would offer free sandwiches, or pizza slices in trendier city venues. It was all rather more low key at The Travellers. You'd pick up a question sheet at the bar, fill the latter in, and then you'd be given the answers.

But one night when I asked for the questions I was given the answer sheet instead. I didn't realize until I got back to our table, and without hesitation, Neil, Pete and Andy all told me to keep quiet and write the answers in. I obviously looked a little shocked, because Andy said calmly, 'Thy're in Yorkshire now', as if to say

'Welcome to the real world'. I asked if they were serious and they didn't find it difficult to find rational justifications for cheating: 'It's their mistake,' said Pete, 'we've done nowt wrong. *Nowt.*' I felt as if I was back at school cheating in a maths test.

However, as time passed, people slowly changed their minds. Their initial instinct may have been to take advantage, but they soon realized that, actually, this would offend against the norms of fair play. Not because it broke the rules – who cares about them? – but because it would be unfair on the other teams. I think they knew that many of the other teams would have owned up. Had they thought otherwise, then I don't think they would have had any qualms about keeping the secret. Not cheating if others are at it is not honourable, it's daft. I'm not sure what they would have done if it had happened in a pub full of strangers.

By the time the consensus had settled against not cheating, it was too late to take part honestly anyway. So we decided to have some fun and see how far we could go without being caught. When the quizmaster came round – an affable bloke who never failed to greet me with his best Dick Van Dyke cockney voice – we told him that Andy's visiting friend was a trivia genius and so we were bound to win. This made the friend extremely uncomfortable, as he actually thought we were going to go through with it. To make it easier to spot our devious ways, we didn't throw in a few wrong answers and we gave away a clue in our team name. But despite scoring an unprecedented 30/30, the quizmaster still announced that the 'Cheating Bastards' had won. I broke the bad news to him and said, 'Remember this next time you take the piss out of Londoners', to which he replied, 'You're a tosser for telling me!' (I'm not a Londoner anyway, but it's all the same south of Nottingham, isn't it?)

A sense of fair play, therefore, is not about following rules, which is why it is compatible with rejecting the liberal assumption that treating everyone the same is a fundamental human duty.

Being fair is giving and getting what is due, and your responsibilities and entitlements are defined not by your membership of the species but by your place in society. If that sounds conservative, that's because it is. Orwell got it right: progressive socialism is alien to the working-class culture which still forms the bedrock of the English mind. The attraction of the left is simply that it promises to give working people a fair share of what they feel they are entitled to, not that it might distribute wealth equally to all, irrespective of how hard they work.

If the English political sense is indeed conservative and communitarian, is that a good thing? So far I have only argued that it is coherent and understandable, not that it is right. And there are indeed many reasons for thinking that it must not go unchallenged. The combination of conservatism and communitarianism can create a stifling conformity that creates an exaggerated sense of 'them' and 'us' and which also leads to the marginalization of anyone who does not sign up to mainstream norms. Homosexuals know full well what the implications of this are, which is precisely why so many move to cities, where life is different from the rest of England.

It's easy to think that homophobia is a thing of the past, like racism. But both assumptions are demonstrably false. Things have certainly got better, but true equality is still elusive, Britain didn't get an openly gay member of parliament until Chris Smith in 1984, and it is still common for gay politicians to hide their sexuality. Nor can you blame them. A BBC poll showed that 39% disapprove of homosexuals in high office, and only 48% approve. There is clearly a religious factor here: 44% of religious people disapproved compared to 26% of those with no religion. But either way, that is a very large number of people for a supposedly tolerant society. I find it hard to imagine what it is about being gay people think is incompatible with high office. Perhaps it is no more than a vague sense that such people are 'dirty': at Station

News near the Rotherham Interchange, the *Gay Times* is on the same shelf as the pornography.

Although expressing hatred towards homosexuals is now taboo in the mainstream media, there is very little positive representation of gay life, which is often dismissed as something a bit, well, queer. Sometimes this plays out fine, and the laugh is shared. In the first *News of the World* I bought, the letter of the week in its Sunday magazine was from a man who went to a car dealer and was eyeing up an open-top VW Beetle. The dealer said, 'Only women and gays buy them.' The punchline was that the male letter writer was with his boyfriend.

But more often it's a case of laughing at rather than with. When *Star Trek*'s Mr Sulu – George Takei – came out as gay, the *Sun* came up with the headline BEAM ME UP, BOTTY. The same hilarious punsters must have been responsible for another headline after it emerged that the first gay couple to win the National Lottery jackpot had stroked a 'lucky duck'. 'OOOOH DUCKIE, WE GOT LUCKY,' it laughed. The assumption is still that being gay is not quite right. When *Big Brother*'s Anthony was 'suspected' of being gay, the *News of the World* reported that his mates 'have rallied round him and claim he has bedded a string of girls', suggesting that being thought of as homosexual is some kind of slur.

The trouble with conservative communitarianism is that it narrows people's focus too much. This finally hit me when I realized what it was that really bothered me about Neil's apoplectic rants. It was on a day when he was in the mood to make Richard Littlejohn look like Mahatma Gandhi. First he was complaining that the only policeman he had seen in his area over the last six months was catching speeding cars. What's more, Sheffield traffic wardens had been arriving en masse to slap tickets on loads of cars for parking where people have always parked on match days. There was too much emphasis on collecting fines and not enough on catching the real criminals. He went on to describe a recent local authority job interview where they were too concerned with making sure he could parrot their diversity agenda back to them and not enough on whether he'd do a good job. Finally, he complained that public services have the kind of inefficiency that would never pass muster in the private sector. I'm paraphrasing, of course: the rant lasted the whole drive from Bramley to the ice hockey.

On every specific point, he was almost certainly right. So why did I get fed up hearing it? Because I did not see why he should be worrying about all of this when there are far more serious political problems to sort out. He's right about the facts, it's just that his priorities strike me as wrong. It's not so much a case of whether you see the glass as half full or half empty, it's whether you're more concerned you've only got half a bottle of champagne when others have only got half a glass of lukewarm water. Perhaps the police do spend too much time nabbing people who speed, although since speeding is a major cause of road accidents, I'm not convinced they do. But they also do other things Neil wants them to do, like respond to armed robberies, as the policewoman shot dead in Bradford the very same night as our conversation did. Perhaps local authorities do get obsessed with ticking boxes to show they are fulfilling their equality agenda, but if that's an unintended consequence of all the good work that is being done to help counter prejudice and get disabled people back to work, I don't mind that much.

The world is imperfect and politics is partly a question of what you prioritize and focus on. Left-liberals prefer to worry about such imperfections as inequality, lack of opportunity, global justice, the damage to the environment, the causes of drug use and crime as well as those activities themselves. These are 'them' issues, not 'me' ones. Liberalism aspires to a universal vision in which things like rights do belong to all precisely because it sees our common humanity as being more important than our national, class or gender differences. The conservative communitarianism of the English, reflected in the *Mail* and the *Sun*, is not the naked self-interest of 'me, me, me', but it is the parochial wider self-interest of 'we, we, we'. Historically, the left has been as willing to play up to this as the right. Trade Unions, for instance, thrived when workers felt that they belonged to a real 'we' of brothers and sisters whose interests needed to be protected against those of the management 'them'.

I would prefer liberalism's universalism to conservative communitarianism's parochialism. But in order to further a liberal agenda successfully, you have to recognize that you are going against the instincts of the majority. And you also need to realize that these illiberal impulses are natural human responses. The people who worry most about the disadvantaged are usually either among them or very far removed from them. For the majority in between, you just want to make sure your life doesn't slide backwards to their level. This is why the *Daily Mail* feeds on fear. It speaks to a class that has a comfortable life but is close enough to the high tide of what threatens it to feel a little frightened. Areas of crime are close enough to you. Some of these delinquents even go to your kids' schools. The drunken youths and discarded needles at Flash Lane recreation ground, in the heart of comfortable Bramley, bear testament to that. It's not that the English lack compassion, it's simply that they are too busy watching their own backs to rush out and rescue others. As Reg put it, talking about the Live 8 concerts to 'make poverty history', 'Don't get me wrong,' he said severely, 'I hate to see anyone starving. But charity begins at home.'

If this thesis is right, then the literary, academic and professional left in England is out of tune with its traditional working-class allies. It can frame its own self-image in terms of concern for the interests of others because its own status is not under threat. This security is often in part financial, because left-wing lecturers, lawyers and the like rarely have to live on anything close to the national median annual income of around £23,000. But the security is more fundamentally cultural. Although recently commentators like David Goodhart have called for liberal nationalism, the professional and intellectual left does not generally define itself in local or national terms. Their way of life is not under threat because it is already removed from the mainstream culture. That's why the intellectual left has traditionally been baffled by patriotism and was late to see any problem with multiculturalism, other than simple prejudice. Its members see themselves as citizens of the world, above parochial concerns. When your values and way of life are not firmly rooted in the culture of your own country, they cannot easily be threatened if that culture changes. Only when they thought that liberalism itself might be under threat did some become worried.

Whether I've got this sector of the left correct I am not sure. But I am far more certain that the conception of the English political philosophy as conservative communitarianism is broadly accurate, and that to see that is not necessarily to endorse it. What I do think, however, is that it has to be respected as a position which speaks to people's instinctive needs and desires and which can be defended in an intellectually coherent way. Progressive politics can never succeed if it doesn't engage with the dominant political philosophy implied by the way the mainstream English mind works.

There is, however, clearly a conflict between what seems to be the relatively narrow outlook represented by the traditional English philosophy and a more open way of thinking. This alternative outlook is exemplified in more welcoming attitudes to multiculturalism, encouraged by the increases in opportunity which education and social mobility have provided, and advocated by the more liberal alternative to conservative communitarianism.

Is it possible to simply describe these as two alternatives, or is one better than the other? It's obvious where my own sympathies lie, but the case for the defence of the English philosophy has not yet been fully made.

4

The Good Life

Beer

A few days after I moved to Bramley, the Live 8 concert climaxed with the re-formed Pink Floyd performing 'Comfortably Numb'. At that point I thought the song might be able to give my book its title. My early perceptions were that the average English person's life was one of neither high excitement nor grinding misery. People were comfortable and didn't seem to aspire to much more. And who could blame them? Most human beings who have ever lived have had to struggle merely to survive, while those who are materially secure still have trouble warding off depression, stress, relationship breakdown and family strife. Given how tough life can be, preserving modest contentment is something of an achievement.

Everywhere I looked I saw signs of people who had no interest in broadening their horizons and who even failed to take advantage of things that were right under their noses. On a stroll during the town's walking festival, the organizer told me about the problem of making local people appreciate what they have on their doorsteps. All the locals that I spoke to on our short, central four-mile stroll discovered parts of the city they never knew existed, even though most had lived in Rotherham for years, sometimes all their lives. And these were the few adventurous enough to go on this walk in the first place. At home we fall into routine, comfort, and cease to be curious.

Over time, however, I came to see that this wholly negative diagnosis missed something. Almost all lives look bland from a distance, and it's only in close-up that you get to see their richness and distinctness. People do like to live comfortably, but they are not numb.

Everyone wants to live what they would see as a good life. Philosophers have had plenty to say about what this comprises, but their answers have tended to reveal an unsurprising bias. As people who value thought and contemplation, they have tended to come up with the idea that the good life is one of thought and contemplation. For some reason this answer has been granted a great deal of respect, even though it looks as objective as a panel of butchers telling us we should eat more meat. What do the English think the good life is? Some attitudes are expressed more clearly by actions than words. We cannot always live how we'd like to live, but we still have choices as to how we organize and prioritize our lives, and it is in these choices that we reveal our values.

Consider, for example, two people I knew who had enough money to buy a house more or less anywhere. Where they chose to live really was a matter of choice, and both chose to stay in Maltby, close to where their friends and family were. In so doing they chose just as positive psychologists say they should, since social networks are one of the main determinants of happiness. That's one reason why if happiness is your priority, expanding horizons is usually the least of your concerns. What I first saw as comfortable numbness was something far more rational, and it is deeply embedded in the English philosophy. Both Trevor at the truck stop and Reg from The Travellers told me that they wouldn't move away even if they won the lottery. Happiness for most of us cannot be bought by accumulating wealth or experiences, but is to be found by finding your niche in society and staying in it.

It sounds so unambitious (that great modern sin), but those like me whose instinct is to tell people to get out more, see more of the world, are often lecturing people who are far more content than ourselves. The restless desire for the new can become a hunger that cannot be satiated. As soon as a new experience is done, you're back to square one, in need of the next fix of novelty. Such a life is certainly tiring. I even found six months of heightened awareness in Rotherham exhausting. A couple who had retired to Benidorm complained of the life of barbecues, parties and tennis there: 'It's hard work, this enjoying yourself.' Building a new life in the sun is certainly more of an effort than settling into your old one in the grey. Is it any wonder that most people find a few things they like and do them again and again? If it's happiness we want then being satisfied with the familiar is a distinct advantage.

We have come back again to the narrowness of the English philosophy, which is perhaps best illustrated by the value that seems to drive the majority of what we do: convenience. Quality, value, distinctiveness, originality, enjoyability and virtually every other positive attribute you'd care to name are all frequently trumped by convenience. This was evident before I even arrived in S66, when I stopped off at the Tamworth services on the M42. In many ways, the much derided motorway service stations have come on a lot since the old days. This one is a clean and smart tribute to plastic, like a small airport departure lounge. Moto even won a Loo of the Year award. But everything was absurdly overpriced and the food was mediocre at best. Still, there was a swift trade in all-day breakfasts, doughy pizzas and huge bags of sweets. On every table you read about their quality assurances and 'no quibble money back guarantees', yet I've never seen anyone say 'No way was that sandwich worth £3.95. I want my money back – no quibbling!' People put up with the low quality and high prices because it's easy and *it will do*.

The service station is a good example, because it serves our needs as drivers, and our love affair with the car shows just how much we're prepared to pay for convenience. In 2006 it costs an average of £5,539 a year to keep a new car on the road – a quarter of household expenditure – compared to the average mortgage repayment of £5,112.

Given cars often take more of our cash than homes, it should not be surprising that we let our motors drive our house-buying decisions. The house I'd rented on Flash Lane was proving hard to sell, and I thought the reasons were obvious. First, it was advertised as three-bedroomed when the third room would hardly accommodate a dachshund. Second, it was on the junction of two main roads, so if you opened your windows you got endless traffic noise. But I was wrong. Everyone I spoke to – the owner, the estate agent, the neighbours – all thought the biggest stumbling block was a lack of off-street parking. Even the neighbours, who were also selling and had a garage, thought the fact their driveway was shared with mine would put people off. So it was that, soon after I'd sorted the front garden out, making an attractive display of flowers, grass and ornamental bushes, a team of builders arrived to flatten and pave it. One of the workmen pointed out that many people were moving to low-maintenance gardens, but this was a little extreme. His boss was more brutal: 'Let's be honest: it may look pretty with a garden, but how much time do you actually spend enjoying it?' For a country seemingly obsessed by garden makeovers, we actually have very little time to spend in them.

But he had missed the point. When Pete and Johnny had lamented the decline in well-maintained front gardens they weren't concerned that people weren't using them. Such gardens are a contribution to the collective well-being. If all the front gardens in your street look nice, you feel more content in your environment. No one garden brings significant pleasure, but if everyone does their bit, a street of them benefits everyone. The rise of individualism and the decline of community may have been exaggerated, but it has gone far enough for us to care less about what the neighbours think. While that's good in that it liberates us from the oppression of peer disapproval, caring is a two-way business, and when we all worry less about how those around us feel, we stop doing things that contribute to the general welfare of the area.

My home 'improvement' was therefore a social trend in miniature. We see less of our neighbours partly because when we go out we are less likely to see them, since instead of walking through our front gardens and down the street we go straight from our front doors to our private off-road parking and just drive off. And cars don't just weaken our attachments to where we live, they are also killing the town centres. Like many local authorities, Rotherham had adopted the apparently sensible policy of trying to reduce car use and congestion by encouraging people to use public transport to come into its very pleasant town centre. Rotherham Minster (formerly All Saints' Church), which dominates the main square, was described by the architectural historian Nikolaus Pevsner as 'the best perpendicular church in the country'. Although it is largely of 15th-century construction, parts of the building date back to Saxon and Norman times. The old town hall is now a small arcade of considerable charm and character, though it lacks the quantity and quality of shops to show itself off in its best light. The Imperial Arcade, on the hill on the way to the new town hall, is similarly blessed and cursed.

The town has plenty going for it, yet it is struggling, mainly because of the huge Meadowhall Shopping Mall in Sheffield and the Parkgate Retail Park, just outside the town centre. Parkgate is like a supersized high street, only instead of a road there's a huge car park in the middle which takes several minutes to walk across. The shops are sheds and there is no attempt to pretend it's anything other than functional. Malls at least have food courts and cafés. Here, there is a café in the Morrisons supermarket. People complain about the death of town centres but they wouldn't be dying out if people didn't prefer places like this. Why? Convenience. It's easy to get here, park, shop and sod off again.

Any attraction the town centre might have has been nullified by the policy of discouraging people from driving into town. If you make it hard for people with cars to drive somewhere, they don't take the bus, they drive somewhere else where parking is plentiful and free. Those without cars simply have to put up with a town centre deprived of the better stores that attract the affluent, leaving them with pound and charity shops that are not going to tempt the crowds back. Hence a policy meant to promote the environmental virtues of reducing car usage actually encourages people to use their cars even more, and leaves those who rely on the bus worse off. How many councils, however, are going to adopt policies that are seen to encourage people to drive into town centres?

I was in a privileged position to observe the effect of the car on our behaviour, because up till a few weeks before I went to S66, I didn't even have a licence. However, I knew enough about typical English town life to know that in somewhere like Rotherham, I'd be very limited without one. Although I passed my test, a tick on one of the medical questions held up the licence being approved, so that for the first two months I relied on public transport. When I finally got my wheels in September, I could see the difference it would make to my quality of life.

Even buying a car was itself a reminder of how much you are out of the mainstream if you rely on public transport, since it took about an hour on buses and walking to get to the dealer. I knew nothing about cars and didn't want to spend much time or money choosing one. After checking out a few adverts and websites, I went with my sister to a garage at Darnall, Sheffield, which had a promising stock list. (Later in the pub they laughed when I told them where I had gone, asking if it had been stolen.)

The garage's online stocklist turned out to be a fiction, so I ended up with a shortlist of three, shortened to two when one car's door wouldn't open. Oddly undeterred, I test-drove an M-reg Vauxhall Corsa with 113,000 miles on the clock, going for £500. 'I've never sold a Corsa for less than a thousand,' the dealer told me, 'you'll never see a Corsa under a grand.' Either he was a very bad salesman or being told something is too good to be true does not generally have the effect of leading people to conclude it is therefore not true.

On my test drive, I was so pleased to get it up the road and back without crashing that I failed to notice that I hadn't got it above third gear, tested the lights or made any number of elementary checks. The engine purred, the clutch was smooth, and it was £500. What more was there to say? Even the dealer advised against trying out a more expensive VW Passat estate turbo diesel, since as a new driver I'd be better off with the small car. I took that as a good sign that he was not just trying to take as much money off me as possible. The deal was done. A new era had dawned. Would I become a believer in the principle of four wheels good, two legs bad?

The short answer, in case the suspense is killing you, is no. Still, I surprised myself by how much I enjoyed the feeling of independence it gave me. I found myself wanting to just take off somewhere, anywhere, like Butch Cassidy and the Sundance Kid, only without being butch or having the Kid in tow. Not that the renegade cowboy theme would be pulled off very effectively in a ten-year-old, three-door, 1.2 litre, burgundy Vauxhall.

The car was certainly liberating and though we complain about its pernicious effects, in towns where little of interest is within walking distance, it certainly improves your quality of life. For example, I went to the Rother Valley Country Park, 300 acres of lake and countryside with 11 miles of trails. I wondered why I hadn't been before, but the reason was obvious: without a car it was virtually impossible. In much the same way, the car enabled me to go walking with the Dearne Valley Ramblers. I had tried a few times before, but the few starting points accessible by bus and train took hours to reach and lifts weren't always available. This is another paradox of car ownership: access to countryside and nature is made much easier by having a polluting hulk of machinery. People without cars are not closer to nature; they're stuck in the towns. It's not as though they ride horses instead.

Exercise also became easier. I had been swimming at Maltby baths, but it was too far to walk and time-consuming by bus. With the car, the exercise routine fitted much more easily into my day. Just as long as I didn't use it when I would normally walk – which I didn't – having it would even make me fitter. Mind you, it also made it easier to pop to the truck stop afterwards for a hearty cooked breakfast.

But I paid for all these benefits. There was a chip in the windscreen, I got a flat tyre and found none of the other three were legal, the brakes stuck when left parked and so on and on. There was a community dividend that reduced the costs. The neighbourhood mechanic, Kenny, is the salt of the earth and wouldn't dream of charging you any more than strictly necessary. Once he replaced a back light with one he had lying around and just told me to get him a drink one day. On another occasion, a pub conference correctly diagnosed the cause of some stalling as a dodgy distributor cap. But even with Kenny and friends in the know, costs add up. Over the four months I had the car in S66, I spent nearly £2,000 on it, albeit some of that covered tax and insurance for the rest of the year. It sounds a lot but studies suggest that, if anything, I got my driving on the cheap. Still, I hadn't ever spent that much on anything that doesn't have walls and drains in my life.

But is not having a car a realistic option in a country that is now effectively built around it? Down The Travellers, everyone agrees that cars are a terrible expense, but no one can imagine life without one. You can be a proper adult without marrying or having kids, but not without a motor. That's why it takes me months to find out that when Pete talked about 'his car' he was not talking about one he drives. He hasn't got a licence, his wife has. It's not something he lies about, but he does tend to gloss over this embarrassing fact.

Now that I had a car, however, I too could enjoy convenient England, and what could be more convenient than an out-of-town mall? Shopping is now a major leisure activity and places like Meadowhall are leisure destinations in their own right, suitable places to spend a day out. The *Mail* reported that on average we make 61 trips to shopping centres every year, spending around £2,000 and the equivalent of seven days in them.

I had already been on a bus that leaves once an hour and takes 25 minutes on a good day. How much easier it would be in a car that leaves when I want to and takes less than 15 minutes. If I felt as though I needed to save even more time, after I pulled up and parked, I could have taken advantage of Café Express's £3.99 'grab and go' offer of a sandwich, a bottle of pop, a chocolate bar and a packet of crisps. (As far as I'm concerned, a country that sees being able to grab and go as being an advantage has serious quality-of-life issues.)

I headed to Next (which instantly reveals something about my demographic profile, showing attempts at genuine individuality are futile). A sale rummage exhausted me, so I went for a cup of tea and a sit-down in what is perhaps ironically called the Oasis food court. Dominated by a huge video screen which alternates promotional plugs for stores and music videos, it's possibly the least calm place for a drink in Yorkshire.

After a browse around the small book stores, I went to the cinema to catch up on the latest blockbuster and saw another example of how people are prepared to pay over the odds for something because it's where they want it. I'm not talking about the ticket prices, but those of the 'concessions'. A regular soft drink was £2.30 and huge. Regular nachos – a measly bunch of them with gooey, synthetic-tasting toppings, was £3.20, as was a hot dog. A regular soft drink and regular popcorn 'deal' was

£5.65. Cinemas now actually make more money from the stuff they sell you than they do from tickets.

After that, I did a bit more shopping and then took another break. I went to M&S's Café Revive. I ordered a jacket potato, with the tuna and sweetcorn mix and butter portions served on the side in sealed containers. They were so keen to reassure me there was nothing scary about the meal that they made me put it together myself. It was a horrible place. The noise, the clatter of pots and cups, the rows of screwed-down, plastic tables. Just as the Oasis was nothing of the sort, so this was no place to revive. Others seemed to disagree: it was heaving. After all, it's convenient and you know what you're getting.

As I walked around the mall there was one section where the ceiling panels were off and all the pipes, vents and wires were exposed. It was too neat a symbol, perhaps, that the attractiveness of this place is all veneer. Peer beneath and it's a seething, ugly mess. The white pillars and fountains evoke antiquity, but it's all panelling and plastic.

By the time I got home I'd been away for seven hours. I'd bought a load of sale clothes, the new phone for downstairs I 'needed', seen a diverting film and fed myself. Is that or is that not a grand day out? Well, not really. Except for the duration of the film, I wasn't really enjoying myself at any time. But if people didn't like it, they wouldn't go, would they? I'm not sure: survey after survey shows that people find shopping stressful. They may enjoy their purchases once they've got them, but in this case the chase is definitely not better than the catch.

But what exactly is it people are chasing? 'Nice things' is the simple answer, but it's not the only one. I got one clue when I went to Meadowhall on a bus and eavesdropped on a conversation between two women, one of whom was talking about a recent trip to Harvey Nichols. 'I thought I'd only be able to afford a card,' she said, 'but I saw a Dolce & Gabbana T-shirt, for £39, and

I thought, if it's good enough for the Beckhams' kids, it's good enough for my daughter's. I told the girl at the cash desk that it was for my young granddaughter and she wrapped it up all lovely in Harvey Nicks paper and popped it in a Harvey Nicks bag.'

To have something wrapped in Harvey Nichols paper doesn't tell me the present is great, it tells me you couldn't be bothered to choose paper and wrap it yourself, and that you're daft enough to pay over the odds for a logo. But then I'm a philosopher, not an anthropologist, and what the woman's story would tell them is that she is just like people the world over, from remote South Pacific islands to sterile South Yorkshire malls: she is interested in status. And in the West, money may not be able to buy you love, but it can often buy you status, or a pretty good proxy for it. A £39 child's T-shirt is absurd, but a £39 D&G T-shirt, from Harvey Nicks, sends out all the right social signals: we're as good as the Beckhams.

Some individuals manage to avoid the status trap, but among all social groups, it is a concern of the majority. Status is not always about money. For the upper classes, buying anything is a bit vulgar, as Alan Clark demonstrated when he talked about Michael Heseltine as the kind of person who 'bought his own furniture' (rather than inheriting it). Status is really about showing to the world signs and markers that you are the kind of person you think your peers will look up to, or at least not down on. At certain dinner parties, for example, you will be reassured that something is 'organic' or, even better, from the local farmers' market. Officially this is because it's better for you and the world, but it's also a way of showing you're not the kind of unhealthy, environmentally unsound ignoramus who believes that there is no connection at all between dying of horrible diseases very young and shopping at Tesco's. Of course, if you are one such person you would deny this, but it is of the nature of status symbols that people are rarely aware of their motivations for acquiring them. No man buys a sports car thinking of it as a penis substitute.

Central to the idea of status is that of hierarchies, and these are found everywhere you go. In S66, for example, Maltby was definitely at the bottom of the scale, though there were grades of difference within the village, too. Interestingly, some of the people who were most blunt about this lived in Maltby themselves. 'People in Rotherham tend to consider Maltby a bit downmarket,' said the landlady of Maltby's only b. & b. The waiter at Maltby 's only restaurant described the area as 'below average'. Sometimes this amounts to the charming English habit of self-deprecation. Waiting to get on a train at Rotherham from which many people were alighting, one girl said, 'A lot of people want to come to Rotherham. I don't know why,' to which her friend quipped, 'Charity shops!'

In Bramley, if ever there was trouble in the pub, it would be attributed to Maltby boys. The local hairdresser also said that Friday night was 'Chav Night' as a group of 'boy racers' from Dinnington another down-at-heel area – raced each other there to get their hair sorted for the weekend. The irony was that to many readers of the *Mail* and *The Times*, she would have matched their idea of a chav herself. The social strata of England are layered and nested very deeply.

There are even hierarchies within the fishing fraternity. Peter and Andy once complained about how, when they were fishing in North Yorkshire, the snobs there looked down on them for maggot fishing, not fly fishing. I'm reminded of Freud's observation that 'Intolerance of groups is often, strangely enough, exhibited more strongly against small differences than fundamental ones.'

Of course, it would be great if we could all free ourselves from concern with such things as status and just do what we like. Nor should we be deterred from trying by the fatalistic observation that everyone is concerned with status at some level. That may be true, but surely it is better to be less concerned than more concerned. But although status may be insignificant to classical philosophers, it remains important to the English folk philosophy. Hierarchies matter to us. The interesting question is how the English think you rise up to them. The short answer is any way you can. But since things like fame, exceptional talent and achievement are by definition in limited supply, in practice people seek to buy status. That's what makes those stressful shopping trips worthwhile.

The trouble is that society is now generally quite affluent, so the acquisition of things to get status has become an inflationary and futile pursuit. Instead of using increases in earnings or a windfall to buy us freedom, we tend to simply increase our spending, always living at or beyond our financial limits, buying ever bigger houses and filling them with more expensive things. People will do this even if it makes their lives worse. One couple lived in a listed cottage, yet the building required so much maintenance, and they filled it with so much stuff that also needed looking after, that it seemed more of a burden than a bonus. Instead of enjoying their comfortable retirement, they ended up fretting about all that they needed to do to maintain their dream home. I stayed there once and even the bedding illustrated how acquiring more and more things makes life unnecessarily complicated. Instead of a simple sheet and duvet combo, there was a valance, a two-part fitted sheet, a sheet, a duvet with a cover and a cover sheet that went on top of that.

The concern for status is a trap that we fall into, partly because we are being led there so eagerly by advertisers and the media. Newspapers have now become more about lifestyle than news: even if you ignore their adverts, they are constantly selling us visions of how we ought to look, what we ought to eat and drink, where we should go on our holidays, how we should get there, what car we should or shouldn't drive. Yet it would be too pessimistic to think that the status spell is so strong that people are just 'shopaholic robots', as the Oxford Street evangelist Philip 'winner not a sinner' Howard shouts at them as they pass. Shopping for status for most is more of a defensive measure, to ensure their faces still fit in the circles where they want them to fit. But as long as the defences are in place, people have their more personal sense of what matters to them.

All over Rotherham I came across people who pursued their own special interests, which we might even call passions, if that word didn't seem too red-blooded for the English. Peter Thornton-Smith organizes a series of folk concerts at the Blessed Trinity Church Hall in Wickersley. Nationally known acts play, supported by local talent. When I went it was full to capacity, albeit of only 50, and in the breaks you could buy tea, soft drinks, and little home-made cakes for 20p. Similarly, the Rotherham-based Classic Rock Society organizes concerts by world-famous bands, as well as a few lesser known ones. I saw the Dutch prog rockers Focus at the Oakwood Centre, which actually turned out to be a school hall. At the start, the atmosphere was like a school disco. Students' art and project work was hung on the corridor walls, while in the main hall chairs were stacked along the sides while people loitered around the room's edges. But the band – famous for the yodelling on their big hit 'Hocus Pocus' – were brilliant, and were received with real warmth which seemed to be reciprocated.

Go around the town and you'll come across all sorts of small-interest groups. On a walk, I came across a club of metal detectors who had just uncovered a Roman coin. The Stag has a very active angling club, which is the country's top participation sport. At Maltby library, and in others in the borough, there is a monthly reading circle. In the basement of Rotherham's only bookshop, there was an exhibition one weekend by the Friends of the Masbrough Chapel and Walker Mausoleum. The Walkers were a steel family whose cannons furnished HMS *Victory* at Trafalgar. One now stands outside Rotherham Town Hall.

There are many other such individuals and groups doing their own thing in towns and villages all over England. You could use the demeaning word 'hobbies' to describe them, but you should only do so if you're prepared to say the same of going to the theatre, reading or entertaining friends with recipes from your River Café cookbooks. Sometimes, admittedly, people's passions are somewhat odd. Arriving at the Hallam FM arena to buy some ice hockey tickets, I stumbled across 'Camp Cliff'. A group of a dozen or so women had been queuing for a week or more to get the best tickets for Cliff Richard's concert the following year. This sounds less crazy once you realize that a week camping with fellow enthusiasts is part of the fun. OK, maybe it doesn't, but is listening to a pensioner sing about how he's looking for a green light objectively any sillier than watching a bunch of men slam a vulcanized rubber disc around an arena of ice with big sticks?

All these little sub-worlds exist almost invisibly, which is one reason why on the surface suburban life looks dull. In contrast, the cultural life of the cities is highly visible. But I've lost count of the number of people who live in London and say that it's great to have all this theatre and so on, but they never go. In the cities many people have the sense that things are happening, and so they enjoy the buzz vicariously. But all the time they work long hours, spend hours commuting and most evenings flake out recovering; are their lives any more intellectually or culturally rich and varied as the town folk with their quiet passions? Pete plays golf, grows his own vegetables and goes to the ice hockey with Neil, who in turn goes fishing with Andy, who goes to rock 'n' roll weekends at Skegness with his wife. Even Johnny, who is not very mobile, keeps his mind occupied reading and watching natural history documentaries.

Even the highest achievers can end up wanting the simplest of things. One of Rotherham's most famous sons, the former England number one goalkeeper David Seaman, returned to the town to help launch something called Rotherham Renaissance, an ambitious £2 billion, 25-year plan to revive the city. It did have the small flaw that its central development was to be on land the council didn't own and Tesco's wasn't selling, but let's not put a downer on ambition. Taking the stage in All Saints' Square, the chirpy DJ from the Hallam FM breakfast show asked an obscenely tanned David how he was spending his retirement. 'Doing the school run, the shopping, going on holiday, the normal things,' he said. 'Catching more fish than my dad, improving my golf handicap.' Had Seaman become rich, famous and successful simply to do just what everyone else does, but in a bigger house, in more exotic locations and with a deeper tan? Yes, and why not? If we believed the things that make up a good life were only available to the likes of Seaman, most of us may as well go out and shoot ourselves now. Life had better be about the little things, or else we're doomed. That's why we should not dismiss the one big change Seaman noticed about Rotherham since he was a boy: he caught a barbel fishing in the River Don the day before, which you could never have done twenty years ago when it was filthy. Forget the grand march of history: that's real progress.

Looking at how people choose to live and thus how they conceive of the good life made me more willing to accept that what I perceived as the narrowness of the English imagination was not incompatible with living a good life, and that having wider horizons does not necessarily make it better. Rather, there are at least two ways to live, but they are incompatible and the benefits they confer are incommensurable.

The mainstream English vision of the good life is one of comfort, convenience and familiarity. It sounds dull, but it's what enables people to live close to friends and family and do what interests them without life becoming a restless striving for the new and exciting. Of course, variation is required, but in moderation: the something 'a little different' of the jazz club.

The alternative is a life of change, constant development and discovery. That makes it sound more exciting, but you could also call it a life of discomfort, inconvenience and unfamiliarity. It may add spice but it also deprives people of roots and strong social networks, the very things that are actually most likely to make us happy.

Although I would maintain the former way of life is the dominant one, many people believe themselves to be living the second kind. Why this is so is something I didn't come to understand until I followed the English abroad (Chapter 6).

Is either of these lives superior? According to Jeremy Bentham's simple form of Utilitarianism, there is no general answer and it's simply a matter of what makes you happier. That at least vindicates those who do prefer the more settled life. But his successor, John Stuart Mill, was not happy with this analysis. He came up with a different test: what would a competent judge choose? Mill's competent judge was a person who had experience of both kinds of life (or in his original version, all types of pleasure) and who thus could compare the two objectively.

This test, however, is useless because competent judges disagree, and to allow a simple majority vote would endorse the tyranny of the majority. My own inclination has been to think that once you've widened your horizons, there is no going back, but the empirical evidence suggests this is untrue. I know of several people, for instance, who grew up in my home town of Folkestone, went away to London for several years, but who have returned since. The reasons they did so are precisely because they have weighed up the advantages of both kinds of life and have decided that they actually want the settled familiarity of somewhere they can be surrounded by friends and family, and where life doesn't exhaust you with its bewildering array of choices.

Perhaps Mill was onto something after all. The point about competent judges is not that we should accept their verdict, but that we should be allowed to become one of them and decide for ourselves. To paraphrase Sartre, it is not what we choose, but that we are able to choose. This can be hard to do when you grow up among people among whom the narrow, settled view is dominant. If you're the only one who wants to spread their wings, the chances are others won't give you the room to do so. This is how I felt about a woman I used to see behind the counter at the Bramley Spar. Her demeanour was always happy and friendly, but her words were of how dull the day had been and how keen she was to go home. It was like watching someone full of life and vitality having it all slowly drained from her. Selling me a National Lottery ticket once, she said that if she won she'd go off to Greece and set up a business there. Why not go now? I asked. Because her other half won't go unless they win the lottery, which I took as another way of saying he doesn't really want to. I found it sad to think of her with her modest, achievable dream, surrounded by people making her think it was a silly flight of fancy. The point is not that other people should be more like her, it's that she should be as able to live life the way she wants to as they are to do the same.

When you talk about giving people opportunities it's very easy to sound as though you're judging those who aren't able or choose not to take them up. It's not often I find myself thinking that a *Sun* columnist has a very good point, but Fergus Shanahan gave me pause for thought when he wrote: 'Cherie Blair moans that if she hadn't gone to university, she would have ended up serving in a shop. And what's so wrong with that? Some of the nicest ladies I know work in shops. They are cheerful, helpful, patient and provide a vital public service . . . Cherie's education seems to have equipped her to spend her life chasing freebies, mixing with dodgy characters and generally being an embarrassment . . . Cherie also seems to be saying that unless you get to university, you are a failure. What codswallop.'

Let's be very unusual and give Cherie the benefit of the doubt here. She wasn't saying that you're a failure if you work in a shop, all she was saying was that she was grateful to have the option to do something else, and that it is good if we extend those choices to as many people as possible. There are many reasons why this is not in fact what happens, many of which are to do with our social structures. For instance, I have long thought that the greatest advantage that private schools give their pupils is that they instil in them a belief that they can do more or less anything. In contrast, my sister's secondary modern instilled the belief that you would do well to work at Debenhams.

But the English mind is itself partly to blame. There is a historic aversion to education and 'self-improvement' in the working class that still persists. For every parent who actively encourages their children to get good qualifications and do better than they did, there is another who just doesn't think that such options are suitable for 'people like us'. I remember a great line from a TV series I heard years ago. A working-class father listened to the advice of the family's social worker and turned to his daughter and said, 'Did you listen to that? If you work hard and get your qualifications, you could be a secretary to someone like him one day.'

This poverty of aspiration does still exist. Only recently I heard about a mother who actively discouraged her children from going away to university, precisely because she feared that they might never come back. There was also a sign of it in the match-day programme of Rotherham football club in the player Q&A. That week's player was asked for ten of their favourites: TV programme, music artists, film, football team, all-time player, holiday resort, newspaper, car, football ground and most memorable football moment. He was also asked for his three least favourite things: a football moment, a football ground and a subject at school. The assumption underlying this is that school belongs to the category of bad, not good things. The only memory of it worth keeping is of your least favourite subject, so you remember to be thankful your education is over.

My own choice of lifestyle was not changed by my stay in Everytown. There was a lot I came to like and value in life in S66. In particular, I grew very fond of my new friends down the pub. But I always knew I was a tourist with a typewriter. I could never live here because the horizons were too narrow for me, even if not quite as narrow as at first sight. What's more, the narrowness was an integral part of the package. It was what gave you the closer communities, the sense of belonging, the comforts and convenience, it was what let you know who you were and where you belonged and you didn't have to question it. But at least I was now able to genuinely – rather than begrudgingly or conde-scendingly – see what was good about mainstream English life, and how the apparent narrowness of experience is an integral part of the country's philosophy of how to live.

Not everything about the ways of the majority yet made sense, however. The English mind may well have become clearer to me, but the English stomach was still something of a mystery waiting to be solved.

5

All We Can Eat

London prices, English eating ethos

Read the history of Western philosophy and you might be forgiven for thinking that philosophers have not been much interested in food. It's more accurate to say that they haven't been much interested in writing about it. David Hume, for example, was a famously corpulent gourmand whose sheep's head broth was the toast of Edinburgh. But like almost all his predecessors and successors, he never wrote a treatise on gastronomy.

I think the philosophers have missed something here. As a good Humean myself – that is, someone who enjoys food perhaps a little too much for his own good – I think it's time to rectify this oversight. If food is a fundamental part of life, then how a nation eats should tell you things worth knowing about how it thinks. A nation thinks on its stomach, and on this subject the English provide more food for thought than most.

Consider, for example, how our eating habits reflect the centrality of convenience in the English conception of the good life. The national dish of England is often said to be chicken tikka masala, but, in fact, the meal most people eat almost every day is the Packed Lunch. No Soviet-style central state government could impose uniformity more effectively. The core of this meal is a sandwich, preferably filled with some form of cheese or ham, and a packet of crisps. This may be supplemented by a soft drink, a chocolate bar or biscuit, and an apple or banana. According to a statistic I've made up, but which I'm more confident of than any other in this book, this basic template is found in 99% of all children's packed lunches and it is carried on into adulthood. Indeed, more than two-thirds of schoolchildren have a packet of crisps in their lunch box every single day. The only difference is that adults often get too lazy to make their own and so buy theirs from a shop, where inevitably the 'meal deal' will combine a sandwich with a packet of crisps and a fizzy drink. The fruit is likely to be dropped. Of course there are variations. The health-conscious go for wholemeal bread and may swap the crisps or chocolate for a yoghurt and add an extra piece of fruit. But the basic formula is the same all over the country.

The Packed Lunch rules because it is simple and convenient. You need no utensils to eat it. It needs no heating up. You can devour it sitting down, standing up or at your desk while you carry on working, or out on the street while you window-shop or chat on your mobile. The sandwich can be finished in a matter of minutes and the rest picked at throughout the day. And, perhaps most importantly of all, you don't have to think, beyond the choice of fillings. It is the ultimate functional meal for a nation which still sees food more as fuel than as an aesthetic pleasure. Variations of the sandwich may well be eaten all over the world, but in England it is a staple.

The sense that food is functional rather than fun is reinforced by the way in which the English are so impressed by the size and value of a meal. Look at the customers at the Morrisons' salad bars, where the food is sold by volume, not weight. They squeeze as much into every box as they possibly can, and you can often see them having trouble getting the lid shut. And then when you eat it, what you get is a chaotic mix of tastes and flavours, in which the spices of the Bombay potato run into the tuna pasta, which mingles with the coleslaw. Less is never more on English plates. The more flavours that fight it out in your mouth the better. It's the same rationale that makes the Ploughman's Andy's favourite sort of pork pie. Its attraction is that is has, in Andy's words, 'everything in it', including a layer of cheese and pickle.

The same obsession with size and value crops up everywhere. When The Ball first re-opened as Ye Olde King Henry, they introduced waitress service and pushed the food. The food was really good, a regular told me, 'but the portions aren't huge, mind'. A place in Thurcroft has a legendary sandwich, containing – and people really could itemize it this precisely – four rashers of bacon, four sausages and god knows what else I've forgotten. All for £2.50. If this is a working-class thing, then it only goes to show how the majority remain working class in outlook, for the same attitudes are found in supposedly middle-class places. On London's Portobello Road, where house prices average £600,000, a trendy gastropub sports a sign advertising Sunday roast, 'piled high with all the trimmings'. To spend more than you need to on food seems decadent. If you get a large helping, at least you haven't thrown your money away.

If size, value and convenience are traditional English culinary virtues, a perhaps more recent import is that of choice, which simply adds to the list of ways in which food is valued in functional terms. A university lecturer once took me to his favourite restaurant and remarked that it had an 'impressively large menu'. I was taken aback by the idea that this was a good thing, as I thought it was obvious that a very large menu is a sign that many of the dishes are pre-prepared, probably even put in the freezer. He was even more taken aback by my scepticism.

Although choice is not essentially an indigenous trait but is rather the product of late capitalism, it is easy to see why England provides the ideal climate for culinary choice to multiply. When your own traditions do not rate quality as highly as functionality, having more options is an obvious improvement, even though it seems to imply less fresh cooking. Choice is thus primarily an Anglo-American value when it comes to food. In Spain, for example, when you go for lunch from the *menú del día*, you usually get to choose from only a couple of dishes, and sometimes there is no choice at all. But you'll get three courses with wine and bread, for less than the cost of a full English breakfast. They prefer a limited range of freshly cooked meals to an array of options from the freezer because they value food for what it is, not just what it does.

In England, we are so out of touch with good eating that we continually need to be instructed on what to eat and what goes with it. This is why there has been a trend for restaurants to not just state what's on the menu, but to describe and sell it to you. Pizza Express is one chain that has recently gone down this road. Instead of simply telling you what toppings each pizza has, the menu now describes the Giardiniera as 'a fresh feast of leeks, petit pois, peperonata, mushrooms, olives and sliced tomato', while 'creamy goat's cheese and sundried tomatoes create a tasty combination of flavours and textures' on the Caprina. Worried about what else to order? Don't be. 'Anything goes with pizza. Especially when they're made to order,' we are reassured. You only have to look at those sentences for ten seconds to see how idiotic they are, but then again, most people probably think it's idiotic to give them more than a second's thought. I fundamentally disagree. It is a premise of this book that it is by looking more closely at the everyday that we understand ourselves better. Too many writers about the English take as their sources iconic figures, films and artists and don't bother examining the English themselves. Both Jeremy Paxman and Roger Scruton's books on the English are full of references to English films, literature, history and key historic events, but make virtually no reference to the daily experience of most English people. As Elbert Hubbard said, 'Little minds are interested in the extraordinary; great minds in the commonplace.' I may not have a great mind, but I at least want to share their interests. And nothing is more commonplace than eating.

If we have such a poor food culture, why do so many people eat out? It is not as though food serves the social function it does in places like Spain and Italy. Indeed, surveys have suggested that half of all British households don't even have a dining table they regularly use. Whole generations have grown up eating their food in front of the television, using only forks and spoons, or just their fingers. A lack of interest in good food and its social role, however, is not an obstacle to the restaurant industry, but an opportunity, which it has grasped in the form of the 'informal dining' sector. This is what took Mitchells & Butlers, owners of the All Bar One and Harvester chains, to the top of Britain's Most Admired Companies list in the restaurants, pubs and breweries sector (note the grouping) in 2005. The award citation said, 'Its strategic shift towards informal dining has proved a success.' In second place came Punch Taverns, owners of the Spirit Group, whom we will come to shortly.

So what is 'informal dining'? To put it in plain English, it's an out-of-home entertainment and dining solution that fills a broad niche in between the casual impulse-buy fast-food sector and the more formal environs of the traditional restaurant experience. In other words, it's eating out for people who don't like restaurants, and don't much care about food.

I have to confess this trend had passed me by, so when I came across prime exemplars of it in S66 I felt like the old gentleman who walked into Folkestone's first burger bar, which I worked in while at school. The place had previously been a café and, bemused by the changes, he asked where the cutlery was. I was now that man, but about thirty years early. For instance, when I went to a Pizza Hut for the first time in decades, I really didn't know what to do. Pizza Hut has built itself on choice and value, of course. In Italy, people choose their pizzeria mainly on the grounds of how good their bases are. Local people will know which pizzerias are currently in form and they will even be able to tell you which of the pizza chefs – the *pizzaioli* – is best. In contrast, in the UK the whole idea is to make the *pizzaiolo* irrelevant, so you can have the same standardized product wherever and whenever you go. And it's not about having a good base, it's about being able to choose between deep pan, Italian, the edge, stuffed crust or a lighter, low-cal one.

But Pizza Hut has also evolved to fit in more with the informal dining ethos. The last time I had been to one it had all been pretty traditional. This one in Parkgate Retail Park, aptly near a filling station, felt more like a McDonald's with plates. Kids climbed over and under the furniture and everyone treated this as normal, which it was, because informal dining is all about feeling as at home as possible. When I finished eating my perfectly adequate pizza, I didn't even know whether to ask for the bill or go up and pay at the cash till. Observation suggests you could do either, but most go up, and pretty much as soon as they've swallowed their last mouthful, judging from the tables abandoned with plates and detritus strewn all over them.

I had also been missing a similar informal dining destination right under my nose in Bramley. Sir Jack looked liked a pub that served food from the outside. Inside it's more like an 'English pub' than an English pub, with lots of visible wood, brick and stone, very well lit to give it that traditional 'it's dark and wintry outside' feel. Give the designers credit: they really do create a simulacrum of an authentic boozer. Its selling point is that it serves two meals for the price of one, which is actually pretty lame, because it's obvious by looking at the menu that main courses are close to double the price they would be in comparable venues.

But looking around it soon became obvious this was not a pub at all. Almost every table was set for eating, which was what almost every customer was doing. Only a couple were just having drinks. The genius of the place – and it is very popular – is that it allows you to eat out without feeling you're in anything as threatening or formal as a restaurant. The pub vibe is just a device to make you feel relaxed. At the same time, it feels a bit more of an occasion than going to a fast-food outlet. You have to admire it. It's market segmentation done to perfection. The Spirit Group, who own the chain, are experts at this kind of thing. Near my home in Bristol is another one of their brands, Bar Room Bar.

There they do pretty good stone-baked pizzas made in front of you in a wood-fired oven. They know which buttons to press to target different demographic groups, and when they press mine, I'm as much their patsy as anyone else.

The food at their Two for One chains, however, is aimed at a more typical mainstream consumer, which means it's just what you'd get out of your freezer. Like many 'family restaurants', they do their very best to make you feel as though you are not eating out at all, but simply having exactly what you'd have at home, without the need to cook or wash up. Even the sauces come in individual, Heinz-branded little tubs. You don't come for the cooking, but to avoid doing it yourself.

It's a soulless, mechanized environment. There is a standard process of finding a table with a number and going to a specific food ordering point. The young staff then run through their script with you. The first thing they say is, 'Would you like any starters?' When you've finished ordering, they ask if you'd like any side orders, listing several such as onion rings to prompt you. Then you order your drink elsewhere at the bar, and you're asked 'Doubles?' expectantly if you order spirits. Since most of the food comes out of microwaves or deep-fat fryers, you don't have to wait long for your meal to arrive. You don't need to rush to be in and out in half an hour.

Places like Sir Jack appeal because they're perceived to be good value. But value and quality are not incompatible. When I asked people to recommend somewhere good to eat, nine times out of ten I was pointed towards a carvery. At a carvery, you are served meat from a hotplate, carved in front of your wide open eyes and salivating mouth. You usually then help yourself to all the vegetables and trimmings. Carveries are very popular, and the best ones really are pretty tasty. Crucially they are also good value. Currently, the cheapest in the area was a place called The Draw-bridge, which did one for only £3. At that price, how the poor

animals who supplied their flesh must have lived their economi-
cally optimal lives doesn't bear thinking about. People are so keen
on getting their money's worth that they will often bring tinfoil
to wrap up what they don't eat to take home with them. Some,
like carvery devotee Andy, have even been known to ask for foil
and have been given it.

In S66 the carvery that got the most votes was served at The
Millstone at Tickhill, the next village along from Maltby. It was
served all day, £5 before 5 p.m., £6 afterwards and on Sundays,
when the place would be packed. You had a choice of four meats.
I went along a few times, sometimes taking visitors from down
south, and everyone enjoyed it. Indeed, one reason for this is perhaps because in many cities, the one food that is hard to get is the
traditional English roast. A good carvery is a fine thing. If you
could eat one every day, as many claimed they could, there'd be
no problem. And many people are that conservative. The temporary landlords of The Ball told me about a pub they had
worked cover for which started doing Thai food. A regular complained, 'We don't want this foreign food. We want traditional
stuff like lasagne.'

The same landlords, however, also told me a story which
made me doubt that The Millstone was indicative of the general
quality of carveries. They once had to cover a pub that served a
Sunday carvery and when they first arrived, as was their usual
practice, they just observed how things were currently done. The
cook brought out a bucket of veg which had a thin white film on
it. He washed it off, heated it up and it went into the bains-marie
to be served up. It all got eaten, so he brought out some more.
When it was all over, he put the veg that remained back in the
bucket. When asked what he was going to do with it, he said it
was for next week. The thin white film was mould. He was going
to do the same with the gravy, which is actually dangerous.

The new landlords vowed to put a stop to that. The uneaten

veg was thrown out and the next week everything was fresh. The new, improved carvery had arrived. There was just one problem. The customers complained that it was not like it usually was. They actually preferred the week-old mouldy stuff to fresh vegetables. (Mind you, even the landlords telling me this, although they claimed to be chefs, weren't as au fait with food as could be expected. When the chips changed taste because of a new season of potatoes and I asked what variety they were, they shrugged their shoulders and just said they were a 'different make'.)

This would mystify Italians and Spaniards. Good food need not be complicated or expensive, it's just simple and well put together from fresh ingredients. For the English, good food is either cheap and substantial or it's expensive and elaborate, and most shun the latter. Posh food is therefore too often a matter of presentation not substance. At Izaballa's, Wickersley's trendiest café (at least until the arrival of @The Courtyard shortly before I left), they served fruit smoothies in tall, bulbous wine glasses with ice. But the smoothie itself was just out of a bottle. Their mozzarella and tomato panini sounded classy, but had so little cheese that not a single bite even threatened to leave behind a stringy tail of cheese. But it was 'well presented', with a typically pointless 'salad garnish', comprising one slice of cucumber, a slice of tomato and a few leaves and grated indistinguishable vegetable matter. Only in England could the purely decorative concept of the garnish – which is often left uneaten – become one of the most common words on menus.

The classiest restaurant in S66 reinforced the style over substance theory. It would not be wholly fair to describe Galliano's Italiano – or Gallianos' Italiano, depending on what sign you read – as a bad restaurant, especially by English standards. When I went, my starter was actually pretty good, a mozzarella tricolore, with basil oil rather than basil. It was served prettily in a stack, which counts for a lot. But with most starters at £6.95 and fish and meat main courses starting at £15.95, you don't expect basic errors like tomatoes cold from the fridge, or an *insalata di mare*, which apart from also being fridge-cold was heavily coated in some kind of jelly, suggesting it had come out of a jar. Having initially accepted that it was OK, by the end of the meal I had got very annoyed at how the mediocre was being passed off as top notch. But then I was probably the exception. After all, if an open kitchen has Utterly Butterly tubs in full view of everyone, it must be me who's odd to think this is not to be expected of a restaurant with pretensions to class. Others thought it somewhere worth making the effort to come to. When we finished our waitress asked, 'Would you like a taxi ordering?', suggesting it's not just locals who keep it going. Indeed, the restaurant is such a success that the owner, Dino Maccio, has become wealthy enough to join a consortium of local businessmen to take over Rotherham United Football Club and save it from liquidation. To be fair, I think most people saw through the superficial style. Pete said he'd been to Galliano's once and thought it was a rip-off. 'I think we're behind London when it comes to eating out,' he said, '*way behind*', in a rare Yorkshire admission that the capital has anything over it.

All the talk of the transformation of the English food culture is grossly overstated. Jamie Oliver, Nigella Lawson and Gordon Ramsay may be superstars, but their impact on the daily diets of millions remains negligible. Of the 171 million cookery books owned by Britons, an estimated 61 million are never opened, and usually only a few recipes are used from those that are. Cooking is still not something it is assumed any competent adult will do regularly. Most people find it very strange that, as a single man living alone, I bother to cook at all, let alone most nights. I once moved into a bedsit where the young man I was replacing actually didn't know if the Belling oven worked because he had never used it. I got used to feeling a little self-conscious in supermarket queues years ago. I've never yet been behind someone with fewer processed items than myself, and I'm not exactly an alfalfa-munching macrobiotic health freak. Take a random July day when I looked in my basket to see things like wholewheat cereals, muesli, pasta, anchovies, fresh mixed nuts, Cafédirect Fairtrade coffee and Greek sheep and goat's milk yoghurt. Then I peeked into the basket of the man in front of me and saw a pile of 99p frozen ready meals (on special offer at five for the price of four). The contrast was extreme but indicative: Britons are Europe's biggest consumers of ready-made meals.

We don't need to trust our intuitions here: just look at what sells. There certainly is a growth in the 'healthy-eating sector'. The Department for Environment, Food and Rural Affairs conducts an annual survey called Family Food, which shows small falls in the average number of calories consumed per head and the proportion of energy derived from fat. The trend is therefore in the right direction, but the pace of change is very slow. Rises in sales of wholemeal bread and natural yoghurt have to be seen in the wider context of a diet still dominated by much less healthy products. In 2004 children in the UK consumed an average of 2.7 portions of fruit and veg a day, while 76% of men and 73% of women did not eat the recommended five portions. The top food brands in the UK by sales value puts Walkers crisps first, followed by Birds Eye, Kellogg's, Cadbury, Müller, Heinz, Coca-Cola, Matthews (of bootiful intensively reared poultry fame), McVities and Stella Artois. Another survey identified the brands Brits would miss if they were unavailable. The top food items were Heinz beans, Heinz soups, Kellogg's cereals, Nescafé, Walkers crisps, Heinz ketchup and Robinson's squash.

Even attempts to educate children have to battle against the ingrained habits of their parents. One of the most memorable scenes in the television series *Jamie's School Dinners*, in which the celebrity chef tried to improve the quality of school meals, was of parents passing their children fast food through the school gates in defiance. In the autumn of 2006, these scenes were replicated at Rawmarsh Comprehensive School in Rotherham, after it introduced a new, healthier menu and banned pupils from going to local takeaways. Two mothers, Julie Critchlow and Sam Walker, came to the rescue, taking orders from up to 60 children for food from local takeaways. Talking to the *Sheffield Star*, Walker said of Jamie Oliver, 'I don't like him or what he stands for – he is forcing our kids to be more picky about their food.'

It's hard to change the eating habits of the young when their parents often just don't get it. In Morrisons' café, I once saw a young boy examine the label of his bottle of Lucozade. 'Not one E number,' he said, demonstrating impressive nutritional awareness for a pre-teen. His mum was dismissive. 'There are, they just don't tell you.' She took a look at the label. 'There, look, colouring. That'll be an E number,' she said triumphantly, handing it back. What she was teaching her son was not to be more careful, but not to bother: all this worrying about what's in stuff is pointless, just get it down you. Another time in a Morrisons' café a mum offered her young daughter a choice of how to complete her kids' club menu: with an apple or a KitKat. The girl chose an apple, only for her mum to overrule her: 'You don't like that sort,' she said. This is not untypical. I was always seeing young children being given chips. I lost count of the times I saw kids in pushchairs unable even to talk being fed chocolate, biscuits and other sweet things. Is it any wonder that by the time they get to express preferences, they refuse to eat anything else?

You may have noticed, by the way, frequent mention of Morrisons' cafés. There is a good reason for that: if you want decent, keenly priced, basic food in S66, you can't do better. When I asked people where a good place to eat was, although a carvery was usually their first thought, they'd often come back to me later and say, 'Actually, Morrisons is very good for a cheap meal.' Their meat-free breakfast (not vegetarian, note – I think that would scare people) was as good a cooked breakfast as you could get, with the exception of the truck stop, of course. My nearest Morrisons was a ten-minute walk away and I would sometimes go with the sole intention of visiting the café. Such eccentric behaviour became all too common while I was in Everytown. Once, to my own amazement, I actually found myself stopping off at Doncaster North services, only a few miles from home, because I wanted a coffee and realized I wouldn't be able to get a ground one of any description near my home at that time.

This surprised even me, but I had learned my lesson a few years back when I lived for a while in Sale, a seventies theme-town south of Manchester. I discovered that the only place you could pop into all day long for a decent fresh ground coffee was The Hogshead pub. That was also the only place to get a sand-wich that was at all 'different', with such exotic fare as ciabatte with goat's cheese. It was then that it dawned on me that people who complain about the insidious effects of chains are usually the people lucky enough to live in affluent cities with thriving inde-pendents. Bristol is like that. When I'm there, I never go to a chain coffee bar. But when travelling, I will go to a Caffè Nero because the chances are it is much better than what is served up at a random independent. In Sale, as elsewhere, chains can help drive up standards.

But isn't a good English caff just as good as a continental café in its own way? Well, yes, but there was a distinct lack of the former in S66, and there had been for a long while. Reg at The Travellers, for instance, reminisced about the good old days (again) when there'd be an all-night lock-in and they'd finally emerge to go for breakfast – at the Little Chef. Look in the broadsheet food pages when they eulogize the great British caff and you'll find the ones they love are usually located in upmarket areas of cities. Bristol's legendary York Café, a winner of national awards, is in BS8, the poshest postcode district of the city. London institution Alfredo's (which closed a few years ago) was situated in Islington, close to the former home of Tony Blair. For the most part, however, the traditional English caff is neither great nor charming. In Doncaster, with time to kill waiting for a bus, the caffs I found were rather decrepit remnants of what once must have been new, fashionable and exciting meeting places. Around 1972.

There is no getting away from the fact that England remains culinarily impoverished. We like our food to be cheap, substantial, familiar and convenient. Not all of it is bad by any means. The Millstone did an excellent carvery, Ye Olde King Henry offered more than decent pub food, as did The Travellers, which introduced a Sunday carvery that did so well they ran one midweek too. Bramley even had a surprisingly good Cantonese Restaurant called the Shining Star, which you would never guess from the outside: a tatty-looking conversion of a pair of terraced houses. At The Horseshoes in Wickersley, the fish and chips on Tuesdays and Fridays is superb, because the cod comes direct from a van down that day from Grimsby. But for every food highlight there are just too many lowlights.

However, if you really want to understand the place of food in the English mind, you need to look at how we choose *not* to eat, as well as how we do. Slimming is a national obsession, and almost every day there is some kind of weight loss feature in the tabloids. In 2004 a quarter of men and 43% of women were trying to lose weight. How they do so, however, depends on ever-changing fads and fashions. Another study showed that in the same year around 10 million Britons were on a diet at any one time, including 3 million on the Atkins bandwagon. A year later only 2.8% were on low-carb, Atkins-style diets and Atkins Nutritional went into bankruptcy.

Why is the allure of the diet so persistent, and the ability to learn that fads are fads so limited? One reason, as I know from personal experience, is that it is a constant battle to avoid getting fat if you have a sedentary job in this land of plenty. The second reason is that the media keep presenting the latest diet as though it were 'different this time'. This isn't just a tabloid crime. *Observer Food Monthly* once ran a totally uncritical piece on the GI Diet as its cover story, suggesting that scientists had finally found the key to permanent weight loss.

The dieting obsession reflects a binge-and-purge culture that seems deep-rooted in our psyche and is most evident in our drinking habits. My feeling is that this reflects our Protestant puritanism, in much the same way as our food-as-fuel mentality does. The pleasure we get from food is the moral and practical one of having refuelled fully at a good price. Enjoying food purely for its own sake is a little decadent, a bit too carnal. Dieting fits this mindset perfectly, since it is all about making the most pleasurable foods prohibited, forbidden and wicked. In a similar way, we enjoy alcoholic drinks more for their effects than their taste. This is reflected in the way advertisers sell food to us. They frequently use the language of temptation, being a bit wicked, 'naughty but nice', giving in, indulging yourself. To enjoy food and drink is a little sinful. In contrast, the south European Catholic cultures don't have these issues. Food and drink are to be enjoyed guilt-free, which is why they consume them without needing to go to excess.

When we do give in to temptation, we give in completely. We might as well, since the sin has already been committed. But then we're left with the guilt afterwards. These attitudes feed the binge-and-purge cycle. Consumer trends reinforce this analysis: growth in the food sector is now strongest in both the healthy eating and 'indulgence' sectors. As one analyst put it, '[We] are choosing more wholesome foods; but we feel the need to then reward our good behaviour with a treat.' I noticed that sometimes in people's houses, someone who at the start of the evening is claiming to be moderating their intake is, by dessert, an unstoppable eating machine. Even after three courses, they dig out boxes of chocolates and liqueurs and by the end of the evening, everyone's bloated and uncomfortable. In England, you haven't had a really good meal if you can stand up at the end of it.

As a society we are bingeing more than ever, and so in turn we must purge like never before. So I thought I'd better join in. I had lost weight in the past, and life in Rotherham was certainly not helping my waistline. So I decided to follow the régime du jour: the GI Diet. This one, newspapers and magazines assured us, really worked. So I ordered two best-selling books on the GI Diet by the movement's guru, Rick Gallop. And when they arrived I was genuinely quite excited. The prospect of losing weight is an enticing one. Even though I was not exactly fat, I was technically overweight and having to buy size 36 trousers was galling. I'm not immune to the warped values of the dieting culture I dislike.

I wanted to believe this would work. Indeed, there was every reason to suppose it would – if I followed it. After all, if you limit your calorific intake by whatever method to fewer than you expend, you will slim down. Diets are just methods to help you achieve this. The trouble is that diets are difficult to sustain. They don't fit in with normal life. They leave you hungry. They exclude things you really like, such as alcohol. I had lost weight about a year before, following a self-devised programme called the Covent Garden Soup Diet™. It comprised a normal breakfast, a normal lunch, and soup for dinner. The only, tiny problem was it left me feeling starving, dreaming and thinking of food all the time. And of course once I finished it, the weight slowly crept back on.

But this is where the GI Diet promised to be different. You don't count calories, but simply eat as many 'green light' foods as you want, and avoid the 'red light' ones. It is designed to stop you getting those hunger pangs and to change your eating habits for the rest of your life. Great! However, reading the books later, I soon had reason to be less optimistic. It may be very sensibly long term but that also means sticking to the regime for months before hitting your target weight. Given the central place the pub had come to occupy in my life, and that this weight-reduction Phase I includes no alcohol, that could be a problem. So I decided to do what you're allowed in Phase II and have one glass of red wine when I went out.

But other details were even less enticing. If I had a sandwich, I was supposed to take off the top bit of bread and have it 'open-faced'. That's asking me to defile our national dish. As for the 'red light' foods to almost always avoid for the rest of your life, they included such essentials as cheese, full-fat yoghurt, bagels, muffins, croissants, chips, butter, gnocchi, pizza, melons, mayonnaise, tortillas, and more than one alcoholic drink. It is indeed a diet fit for puritans. I realized that I was going to have to cheat, and that there was no way it would ever become a long-term template. So just reading the books took me through the complete psychological cycle of the dieter: allure of the thinner me, belief in the cure, baulking at the medicine, cheating, then abandoning. Still, the experiment had to go ahead, so I gave it a month. For 28 days, I would join millions of my compatriots losing weight.

It started off quite well. Breakfast became a little duller than usual, as my skimmed milk porridge was not sweetened with the usual dollop of honey. But in some ways the diet was a bit of a liberation. I was eating more like I did pre-S66, enjoying more fresh vegetables and fruit, and eschewing pies, cakes and chips cooked in beef dripping. It also seemed to be true that the regime keeps hunger under control. I felt slight low-level pangs, but it didn't get worse and it was quite easily faced down. But perhaps that was just the positive thinking of being on a diet.

However, one unhealthy thing about dieting is surely that it makes you think about food even more than usual. By day two there were early signs of delirium as I dreamed of food. I found myself in a branch of the sandwich chain Subway, which was unusual for me, but it's actually one of the few fast-food places the GI Diet recommends. I was trying to get a sandwich and I was asking about GI-approved wholemeal bread. But the guy serving me kept failing to understand and offering me white baguettes. At one stage he trimmed the end off one, put it in a machine which cut it to the right length, heated it up, made slits in it and inserted lashings of garlic butter. It smelled delicious. While I was waiting for him to get me what would inevitably be yet another incorrect bread, I began to panic about whether any of the fillings available were actually GI approved anyway. Was that tuna mixed with mayo? Red light! He was foreign, which didn't help the communication, so in the end I asked him where he was from. 'Peru.' '*Ah, entonces hablas español?*' I asked. '*Sí.*' '*Pan integral! Esto es lo que quiero. Pan integral!*' He replied (in English, because the Spanish was getting too advanced for me) that he could do that, but because he wants to give his customers the best, he usually doesn't offer it. I woke up. This couldn't be good for me.

On day five I came across a survey on why people lose weight. 'Looking good' was the number one reason, while 'to wear the clothes I want to', 'to look more attractive' and 'to feel less self-conscious' came above 'to reduce risk of heart attack' and 'to lower my blood pressure'. This rings true, though perhaps a more general 'to improve my health' option would have got a higher score. We have become very anxious about how we look, which is why even anti-cigarette and anti-drug campaigns have recently focused on what they do to your skin, as this seems to scare young people more than dying.

After a week, I went for my first weigh-in. These have to be at the same point of the day and I'd chosen after my swim, because the baths have scales. I felt real tension and anxiety as the verdict approached. I needed the motivation boost of having had some success, but in any given week there's always a chance you'll register as having lost nothing, or perhaps gained a little. The nervousness led me to have ridiculous thoughts: will how much water I drink make a difference? A litre weighs one kilo after all. Or the heaviness of my wallet? And I'm wearing a long-sleeved T-shirt this week. Wasn't it short-sleeved last time? When did I last evacuate my bowels? The Subway dream was no one-off: I was clearly going insane. But when I finally stepped up and dropped the 50p coin in the slot, I got the result I wanted to see: 3lbs (1.2 kilos) down on last week. That was actually suspiciously good, since I hadn't been totally strict. It felt good, but was it wise that I was investing so much of my happiness in how I performed on a weight-loss regime? After all, if losing weight that week made me feel great, wouldn't failing to lose it have made me feel terrible? I felt that just by following the diet I was acquiring the English tendency to somehow imbue what I eat with a moral significance it doesn't really have.

Keeping up the diet wasn't too difficult, but it did require some effort, and forward planning when travelling. The sandwich selection on most trains, for instance, will often have no 'green light' options. But in a way following the diet was almost fun. It became a kind of game, and because the rules were set, I didn't even need to think. I could stop wondering if I should go ahead and have something 'naughty' because the rules told me it was just not allowed. Jean-Paul Sartre would see the appeal, as he knew how difficult we find confronting our own freedom. When we choose to go on a diet, we are of course responsible for our choice, but we only need to make the one initial decision to go on it and thereafter we place ourselves in the hands of the diet book. Ironically, though it is about limiting our options, it feels liberating.

By the end of week two another 2lbs had fallen off. Perhaps

this GI thing really did work. But even if it did, fashions move on and the papers were already pushing the latest fads. The *Daily Mail* showcased 'the perfect winter diet. It will boost your immune system, lower cholesterol, beat the chill AND help you drop a dress size for the party season. The soup-only diet that could lose you 10lb in a week.' Clearly my Covent Garden Soup Diet had been ahead of its time. The fact that medical experts recommend losing no more than a steady 1–2lbs a week was not mentioned.

In week three my cheating was getting more frequent, as I was getting quite bullish about how effective the diet was. And indeed, at the end of the week, another 2lbs had gone, which meant I had lost half a stone in three weeks. However, the final week was not such a success. I was in a number of social situations where not to have a drink would frankly have been rude – or at least that's what I told myself – and when I did a bit of maths I discovered that I had actually consumed 2,000 calories in alcoholic drinks alone, which is about what I should have been eating in one day. So I put on 1lb. Still, it had been a success, hadn't it? 6lbs lost in four weeks?

You can guess what happened next. By the time I left Rotherham all that I had lost had been put back on again. Old habits die hard, and it's especially difficult to keep the weight off when you're living the typical life of the English. My local shop, the Bramley Spar, for example, was a decent size, but the only fresh produce it stocked were bags of potatoes. The link between health and food still eludes many. It's always been a mystery why sports centre cafés up and down the country always tended to specialize in sausage, egg and chips. At Maltby baths, alongside the vending machines full of sugary drinks, chocolate and crisps, they even have one dispensing Pot Noodles. There's joined-up thinking for you. It's almost as bad as seeing the ice cream vans outside Wickersley and Maltby comps.

The dieting culture reinforces this disconnect. Look at the supermarkets with their 'healthy eating' and 'Be good to yourself' options, as though the healthiness of food is determined solely by their calorific and fat contents. But read the labels and you'll see they are often highly processed. The *Daily Mail*'s 'Meal Maths: How to calculate a healthy lunch' also told me that one Waitrose chicken and bacon sandwich contained 494 calories; while one Waitrose roast chicken sandwich with lemon crème fraîche, plus a packet of Skips and a Special K chocolate chip bar had only 477 calories. I was left asking how we were supposed to know from this information which was the healthier, but in a culture where calories are all, I suppose it should have been obvious. Not to me it wasn't. One decent sandwich is almost certainly more nutritious than a lunch containing a highly processed cereal bar and a packet of crisps made from maize, vegetable oil, potato starch, sodium diacetate, lactose, dried whey, dried yeast extract, dried onion, paprika extract, curcumin, sugar, salt, annatto and carminic acid.

Does any of this really matter? I have a friend who's a 40-something man with the palate of a ten-year-old boy. His diet is based around white bread, pizzas, chocolate, omelettes and ice cream. The way he sees it, all these people like me who bang on about how bad the English food culture is are just snobs. We talk about our bad diet as though it were a moral failing rather than simply a difference in taste. He has a point. In moralizing the deficiencies of the English diet we are simply persisting with the fundamental English error of thinking that food is primarily a moral matter in the first place. Indeed, what is most talked about today is not how much better our cooking could be, but how much better for us it should be. Health is the issue, and that is just another issue of functionality.

Food matters for the English philosophy, not because it exposes our moral weakness, but because it helps reveal our attitude to life. Our relationship with food reveals a kind of

Protestant puritanism and utilitarian functionality. Despite our apparent embrace of hedonism, our binge-and-purge mentality makes us very different from the ancient Epicureans, who understood that real happiness required moderation. It is better to savour less than wolf down more. If we learn to have a less moralized relationship with food and drink, so that it is not something we either shun or indulge in to excess, it will be able to fit in as part of the mixture of factors which can make everyday life a blessing. The new food fascism, however, is simply a continuation of the old moralizing of food in a new form.

However, this is not the same as saying that the English should have more of a food culture. We could cure ourselves of our moral delusion about food and yet still find the majority prefer convenience and functionality over quality, and there would be nothing wrong with that. People who accept what I judge to be poor standards at motorway service stations may not be mistaken, they might just not care. Andy, for example, genuinely loved his pork pies and carveries, and remained lean despite, or perhaps because of, this. It is my priorities that might be warped. The English have better things to worry about than whether or not their sandwich fails to meet the high standard set by the award-winning Chandos Deli in Bristol. In that way, the English emphasis on convenience might be a virtue: it means that they can worry less about the things that matter less, and save their time and energy for what they really like, be it fishing, gardening, reading or walking.

To those like me for whom food is a basic pleasure of life, it looks as if people would be missing out. That's how it seemed to me towards the end of my stay in S66, as I tucked into my Whitby breaded scampi at Sir Jack (their 'best ever', I was pleased to note from the menu). Then I realized that my attitudes had gone full circle. When I first arrived, I was a bit of a food snob, keen to avoid bland, pre-cooked processed food. Then I learned to relax and get on with it. Usually what's on offer is not expensive, it does the job, and it's frankly more effort getting uptight than just eating it. I would no longer fret if the only option was a McDonald's. Some of that attitude has remained with me. But eventually I began to get annoyed again. Places like Sir Jack are not evil or terrible, they're just unnecessary. We can and should have better. That we don't is supremely annoying.

But I ought to keep my indignation in check. We often find it hard to imagine that things we love, others care little for. My lament about English food is simply a partisan complaint from one of many who find their own preferences are not adequately catered for, and who look at Spain, Italy and France in envy (though not at Holland, which has even worse food than we do). Wittgenstein once wrote that without music, life would be a mistake. It's oft-repeated but clearly utter rubbish. Are the lives of the deaf or tone-deaf a mistake? In the same way, life without *risotto milanese* would not be a mistake, unless you were the kind of person whose life really would be enriched by it. Again, it is a matter of giving people the opportunity, not demanding that everyone take it. And what holds us back here is a puritanical, functional attitude to food that acts as an obstacle to its proper enjoyment. Set our taste buds free, however, and I wouldn't be surprised if many still opt for whole-tail Whitby breaded scampi, and good luck to them.

Thinking about food had therefore helped me to get a better grip on the English ideal of the good life, and how we can plead for greater openness to alternatives without hectoring people to change their ways. But there were still more pieces of the puzzle to find, and to get some more of them I needed to see the English outside of their native environment. It was time to see the English abroad.

6

Hefted Holidaymakers

Holidaymakers at Cala d'Or, Mallorca

'I'd like to go where everyone else is going, please,' I said as breezily as I could to the consultant at the Co-op travel in Wickersley.

'And where's that?' she replied, as though I had simply named a resort she hadn't recognized.

'You tell me!' She looked understandably flummoxed by this, so I tried again. 'What's your most popular destination?'

'Oooo, I don't know,' she said, as though she was the last person in the world who could be expected to know the answer. 'Greece, I'd say.'

'Greece?' I replied incredulously. 'Noooooo.'

'I didn't know I was doing a quiz!'

I was being a little unfair since I already knew the answer. At least, I knew where most Brits went abroad for their holidays: Spain remains Britain's number one holiday destination. The gap between it and second place France varies according to different studies, but it seems that it would be huge if it weren't for the popularity of weekend breaks in France. Within Spain, the Balearic Islands are the most popular areas, and of these, the top resort is Mallorca. What's more, most people going to the island still opt for traditional package deals. Once again, although we are often presented as a country whose tastes are rapidly developing, the reality is that England is much as it was.

So I had to break it to her: I wanted to go to Mallorca. After a cup of tea and a browse through some of the options I settled on a hotel in Cala d'Or which I was pleased to see had a 100% approval rating for its food. Maybe it did a carvery. I noticed the swimming pools and tennis courts and imagined myself spending an invigorating healthy week not going very far. There were some optional extras I could order, such as a 'celebration cake' or a 'celebration pack'. I declined.

For most people, their annual trip is something they spend months planning and looking forward to, not to mention saving for. The average family now spends close to £3,000 on its holiday. Arriving at Birmingham International Airport for my break in the sun it was hard to see why they bothered. Long queues, exceptional these days on scheduled flights, are still routinely suffered by charter passengers, who are expected to check in two to three hours before departure. Five minutes after my check-in desk was announced the queue was already so long that I gave up and went for a coffee. I came back 50 minutes later, the queue was still enormous and the person behind me when I quit had only just checked in.

Many people loathe airports, but I usually like the buzz of anticipation, and the sense of being surrounded by people coming and going from all over the world. But here in charter city you couldn't move for white Anglo-Saxons and the atmosphere was more like Victoria Coach Station on a bank holiday weekend. It was much the same on the plane, which felt like a bus trip to the seaside, without the singing.

I began to feel like a live animal export. I was just a body among many, all being herded the same way, all travelling for the same purpose. At Palma airport the arrivals hall was packed with tour operators' booths. I reported in and was told to go to coach number 624. It wasn't difficult to find: transfer coaches are allocated the prime place closest to the exit, as they are the main form of transport out of the terminal.

On the coach our 'holiday consultant', as reps are now called, greeted us with a familiar 'Hi guys!' It later transpired that Eileen speaks Spanish like a native − of Liverpool. In front of me a young girl was playing a memory game with her family. 'Who was the last person to get drunk?' she asked.

I arrived at the hotel. My room was basic, but clean, and I had a nice view of a wall, over which I could see the sign over a bar reading 'Fast food'. I was surprised there was no TV, since this is now mandatory in virtually every hotel room or b. & b. in the UK. It was 9.30, and in Spain most people hadn't even started their dinner yet. However, I was told that the hotel finished serving hours ago. There were two dinner sittings, determined by the colour of your meal card. This week mine would be between 6.30 and 7.30. The first rule of the English on holiday was already evident: when in Rome, sod what the Romans do. Still, I was offered a 'cold plate' from what looked like a leftovers buffet, including such delights as boiled baby carrots and potatoes in a not particularly cheesy sauce. I ate all I could, which was very little. Perhaps there was more enticing fare on the streets, so I went for a wander.

High season was over and at the tail-end of summer it was all fairly quiet. Still, I got to see what was on offer: English and Scottish pubs, such as The Tartan Arms, which had bingo and a fun quiz and showed 'all your favourite soaps'. Other places were showing Sky Sports. Italian joints were also plentiful: pizza and pasta are international safe food. Full English breakfasts were served. There was a large Wimpy and a Burger King. It was therefore something of a shock to eventually find a small bar which seemed vaguely Spanish. They did me some *calamares* and a beer, though the barmaid asked '*Grande?*' when I ordered, obviously having learned that people who look like me will probably complain if served the smaller, typical Spanish measure.

I returned to the hotel somewhat disheartened. Remember that I was not looking for the tackiest, cheapest, nastiest holiday around. I could have gone to Magaluf (or Shagaluf as it is affectionately known) on the other side of the island and reported on trashed hotel rooms, vomiting gangs of drunken Brits and sex on the beach. Instead I was at a typical, mid-market resort finding out that the traditional package tour is still based around the key principle of protecting holidaymakers from anything too foreign.

It confirmed my growing impression that mainstream English life is much more as it used to be than many people believe and is solidly working class in culture. It also confirmed how much people like me had lost touch with mainstream England. My assumption – born out by conversations on my return – was that people I knew would find the details of my trip odd or funny, that they would be surprised to hear that people still went on these kinds of holidays. But, of course, statistically speaking, we are the odd ones. The only thing normal about us is that we tend to disapprove of how our fellow countrymen behave abroad. One survey showed that 98% thought that Britons let the country down in the eyes of foreigners. Either very few people are embarrassing or a lot of people are in denial.

Despite my initial disappointment, I did quite enjoy my week, and over the course of my stay several aspects of the English mindset became much clearer to me. Impressions that had built up over the first few months in S66 finally took a more precise shape. And the catalyst for this was a realization that I had missed a fundamental distinction between types of travellers.

I've never had much time for the alleged contrast between travellers and tourists, which, according to an old joke, is that tourists go to McDonald's for the food and travellers go there for the toilets. Tourists are the inferior beings in this hierarchy, who follow itineraries set by others and never see the 'real country'. Travellers, in contrast, are free spirits who do what they like and get real with the locals. Of course, this is hogwash. Travellers go where all the other travellers go, following the Lonely Planet Bible. They may stay in more basic accommodation, but that doesn't make their experience any more real, just less comfortable. After all, it's not as though locals live in youth hostels. Sure, they'll come back with at least one story of how they found somewhere that 'tourists never go' but that's often because there's no reason to go there. Tourists never go to Bramley, but would you recommend they did? Travellers are just deluded tourists with pretensions.

But having collapsed the tourist/traveller distinction I realized that there was another genuinely different category: the holiday-maker. Whereas the tourist travels in order to see new places and try new things, the holidaymaker goes away simply to have a good time where the weather is better and the problems of home are forgotten. Once you see this, and understand that Mallorca is for holidaymakers, not tourists, everything that made me despair about the place makes perfect sense.

Take the pubs, bars and restaurants. Of course they serve full English breakfasts, Sunday roasts, pizzas, chicken and chips. You're on holiday, not an anthropology field trip. Of course the evening's entertainment revolves around the television: 8–9 is the soap hour and after that it's Sky Sports. You've come to get an extra dollop of your favourite pleasures, not to deny yourself them. That's why come the night-time the bars are full of karaokes, quizzes, top turns such as tributes to Robbie Williams and Westlife in the Tropical Gardens and, in the nightclubs, such monstrosities as the 'dentist's chair', a wacky way of administering large quantities of alcohol in one sitting. You're getting generous helpings of all that you like, but you're sitting outside, not in a dingy pub on a cold night, and you're up late, with no worries about the morning. It beats what you'd be doing at home, even if it's only a matter of doing the same things, but to excess.

This wasn't simply how the majority spent their holiday: there was no other way to be. Different venues catered to different age groups, but it was relentlessly British. I saw a British mini-market, selling only tabloids, with the owner standing watching Newcastle v. Blackburn on a portable television while munching on crisps. There are several fish and chip shops, fitted out exactly as they are back home, with the glass-fronted hotplates above the long deep-fat fryers. Walk around while the football's on and you need never lose track of the commentary on Sky Sports wafting out from some pub or other. Even at one of the few restaurants to have an extensive selection of Spanish dishes on its menu, the waiter tells me that the most popular dishes among the Brits are kebabs, roast chicken and prawns.

I didn't feel I was even in Spain until I went on a day trip to the capital, Palma, where half of all Mallorcans live. I didn't do anything exceptional there, I just enjoyed being somewhere different. At the Mercat Oliver, I bought some marinated *gordal* olives, and stopped at one of the bars to order a *mosto* with a tapa of tortilla, with slices of fresh bread offered in a basket for me to help myself. Down by the harbour I had a *café con leche* with an *ensaimada* – a local light, quite plain pastry. I then walked up to the fourteenth-century Castell de Bellver, so called because of its good views over the bay of Palma, which alone make it worth the walk. Back nearer town I had a *manzanilla* and a plate of three *pimientos rellenos de bacalao*. I wasn't 'getting away from the tourists' and nor was it morally or culturally improving. It was just different to my normal life, if not from my whole life's experience. This is the stimulation I seek as a tourist. In contrast, holidaymakers seek relief and respite. 'Difference' is something they are suspicious of, which is why the English value comfort and convenience and merely tolerate the different.

Although people came primarily as holidaymakers, they would do a little tourism, but almost always on organized coach tours. This led to some absurdities. Only a few miles outside Cala d'Or is the medieval hermitage of San Salvador at Felanitx, perched on a hilltop at 1,400 feet with wonderful, expansive 360° views. But I'll have to take the word of others on that, because as the woman at the tourist office confirmed, there was no way to get to it other than by taxi. However, I could see it from a distance on an organized tour, on the way to an authentic twentieth-century leather factory, where our tour comprised a look over the shop floor from one roped-off end, followed by an opportunity to buy stuff from their shop.

The inclusion of some kind of 'factory' visit in every tour really irritated me, as they were obviously just excuses to herd a load of tourists with Euros burning in their pockets into big shops. I'm sure that the factories must pay the coach tours to stop there. Although I saw one man clutching a canvas organic and wholefood shopping bag fume indignantly 'It's a waste', the vast majority seemed to appreciate the stops. After all, shopping is a leisure activity, and most did indeed buy something.

It was because Mallorca was for holidaymakers that I felt so awkward there. I've taken plenty of holidays by myself and thoroughly enjoyed them. But that's because being a tourist is about discovering new places, and you can do that perfectly well alone. Holidaymaking, in contrast, is something you do in groups, or at least pairs.

Once I had hit upon the holidaymaker/tourist distinction, however, it took on a wider significance. It seemed to me that it applied equally well back home as it did over here. You can approach life in general as a holidaymaker or a tourist, and the English mainly do the former. Comfort, convenience, familiarity, being among people you feel a part of, finding what you like and sticking with it: these describe both the vision of the English good life I had observed in Everytown and the values of the holidaymakers in Cala d'Or. Tourists are the exception. They're prepared to move out of their usual comfort zone, dispense with some of what is convenient, actively look for the strange and different, do things by themselves, and instead of sticking with what they know they like, they want to find other things they like too. In reality, most people are neither pure holidaymaker nor pure tourist, but it's obvious to me which usually dominates.

Quite a few become tourists once or twice a year, but very few manage it all year round. The reason for this is, I think, that we remain for the most part highly social animals, and the tourist ethos is just too individualistic. If we are too adventurous, we cut ourself off from the group, and that is something very few are prepared to do. This contradicts one of the great givens of contemporary social analysis: that we are becoming much more individualistic. The evidence for this, however, seems to me slim, and when you look more carefully, you'll find that the individualism we're buying into is somewhat superficial. The reality is that people fall into three broad categories: the herded, the hefted and the individualistic.

Herded is what I felt like throughout my holiday, especially during the full-day 'best of the west' excursion, which started with the leather factory. But it did improve. We had a dramatic drive over the mountains, via the kind of snaking roads favoured by directors of car adverts. In the shadow of Mallorca's highest peak, Puig Major, the views of forested mountains and valleys were beautiful. At Sa Calobra, there was a stunning ravine, Torrent de Pareis. From there we took a 45-minute boat trip along the rocky, coved coast to Port de Sóller, from which we were whisked to Sóller town. We could perhaps have used more time here to enjoy the relaxed central square, the modernist architecture and the charming old tram, but our train could not wait. As we went through the mountains, the views from its old wooden carriages which date back to the opening of the electric line in 1912 were glorious, even though the journey ends at what is basically a coach park outside Palma. This train is only really for the tourists. Then, it's the coach back.

I saw some lovely places, and this just wouldn't have been possible independently – there were two one-way trips, for a start. But like many, I don't like being herded, spending so much time in a coach and wasting too much time in a leather factory. It's a case of balancing pros and cons. I have more freedom if I travel independently, but the easiest way to see this much in one

day is to go with others. The trend, however, is for more independent travel, reflecting, so it said, the rise of individualism.

But this analysis is too quick and superficial. Sheep need
not be herded, they can also be hefted. I first came across this
word when I watched Johnny's favourite television programme,
The Dales Diary, which was all about rural Yorkshire life. A heft is
the unfenced area sheep learn to keep themselves within. This was
originally taught to them by shepherds, but as time goes by, they pass
it on to each other and need no shepherding. Sheep who learn
this are called hefted, and in much the same way, so are people.
Their territorial boundaries are more complicated and flexible,
but they too rarely stray beyond them, without a shepherd, even
though there are no fences keeping them in. Individualism is a great
myth. All that has really happened is that we have dispensed with the
sheepdogs and have become hefted.

One of the most regulated hefts is the pub. Not only do we
tend to confine ourselves to the same pubs, we also stick to the
same bar, and often the same table. We'll do this even if the grass
isn't just greener on the other side, it's non-existent on this one.
When I first met Reg in The Travellers he was grumbling because
the night before they had switched off the Live 8 concert at 11
p.m. sharp. It's just typical of these new managers, he complained.
The old landlords would never behave like this. 'I'll just sup my
pint and go,' he said. 'I'll have no more of it.' I just knew there was
no way he would have no more of it, and sure enough, he didn't
even manage to leave without having a second pint. He would be
back, for sure, because this is one of his hefts.

The greatest example of the self-deceived hefted human is the
independent traveller. For instance, the one day I felt like a tourist
and not a holidaymaker was when I took off to the capital Palma
for the day. How I enjoyed the 'freedom' of doing my own thing
on my own terms. The reality was that I had a guide book, and I
saw what I was told to see, ate where I was recommended to eat.

Sure, I had some choices to make, but essentially I was just roaming around a heft, not wandering free. The same goes for round-the-world gap-year students, who follow the same old itineraries, hang out on the same beaches, drink in the same travellers' bars and return with the same old travellers' tales. The freedom of the independent traveller is a kind of autonomy-lite: we take a little more control but we don't use it to do anything too radical. And that is the freedom of the modern Western consumer in a nutshell.

The kind of individualism and choice which is apparently on the rise is of this same, hefted variety. Most people remain firmly within their own hefts, choosing only where to wander around the limited space within them. So, for example, if you belong to a certain affluent professional class, you might consider whether to go to Tuscany or the south of France for your holidays, but you wouldn't try Magaluf or Marbella. In the same way, we need no sheepdogs to define the limits of where we can shop, eat, drink or go out, yet if we are honest we will admit that when we do all these things, we're sticking with our flocks. Most fundamentally, as we saw in Chapter 2, it's also true that people choose – they're not forced – to live in areas where they feel as little like the black sheep as possible. You don't need to herd Bangladeshis to Brick Lane, or liberal middle classes to selected areas of North London, they happily find their own way there.

This is not the official story. The modern liberal individualist is supposed to rise above the group and seek value in individual growth and accomplishment, and be opposed to the conservative communitarian view that what is of value is found only within groups, and that to 'transcend' it is really to cut oneself off from your fellow human beings. Self-enhancement for the liberal individual does not mean, as it does for most English people, having more and better of what the group values, but something else, special to you. All this sounds very noble and self-aggrandizing, which is why most of us like to think we're true individuals. In reality, we're like the crowd in Monty Python's *Life of Brian*, who are told that they are all individuals, and reply 'Yes, we're all individuals!' as one. The gag is made perfect by the one person who then pipes up, 'I'm not.' This is as acute an observation on the shallowness of modern individualism you could wish for, and perhaps the punchline suggests that the only way to be truly individual is to start by accepting just how much like others we really are.

Individualism only seems to be on the rise because it is confused with other superficially similar-looking phenomena, notably individualization. It's true that we seek to individualize or personalize more and more of what we own and do. This can range from simply painting your front door a different colour (which for decades wasn't an option for council tenants), buying a bespoke suit, through to having your own personal trainer or life coach. However, this is not profound individualism since almost all these are essentially ways of enhancing your status within the group or of distinguishing yourself in terms that the group approves. Having a different ringtone from your mates is not a mark of true individualism, since you are marking out your difference in exactly the same way that everyone else does. Personalized number plates do not enhance your driving experience or autonomy, they are simply a marker for others to see.

Once you begin to question accepted wisdom about the rise of individualism and take a look around, the evidence that group and collective identities are still very important becomes obvious. Look at the number of crosses of St George on display during the World Cup, or the euphoria over winning the Ashes. Consider the power of the myths of togetherness clung onto by people who romanticize the 7/7 silences or the huge anti-Iraq war demonstration on 15 February 2003. Observe how young drinkers move in packs, especially on hen and stag nights. And what about the durability of the family? It has endured better than conservatives feared and radicals hoped, celebrated in such unlikely places as Radio 4 – where *Home Truths* was one of the most popular programmes for close to a decade – and the *Guardian*, which launched a Family section unthinkable in a left-leaning paper only ten years ago. Far from being a thing of the past, the family has been totally rehabilitated. Togetherness remains what people prefer; think of how negative words like 'separate' and 'apart' sound.

I'm not saying that we have failed to be the true individuals we should be. Rather, we should simply recognize that when we are given the freedom to in theory live as we wish, almost everyone chooses to live within a heft and not strike out alone. That's not a bad thing: humans are social animals. But what it does show is that the conservative communitarian ethos is far more deep rooted than we might think. In this respect, the lives and aspirations of the mainstream English majority have a kind of honesty that many self-avowed individualists do not. For the latter have more illusions. They think their lives are better because they make more choices, they do not conform and their horizons are expanded. Accepting that their choices of car, school, home, food, holiday destination, career, partner, books, newspaper, toilet paper, films, plays, clothes, shoes, political heroes and villains are all, more often than not, the same or similar to those of their heft is therefore difficult. Once we see that almost everyone in England today is part of some kind of a heft, it is much harder to take a superior view of the herd-like instincts of the masses. We are just sheep pointing fingers at other sheep, not bothering to look around and find we're in a flock too.

I'm sure that living as a hefted human is the norm across almost the whole world. What makes the English a little different is that our self-assurance about our own historic greatness tends to give us a certain arrogance that stands in the way of truly opening up to the countries we visit. Our imperial past has not made us more open to foreign cultures, it has actually made us even narrower in our outlook because we expect the whole world to revolve around us. For example, when I asked our hotel receptionist if there were any differences between the English and the Germans (the other main visitors to the island) he said, wearily, that he could go on all night. Asked not to, but to say something nonetheless, he volunteered that the Germans were *más simpático* and *más educado*. '*Educado*' doesn't mean educated in the formal sense. Rather, it is the opposite of what we mean when we call someone ignorant because of their social behaviour. Given that the English are famously polite, this may seem odd. But overseas, our refusal to make any concessions to the fact that we're not in England makes us extremely rude. In one café I heard an English woman ask the Spanish *camarero* who had just served her tea, 'Can you pop some milk in?' The phrase was formally polite but the casual assumption that a foreigner will understand her speaking colloquially, just as she would back home, is very common, and indicative of English arrogance and ignorance.

Although this is clearly a fault, I'm not convinced that overall the life of the hefted holidaymaker is inferior to that of the hefted tourist or the rare true individual. By the last night of my holiday, all I knew was that I had surrendered to the flock. All through the week I had found myself tugging against the holidaymaker ethos, but now it was time just to do what everyone else does. So off I went to The Tartan Arms quiz night. In fact, it was quiz night every night, except for the twice-weekly bingo and fun quiz and Monday's race night.

When I arrived most people were engrossed in *Coronation Street*, the episode where Les Battersby gets thumped by Status Quo's Francis Rossi. The pub was decorated so as to declare its Scottishness with all the subtlety of a Mel Gibson movie. Those faux Irish pubs in England actually reflect the truth that ex-pats often go over the top to keep alive their links to their country of origin. The Tartan Arms even sold Irn-Bru. I asked the landlord if this was the only place you could get it here but apparently lots of Scots come to this resort and other bars had caught on. I ordered a pint of John Smith's and sat at the bar. I had come all the way to Spain to hole up in a corner of Britain. The first language of this pub was English, the staff were Scottish, the beer was British, the crisps were Walkers and the air-conditioning even gave it an autumnal UK chill. But what could be more relaxing? No puzzling over unfamiliar choices or stumbling over stilted communication. You've had a day out or on the beach and all you want to do is unwind.

The quiz was won by a team who called themselves 'Pissed and Broke'. You can guess what one wag shouted out when one answer was revealed as 'the actor who played Victor Meldrew was Richard Wilson'. I didn't believe it either.

The trouble with spending an evening at a British pub is that you tend to get pissed, especially when the single malt whiskies come in such large measures. Hence, the next morning all I wanted was an English cooked breakfast, so I went to Walshies, 'the families bar'. On an island in the Mediterranean I had two small hash browns, toast, mushrooms, fried egg, baked beans and a grilled tomato with a pot of tea. It was the best breakfast I'd had all week. It was just what I needed the morning after. Being English is a package: any single item by itself looks absurd. But live it all together and it makes perfect sense. I went off to buy two bottles of Carlos III brandy and some cigars, and reflected that I couldn't be entirely unlike my countrymen if I was making an effort to bring back fags and booze.

On the transfer bus to the airport, however, I got a feeling I hadn't had before: I wanted to go home. Not to Rotherham, not even to a particular place, but to my world, somewhere I could live as it suited me, my heft. I was homesick for a way of life. Just like these holidaymakers, I have my way which I'm comfortable

with, and that way is actually in part defined by what I'm not comfortable with: groups, a sense of belonging, stability, tightly knit
extended family. I protect my home-world as much as they do.
They 'should' be more adventurous; I 'should' be more accommodating and willing to join in. Or perhaps there is no 'should'
about it. We all seek home, and it is just the arrogance of the person
whose home is different to think it is therefore somehow better.

What is odd, and perhaps even absurd, is that I was finding
typical English life quite tough. I had discovered that it was actually harder than going somewhere really alien. Going to, say,
India, doesn't challenge who you really are. The differences are
too great. You admire the culture, note the striking differences
and see the contrast between us and them. With S66, it's much
closer to home. Us and them doesn't always do it. And you feel
like an outsider where you should be an insider.

By the time I got to Birmingham, delays to my flight meant
that it was too late to get a train back to Rotherham. I had little
choice but to stay at a Travel Inn. I checked in and went to the
bar for a drink. My glass of Campo Viejo rioja crianza was better
than any wine I had drunk in the country of its origin over the
previous week. And what was on the telly? Sky Sports, of course.
Welcome home.

7

Gambling on Reality

Doncaster Races

If you set aside places to refuel (your car or your stomach) there are four kinds of non-residential building which you'll find almost everywhere in England: churches, pubs, bookmakers and hairdressers. The pubs and hairdressers provide some clues as to how we seek pleasure, but the churches and bookmakers tell us something much less obvious. They are clues to the implicit ideas we have about how the world is fundamentally structured, the 'folk metaphysics'. It may sound abstract, but we can no more live without a metaphysics than we can without ethics. Too much of what we do depends upon it.

Of the two, the church reflects the popular metaphysics less reliably. What is preached there is not determined by what people think but by what the local vicar thinks, which could be more or less anything, given the supreme flexibility of the Church of England. For clues as to the English metaphysics, our gambling obsession is a much better bet. And 'obsession' does not seem too strong a word. Bookmakers are now so common that the first one I came across during my stay in S66 was at the Moto service station on the way up. It would never occur to me that placing a bet was as much a priority to travelling Brits as going to the toilet or grabbing something to eat or drink.

According to the official graduate careers service, Prospects, 'Next to eating out, gambling is the largest out-of-home entertainment sector.' The 'out-of-home' activities it is competing with include pubs and bars, restaurants, cinemas, theatres, holiday parks, theme parks, museums, galleries, beaches, the countryside and nightclubs. While 89% of the UK population gambled at least once in 2003, a majority did so between one and three times a week. While the most popular form of gambling was The National Lottery, the other main types were horse racing, greyhound racing, off-course betting, the tote, casinos, bingo, fruit machines and football pools; 5.5 million people attended race meetings in 2003. Official government statistics claim a figure of 6 million for the same year, twice as many as saw a live football match.

The idea that gambling may be more popular than football may seem outlandish, but while football fever comes and goes, gambling runs a high temperature all year round. As a nation we only get behind the England football team at big tournaments. When I went to watch the crucial World Cup qualifier against Austria at The Masons, for instance, the atmosphere was oddly flat. It seemed more like an excuse for an afternoon's drinking. Few people were following the match avidly. But when Michael Owen was awarded a penalty and Frank Lampard stepped up to take it, one table suddenly went berserk. They were shouting, egging him on, and when he scored, there was jubilation. This was odd, because so far most of them hadn't even been facing the screen. The reason for the burst of enthusiasm soon became clear: together they had bet £50 on Lampard being the first scorer at odds of 13–2. Their booze kitty had just swollen to £325. One went off to collect the winnings and they celebrated with a tray of gaudy coloured shots. The World Cup may have been big, but maybe that's because by the time it was over, Brits had bet around £1 billion on it.

Gambling has always been popular, but it has really taken off in recent years after the state sanctioned betting with the launch of its National Lottery and then loosened regulation on other forms of gambling. Catering to the latent demand has seen the sector explode. Betting revenues (excluding lotteries) hovered around £500 million a year through the nineties, but have since rocketed to £2,500 million. Horse racing still accounts for the biggest slice of takings, but its market share is under attack with the emergence of online gaming. But according to *The Economist* the biggest growth areas have been 'football . . . financial spread betting and "novelty betting" on anything from politics to reality TV shows'.

Although sports betting is a mainly male pastime, women also gamble huge amounts in the endless round of raffles and, of course, The National Lottery, on which we bet nearly £5,000 million a year – that's over £80 for every man, woman and child in Britain, of which just half comes back in prizes. No event is complete without a small flutter. There are weekly draws at The Transport Club's jazz night, as there is at the Wednesday jazz at The Horseshoes. There is always a raffle going on in aid of the charity of the year at Morrisons. I took part in numerous raffles but didn't win a thing until my last month in S66, when I won a pair of children's books from a Morrisons tombola. But then, as if to show these things follow patterns, in the same week I won a mini-bottle of Spanish table wine at the Ramblers' Christmas lunch. It was clearly my lucky week.

There are also '50/50' half-time draws at the football and ice hockey, where half the money goes to the winner and half to the club. There was even a draw before the Focus concert. Newspapers run frequent bingo and scratch card games all year round. On one day I got an instant scratch card and a lotto syndicate ticket in the *Mail*; while out from the *Sun* fell the daily lotto and bingo card, plus a Willy Wonka golden ticket game. Both airlines I flew with while in S66 – Monarch and Ryanair – sold their own scratch cards in-flight.

It's easy to miss the extent to which the mainstream media offers gambling services to its readers, because if you don't use them you tend to blank them out. For instance, on Saturdays the *Sun* has a sixteen-page betting pull-out called Favourite, while the so-called quality press still devote a couple of full pages a day to the horse racing cards, with information on form that is not there to help you enjoy the spectacle. And although it's become a bit of a joke, Radio 4's flagship news programme, *Today*, still gives a couple of racing tips every morning.

So what is it about our mentality that makes us so keen to gamble? It's not as though we take risks in general. On the contrary, as a nation we tend to play it safe and stick with the familiar. To see the attraction, I had to take part. My first attempts to become a gambler involved the modest task of taking part in the EuroMillions Lottery, when the jackpot stood at an absurd £55 million. When no one won that, it went up to £66 million, then £77 million. Although I knew my chances of winning were so small I would have been better off just keeping my eye open for a discarded suitcase full of used banknotes, buying a ticket does make you fantasize. When you place a stake you are giving yourself a (tiny) chance that you didn't have before, so it opens up a new possibility. The lottery's advertisers plugged into this with their 'you've got to be in it to win it' slogan. So perhaps what you're buying is a little fantasy, a weekly chance to wonder 'What if?' The unlikelihood of winning actually makes it a safe fantasy. Like the woman in the Spar who dreams of going to Greece but won't make any efforts to go there, the English people like the idea that another world is possible, but not the reality of actually moving to it. There are many stories of lottery winners who either refuse to change their lives or soon go back to their old ones. Tommy Cone won £4.2 million in 2003 but sixteen months later he was reapplying for his old security guard day job, on a part-time basis. It took a similar length of time for the then 16-year-old Callie Rogers to go back to work as a part-time receptionist after a £1.9 million lottery win.

I suspect that wh ile we like to be comfortable, if we get too comfortable, we get bored. Hence we need the frisson of things that are sufficiently different to excite us but not so different as to threaten our basic way of life. Something a *little* different. Fantasizing about winning millions provides one such sparkle of difference, as does getting very drunk in the Balearics rather than in Birmingham, or having an affair with someone you have no intention of leaving your partner for. It is as though we need to pinch ourselves sometimes to make us feel we are awake, even if the pinch ends up hurting us.

The fantasy element may well be one attraction of gambling, but it does not account for the fact that most of the time we bet, we're not going to win life-changing amounts even if it all goes our way. In these cases, I think that the pull of gambling is more to do with the intrinsic psychological dynamic and not the potential rewards. Gambling taps into our feeling that things don't just happen. There is always a hidden purpose or pattern just beneath the surface of life. The week I won the books and wine was a lucky week, for instance, when the hidden forces were going my way. Gambling is one way in which we try to tap into them.

It's not hard to see why people think that hidden patterns are there. In one sense, this is what all human understanding is all about. We would have no science or philosophy if people weren't inclined to look for the underlying order in things. We have evolved to be pattern seekers and once we start looking for them, they crop up everywhere. For instance, three weeks running at The Transport Club I was just one number out in the wine raffle. What are the chances of that happening purely by luck? If there were 100 tickets sold, I could be one number out with two different numbers (assuming I didn't pull 1 or 100), so in any given week the odds would be 50–1. That means the odds of the same thing happening three weeks in a row are 125,000–1. That sounds too improbable to have just occurred by chance. Surely there are forces at work here which we do not know about? If we could only work out what they are . . .

My first trip to the bookies in Bramley certainly didn't make it clear why people would bother if they were in it purely for the entertainment. The place was not full, but around half a dozen men were milling around, studying form guides or watching results come in on the numerous television screens. Despite the turnover of people, most of whom must have been familiar to each other, it wasn't a very sociable place. Without the banter of the two women who worked there, it would have been pretty quiet. I was there for about an hour and a quarter, and in that time just one woman came in. Most punters were there for no more than half an hour at a time. Pete, for example, popped in after his golf round to have a couple of punts and gave me a tip accompanied by an unwavering look of such conviction I could not disbelieve him. He described himself as an occasional better, but the people there seemed to know him pretty well. A few months later he had a heart attack, and the first time he went out afterwards was to place a bet.

Horse racing was the main focus, of course, and despite the fact that it is presented as primarily a sport, everything about the industry puts the gambling in first place. Just look, for instance, at the race times of any meeting. They're often at odd times, like 2.55, or 3.10. Why? Look at all the day's main meetings around the country and you'll see that they are all staggered so that in the bookies you're never more than about ten minutes away from the next race, and no two races start at the same time. The times are to suit the millions at the bookmakers, not the spectators at the track. Further proof of this comes with the times of greyhound races, which most punters put second after the horses. These have start times which look very odd indeed: 1.13, 2.24 and so on, but that's because they're designed to slot in between the main horse races to attract a small additional flutter.

There is some fun in placing a bet and seeing how you do. When you have a stake and your horse is in contention, you get some excitement, or at least tension. It does seem irrational, however, that people believe they can get the better of the book-makers. People study the form and so on, but unless you can assess the odds better than the people who are paid full-time to set them, this can't help. To have an edge you need to see the hidden order of things that often goes unnoticed. The bookmakers only observe the facts of form and so on. But there are more mysterious forces at work, such as the ones which make sure I miss winning a bottle of wine by one number three weeks running.

To beat the system people develop their own systems. Mine was to place low-stake each-way bets on horses with reasonably long odds in short fields. The idea was that this gave me a decent chance of getting something back fairly regularly, as with an each-way bet you win something as long as your horse is placed. I didn't think it was a way of winning in the long run; it should just have made me win often enough to keep it interesting. (What I didn't know was that what counts as a place depends on the size of a field, so my short-fields policy was essentially pointless.)

I scribbled down my first bet on the slip: £1 each way (a total stake of £2) on Surely Truly at the 2.45 at Thirsk. I took it up to the counter not knowing quite what to do, but trying not to look too awkward. I told the young woman serving me that I had never been in a bookies in my life. 'I wouldn't. It's a mug's game,' she replied. 'It can't be much fun working here if you think all the punters are mugs,' I suggested. She and her older colleague explained that they have their regulars who just play a bit for fun and they have a laugh with them. 'But there are customers who lose more in one hour than we earn sitting here all week. That makes your toes curl.' Isn't that just a small minority though? 'There are a few,' she replied, ambiguously.

Surely Truly raced well in a small field of 7 and sneaked in third, not enough to land me any winnings. My second bet was on Peace Offering, an 8–1 shot, at the 2.55 at Doncaster, again each way. He or she came in second, which meant I won £3. A small return, but there was a little kick from winning. Finally, with no small field due to run for a while, I realized that was a daft policy anyway and placed my last bet on the big race of the day: the Stewards' Cup at Goodwood. From a huge field of 28, I picked Fantasy Believer at 16–1, not because it's the perfect name for a gambler, but because Pete had told me the trainer of the two top-tipped horses had backed it. Having been told so confidently it was a hot tip, how could I look him in his probing eyes if I didn't back it and it won? The 'girls' also told me it was a hot tip. Watching the race, I wasn't terribly excited, unlike the man next to me who was clutching his fist and shouting 'Come on' through his gritted teeth. But when it came in third I felt my chest puff out and a grin spread over my face, pleased with myself for having won a fiver. So, over three races, I staked £6 and won £8. I was £2 up for over an hour of, well, entertainment. I left oddly buoyed by this, even though I knew it was pure luck and that £2 is neither here nor there. But that's not the point: I had beaten the system. Somehow, I had tapped into destiny and seen the future. Or so it seemed.

Even more so the next week when I came out £9 up. Two weeks in a row – what were the chances of that? I couldn't help but feel a bit smug, as though I had made smart rather than lucky choices. The next step in the gambler's psychological journey is to think of why you made the choices you did and carry on doing the same. In other words, the feeling that you have a knack, a lucky charm or a system is almost irresistible. That's why people end up with absurdities such as lucky underpants. If you wore them both days you won, it's easy to think that the wearing must somehow have been responsible for the winning. It sounds absurd, but if there are hidden, mysterious patterns, who is to say?

In my case, the fallacy I could have fallen victim to was the one that said because I had a system and won using it, I therefore won *because of* the system. I didn't need to do the maths to know that my system just didn't beat the odds. But the maths would be complicated, and so it would be very easy to kid myself that this was a way to bash the bookies. And so, it would have been tempting to keep the system, but raise the stakes. It was clearly a bad idea and I wouldn't act on it, but I knew the flawed logic was seductive because I couldn't help fantasizing that for reasons I did not yet understand, in the course of two hours I had found a way to win which millions before me had not.

You'll rarely meet a gambler who accepts that at the end of the day it's just luck. Pete thinks that there are ways to beat the odds, either through skill – knowing the form, which stable is coming into a good run, the breeding – or simply by having the right feeling. 'Some days you have the feel for it and some days you don't,' he told me. (Odd then that he hadn't learned not to bet on days when he hadn't got it.) He also thinks you need to be alert to omens or people sending you messages.

Despite the fact that he was the biggest gambler in The Travellers, Pete had no interest in going to a racecourse. So when I did go to Doncaster races, it was with Andy and Neil. The track, which was shortly to be redeveloped, was a bit tatty. Pints were being downed all over the place but there was very little food to soak it up. Outside there were a few vans selling pork roast, burgers and jacket potatoes. Inside the grandstand you could buy crisps and chocolate, or a pie and chips from the grubby seventies canteen-style café. The members' area was doubtless a little more salubrious, since you had to wear a tie to get in. (I'm always amazed at how the English are so adamant that tying a bit of cloth around your neck brings respectability.) There were also stands in the main hall selling framed equine portraits, hats and jewellery.

All the independent turf accountants were gathered near the parade ring, with their stands and boards advertising their ever-changing odds. There was no communicating between them with the traditional tick-tack sign language, nor did they scribble a record of your bet on a card. These days you tell the bookie what you want, a message is passed on to the lackey who puts it into the computer, who then prints out your receipt, which even tells you what you stand to win.

Looking around, it became clear that horse racing bestrides the social classes like no other sport or cultural pastime. Perhaps because, by combining betting and beer, it gathers our two national obsessions in one place. The crowd was cross-generational, with a fair number of women, who would usually be dolled up for the occasion, as though they were going to a wedding. You hear Irish and London as well as Northern accents. Cricket, football, rugby, opera, theatre, rock and cinema all have much more demographically limited audiences.

Andy was determined to get some hot information, and we were hardly inside the enclosure before he heard the magic word 'tip' fall from someone's lips, and he darted off to hear the advice of some bloke with a Benny hat who gave him two names. 'How do you know he's not just some random nutter?' I asked. 'Tha should listen to him, he knows what he's talking about!' Neither of the tips resulted in a win.

Neil thought it was more a case of pot luck, and as a hardened cynic he was politically committed to the view that gambling is yet another ruse for the Exchequer to fleece us. But even he liked to choose horses with names that sounded like they could be omens. He mentioned a friend who had put £20 on a horse called Vic to win at Cheltenham because his daughter was called Vicky. If he had a son called Tribal Venture and saw the horse with the same name running, I might have been more impressed.

All Neil and Andy were doing was entering into the spirit of what makes betting fun. The statistician will tell you that if the odds are fair, then it doesn't matter who you pick: long odds will give bigger wins more rarely, short odds smaller wins more frequently. In the long run, you'll always lose, because built into the odds is the bookmaker's profit margin. The only way to beat the odds is to know that they are not fair, which doesn't necessarily mean they're rigged, just that they do not reflect the true probabilities. And as a punter you are in no position to do this. But if you accept all that and really believe you're doing no more than sticking a pin in a piece of paper, you're depriving yourself of the core pleasure of trying to use all your brain and intuition to see the future. Given that's a key survival skill, it's little wonder we've evolved to be drawn to practise it.

While Neil seemed to play the foresight game for fun, Andy, like Pete, thought he could outsmart the bookies. He enthusiastically jumped on all sorts of information that might point the way forward, even the form description and ratings in the race card, which he clearly didn't even fully understand. At one point he heard someone talking into a walkie-talkie mention a horse's name, so he backed it, thinking he had some inside information. For all he knew, the person could have been saying the horse was heading to the dog food factory. It came in out of the places. When J. P. Spencer romped home in the fifth race at 33–1, he said we were pillocks for not backing him, because he had just been crowned champion jockey. The signs were there all along, if only we had looked for them. This outlook may not have made him money, but of the three of us, he was the one who was revelling in the occasion the most.

Of course, for me to enjoy it fully, I too had to have reasons for my choices. It was the first time I had been to a racecourse since I went with an uncle as a small boy. That time I picked a few winners based on looking at the horses in the parade ring. Ever since I had wondered if I had the knack of spotting a good horse this way. My head has always told me that was ridiculous, since I no more know what a healthy horse looks like than I do one with three days to live, but it seems to be a fundamental human instinct that we constantly keep an eye out for anything that might give us some kind of edge, test it as soon as we can and only discard it if we are certain it is useless. Hence the power of the two sentences which provide the greatest ballast to belief in nonsense: 'You never know' and 'What have you got to lose?'

Once the races started, the spectacle was engrossing. There is a real sense of anticipation as the jockeys mount their steeds and trot off into the distance for the start. There is a three-minute warning, and then on the big screens you see them enter the stalls. When the gates open and the horses spring out, it's like a release of tension. But this is only the cue for it to start building again, tighter than before. As the race progresses you get pointless cheers as people egg on their horses. 'They can't understand you!' I want to say. But it's not rational, it's emotional. You're involved because you literally have something at stake. In most sports that stake is emotional; in horse racing it's financial, which only heightens the emotion. Usually, however, the emotion dissipates towards the end as you see your horse is not in the running. Disappointment is the norm, but that only makes the victories sweeter when they come.

After the first two races, only Neil was up, which would challenge his deeply embedded pessimism. My attempts to spot talent in the parade ring had been so off the mark, I dropped the strategy immediately. Andy was also a little disheartened, as he had paid £1.75 for a small pasty only to discover that he could have enjoyed a piled-high plate of fish, chips and peas for £3.25. We needed a change of luck, so I resorted to the one I had used in the Bramley bookies. And sure enough, in the Startstone Land Rover Handicap Stakes we all backed Don't Call Me Derek at 14–1, who romped home the clear winner. Our horse, the more or less random nag we had plucked out of thin air, had done us proud, and we all felt more than a little pleased with ourselves for making such a good choice. The feeling was reinforced when Makfly won the European Breeders Fund Freeclaim IDC Maiden Stakes to make it two wins in a row. And I got another good win later when I backed Akarem each way at 40–1 and he came in second. By the end of the day, I was £24.30 up. Even allowing for my costs, I had made £15 and had a fun afternoon out. More to the the point, I had second-guessed destiny and won.

Perhaps I had a gift. I had a look at the newspapers' top tip-sters' choices for our meeting. These are people whose full-time jobs are to pick winners. The *Sun's* Templegate ('Britain's No. 1 Tipster') backed three horses, two of which didn't get placed and one of which came second. Likewise the *Times'* Rob Wright backed seven horses, two of which won but five of which didn't even get placed. In other words, three novices from The Travellers in Bramley did better than two of England's top tipsters. We would have been fools to have been impressed with ourselves. During the last World Cup the *Guardian* pitted a sunset wagtail platy-fish called Der Kaiser against the collective wisdom of its readers in a series of bets throughout the competition. The gold-fish, of course, won. Tipsters are just like the astrologers: people read them believing they're onto something despite their terrible track records.

Yet still the sense of pattern and order is irresistible. When I went to another meeting and had a worse run, I couldn't help but feel that I was 'due' a win, even though I understand full well that this is a well-known delusion known as the gambler's fallacy. The principle here is that the probability of a future event occurring cannot be affected by previous, causally unconnected events. If I toss a fair coin ten times and it comes up tails every time, the chances of the next one also being tails is still 50/50. Heads aren't 'due'. The reason we fall for this fallacy is that on an intuitive level we simply do not accept that events are causally unconnected. The cosmos has some sort of order which it imposes, and it will not simply forget what has happened in the past.

You see this in all forms of gambling. The *Mail on Sunday*, for instance, tells you what numbers have and haven't some up in the lottery recently. There would be no point in doing this unless people thought that the draw wasn't really random, but that the numbers pulled out follow some sort of pattern. Never mind that this leads then to contradictory thoughts: numbers that haven't been drawn much recently are 'overdue' but then numbers that have are 'hot'.

The refusal to accept that things just happen lies behind the resilience of what approximates to religious belief in England. Only a small minority are seriously religious. Just 14% attend a religious service once a week or more, while 40% attend once or twice a year or less, and 28% never do. Another study showed that people in the UK are less likely to believe in God than those in any of the other (non-European) countries surveyed. While in the USA 91% believe in God or a higher power, in the UK the figure is just 67%. Oddly enough, while 56% believe in God, 69% identify themselves as Christians, which proves how non-committal that designation is in England. Many don't even seem to know the basics of their national faith. I saw some boys from Maltby amusing themselves on a bus, shouting things at kids from St Bernard's Catholic School, among them 'Catholic!' After a while of doing this, though, one turned to the other and asked, 'What's a Catholic?'

However, it is still the case that the majority hold onto some kind of belief in the spiritual and most people call upon whatever faith they have in times of need. Only a quarter of those polled in the UK said they never prayed, even nearly 30% of atheists admitting that they prayed sometimes. Walking around the tributes to the victims of 7/7 in London, I saw plenty of notes speaking of God, souls and prayers. And 54% of us agree that death is not the end, though with 40% disagreeing, that's a large minority who accept their own mortality. Only 19% would give up their lives for their beliefs, which is perhaps one reason why the actions of the suicide bombers are so incomprehensible.

Normally religion is kept in a separate compartment. It doesn't really affect how we live our daily lives. This allows for apparent contradictions such as one teenage boy who I saw wearing both a WWJD (What would Jesus do?) wristband and an AC/DC belt buckle, thus celebrating both the Messiah and the band who joyously sang that they were on a 'Highway to Hell'.

During my six months in S66, religion was hardly ever mentioned, except in discussions about the trouble of Islam growing in a country which 69% believe has an essentially Christian national identity, and which 72% believe should be based on Christian values. Pete was the only one to ever express an unashamedly religious viewpoint, saying that he was a Christian and, yes, that meant he thought Christ was the son of God. On one occasion, he told me that the advent of global warming and the climate catastrophes had been foretold in the Book of Revelation. But even he hasn't been a practising churchgoer since he was at school. Indeed, central to his faith is not anything specific to the New Testament but personal experiences, which convince him that there is more to life than that which has simply evolved.

The two experiences he cites are of a relatively common kind: a premonition dream which over half of us claim to have had, and a ghost sighting, which one survey suggested 13% of us have experienced. The premonition was a very clear dream in which he 'saw' his third wife years before he met her. She had an anguished look, and she did indeed suffer from severe depression. The ghost he saw when he was a young kid, when he was walking with two relatives near a churchyard. Two nuns, dressed in white, walked past and patted him on the head. But when he asked the others about them, they said they had seen nothing.

When people have had such powerful personal experiences, all counter-explanations seem inadequate. The sceptic often sounds as though he or she thinks he or she is being lied to. That was one reason why I had no appetite to dispute what he had told me. Had I done so, I could have said that there are many reasons to doubt we have genuine premonitions in dreams. First, we dream all the time, and some dreams are bound to find uncanny echoes in what actually happens. Furthermore, the realization that one has had a premonition can only be made retrospectively. And that requires us to remember the dream accurately in the first place. Unfortunately, numerous tests have shown that our memories are terribly unreliable. For instance, one famous experiment found that it was easy to make people believe they had seen Bugs Bunny at Disney World, even though that would have been impossible, since Bugs Bunny is a Warner Brothers character. The fact that we are convinced we've seen something before, or have dreamed about it in the past, does not at all prove that we did so.

However, to explain every detail of why the experience Pete had was not as it seems would be very difficult, if not impossible, and so it is understandable why people prefer the intuitively straightforward explanation – things are just as they seem – to the less complete, complicated one. The same goes for the ghost sighting: people do sometimes see things that are not there, but suggest that to someone in Pete's situation and it sounds as if you're saying he's mad. His explanation is, as he says, just 'common sense'. But common sense sucks. Ironically, it is this readiness to believe the unusual evidence of our senses that leads people to say there is more to this world than that which our senses usually perceive.

Although a sceptic myself, I left S66 more sympathetic to the widespread belief in the spiritual, the hidden and the paranormal than when I arrived. Not because I thought such beliefs might have something to them, but because I came to see that the reasons for disbelieving them are not obvious but are often complex and counter-intuitive. It is not stupidity that leads people to believe. On the contrary, without certain philosophical resources, it is exactly what reason would lead you to believe. One such philosophical resource is Occam's razor. This is the principle that we should not multiply entities beyond necessity, often paraphrased as meaning that we should prefer simpler explanations over more complicated ones. This is a principle of common sense, too, but common sense does not take it far enough. For example, from Pete's point of view, the simplest explanations for his experiences are that they happened just as they seemed to. Alternatives that talk about minds playing tricks and so on look implausibly complex in comparison.

It's only when we take all our beliefs together that the supernatural thesis begins to look the more over-elaborate one. Explaining what happened as some kind of delusion only requires us to accept as true those phenomena which are well understood and within testable experience. We know that the brain is complicated and that the mind plays tricks. We know that thought is sustained by brains and that, therefore, when brains die, there is nothing we have ever found which could continue to keep our minds going. We also know that, despite many claims, there have been no verifiable instances ever of people being able to see into the future. Individual uncanny experiences do not prove foresight, they only prove people believed they had foresight. The distinction is crucial.

In contrast, if we say that Pete did have a premonition or that he did see the ghosts, we are left with a much more complicated and fragmented picture. What are these ghosts made of and why have we never been able to detect them? Why, if seeing the future is possible, is this something that only ever happens fleetingly, in situations where it cannot be tested? Why is it that although there are plenty of people who claim to be clairvoyant, none have been shown to have any special powers, despite their claims to the contrary? How can there be two worlds, one of spirits and one of matter, which interact with each other, when science tells us all physical events have wholly physical causes?

Uncanny events, however, exert a strong hold on our imaginations and it is hard to accept that there is nothing inexplicable about them. In part, that's because we don't realize how unreliable our memories and senses are, perhaps out of fear that if we do, we might think ourselves mad. That doesn't bother me because I think in many ways we are all mad. Another reason is that we have a very poor intuitive grasp of probability. The fact is that all sorts of apparently wildly improbable things happen all the time. For instance, earlier I pointed out that the chances of me missing out on the raffle by one number three weeks in a row was 125,000–1. But what were the chances of the actual numbers that were drawn coming up? That's simple: it was 100–1 each time, so the chances of that exact sequence being pulled would have been a phenomenal 1,000,000–1. But no one would say, 'Blimey, 12, 78 and 32! That was a wildly improbable sequence! There must be some mysterious cause behind it.' Most weeks someone wins The National Lottery, at odds of 14 million to 1. To the winner, it seems too unlikely to be pure chance. But, of course, in a lottery where only chance is a factor, someone will win at those odds. Nothing other than luck is required to explain it.

Every day thousands of things happen to us, and all the time opportunities for coincidences pass. Today, no one rang me within five minutes of me thinking of them. I didn't bump into someone I hadn't seen for years in the street, on the only day they were in town. But over a lifetime, these things, and many uncannier ones, will happen, and when they do, the sheer improbability of it all will be totally expected and will require no supernatural explanation. There is no need to see hidden forces at work.

And yet, this line of reasoning is counter-intuitive. The reason is probably an evolutionary one. As Lewis Wolpert has argued, one of the most fundamental features of human intelligence, the thing that allowed us to develop our mental capacities so far, was an ability to attribute powers of cause and effect to things in the world. We need to do this to survive, and we need to do it without rational proof or direct observation, because neither is available to us. When I turn on the light, I do not see the cause of the light coming on, nor is it purely logical to assume that because this has happened in the past, it will continue to do so in the future. The perceiving of causes is an instinct, a habit, not something that is fundamentally rational. And that means we are apt to see causes where there are none, and we prefer a bad causal explanation to none at all. We are creatures who see hidden powers at work everywhere, when, really, the only powers at work are the random ones of physical chance.

So although belief in traditional religion is not strong in this country, we are only human and so we persist with belief in something less precise. The majority are, as another BBC survey on belief concluded, not religious in any specific way but have 'vague faith'. This nebulous concept of spirituality does two main jobs. One is spurious: people like to think of themselves as spiritual because they think it means they have moral values, and are not just wedded to the purely materialistic. This has nothing to do with being spiritual in any traditional sense, however. Hard-nosed materialist atheists like Richard Dawkins can have strong moral values, love and be moved by the beauty of nature or art. In other words, in this sense of the word, almost everyone is spiritual.

But there is another sense of spirituality which implies some kind of metaphysical view that the physical world is not all that there is. This does not just mean that there is more to be said about life than can be said by science alone: we can all accept that. Rather, it is that there are powers, forces or entities which are outside of science altogether, either out of some necessity or because science has yet to catch up. Perhaps ghosts and premonitions have no scientific explanation at all, or perhaps one day we will understand them. Either way, we are primed to believe in them, because that way the world seems less random than it really is.

So we should not be surprised that York has numerous ghost walks and a Museum of Psychic Experience, set up by the *Daily*

Mail's astrologer Jonathan Cainer, who once successfully predicted that if he opened astrological phone lines that charged 60p per minute, he'd make a fortune. Nor should I have been taken aback by the presence of two New Age shops in Maltby. Bramley, which hasn't got more than a dozen shops in total, is the home of Time for Healing which offers 'hypnotherapy and alternative therapies'. What such shops offer, however, is a rather odd mix. Why, for instance, does Maltby's Exodus New Age store advertise on its sandwich board that it does body piercing? And why the combination in Valentino's Holistic Health, Tanning and Beauty in Wickersley? Spirituality, it seems, really is skin deep.

All this completely transcends social class. The details may change according to social milieu, but the basic forms of belief do not. It took me some time to realize this, since I was initially surprised to see New Age shops in S66, when I associated them more with affluent, Liberal Democrat strongholds like Totnes. I soon realized, however, that what we now call 'New Age' is simply a contemporary manifestation of the timeless hold of superstition. For instance, Michael Collins describes in *The Likes of Us* the common practice of sewing lucky charms into the uniforms of working-class soldiers going to fight in the First World War. In the same book, Collins notes how the Mass Observation studies of the late 1930s identified a public obsession with astrology. I wonder how many of those who pay through the nose for reiki and homoeopathy realize they are simply visiting the modern equivalents of gypsy fortune tellers. The only distinctions that can be made between the kind of New Age nonsense favoured by one class rather than another have nothing to do with proven reliability. You can't dismiss the popular obsession with astrology as mere superstition if you go to a reiki healer. Both are systems of belief that go against all scientific understanding without anything like a sufficient evidence base to do so. Their relative acceptability is purely a matter of fashion.

The newspapers, meanwhile, have extraordinarily uncritical attitudes to the New Age and the spiritual in general, and alternative medicine in particular. The popularity of horoscopes is well known, of course. While it is easy to dismiss these as harmless fun and say that no one really believes them, that's patently untrue. Many people, for instance, explain the way that they are by saying 'I'm a Scorpio'. This is very common, but because people who go to university often learn that this is not considered a very intelligent thing to say, those in graduate professions can easily miss the fact that this is what many people think, or hide the fact that they think it too, even to themselves.

Sometimes it seems no amount of evidence can be stronger than people's will to believe. At Ye Olde King Henry, for instance, the temporary landlords Darren and Karen organized a psychic night. This wasn't a show, but the chance to have a 30-minute one-to-one reading with a 'top psychic' who had been on television, so must have been good. Almost all his £20 slots between 4 and 11 were booked. That's £280 for a night's work – the pub got nothing, except profile and drinks from the punters. One family spent £60 to have three members see him.

Karen told me about their history with this guy. The first time they had booked him, at a different pub, she had asked everyone what he had told them and found he had said the same to everyone: there was a wedding and a baby in the offing. Since most people will know someone getting married or having a baby in the coming year, he didn't need to be Nostradamus to work that one out. Not only that, he had also given Darren and Karen personal readings over the years and she said that nothing he had ever said to them had come true. They were supposed to have come into a life-changing amount of money, so she had bought lots of lottery tickets, but had won nothing. (Give it enough time and of course they will get some kind of windfall, such as an inheritance.) Her sister was supposed to get a man, and she hadn't yet.

Her son was supposed to have met a new love, but he has one of those all the time apparently. Despite the fact that his predictions were so vague and many would probably happen by chance anyway, he had failed to be right once. He even gave them specific lottery numbers once. They didn't win. In other words, Karen had every reason to think he was totally unreliable at best, and a fraud at worst.

And yet, that night he had told her that she and another woman would come into money together. So after having told me all this, she got on the phone to her sister, telling her that they had to buy a lottery ticket together. Still she persisted with the thought that you never know, there might be something in it, and after all, what have you got to lose, except 50p? Or, if you're a punter, £20. Still, on his posters he promised, 'I will not tell you anything bad', so that was one less thing to worry about.

How are people supposed not to believe in this kind of thing when it is not only instinctive to do so, but an uncritical media bombards them with material telling them there is something to it? A self selecting poll by Choices UK said that, '76% said that TV reality shows about the supernatural and films like the spooky *Blair Witch Project* had played a part in convincing them that ghouls exist.' The nature of the poll makes the actual number unreliable, but it would be incredible if the constant media coverage favourable to the supernatural did not have an effect.

The media are even more generous to unproven complementary therapies which are no better than superstitions. You often read statements like this one, in the *Daily Mail*: 'Homoeopathy works on the principle that like cures like, and is a safe and gentle way of treating hay fever.' This is stated as fact, ignoring the actual fact that almost every medical or scientific expert who is not themselves a homoeopath claims it does not work. But still, in the *Mail on Sunday*'s *You* magazine, the health notes column recommends homoeopathic remedies to keep in your first-aid kits. I'm sorry, but there are good reasons why homoeopathic hospitals do not have A. & E. departments.

The *Daily Mail* also runs a series called 'conventional v. complementary' which makes no attempt at all to assess their relative merits: it simply presents both as equal options. In one 'case study' they used 'John Bragg, 57' who 'owns three health food stores', apparently oblivious to the vested interests this entails. But then it seems to go without saying that purveyors of complementary therapies are nice, 'spiritual' people who can be trusted, while conventional medicine is run by a bunch of evil Dr Frankensteins. Still, all the information you need to dismiss the claims is presented in the piece, if you take care to look. We are told that after John took Viridian supplements of hawthorn, co-enzyme Q10 and potassium citrate, he ended up with the blood pressure of a twenty-year-old. However, since we're also told he started going to the gym and his wife stopped cooking with salt, it seems odd to attribute his success to unproven remedies when he also took tried-and-tested measures. Similarly, on another occasion someone who had recovered from cancer said he 'owed his life to complementary therapy' even though he also had chemotherapy and radiotherapy. Interestingly, what he thought meditation, acupuncture, aromatherapy and reiki gave him was 'the psychological strength he needed to carry on', which is pretty close to accepting they were just placebos. Not that the piece itself would dare to suggest such a thing. You don't need to be a rabid opponent of all complementary treatments to see that such reporting is based more on what people *want* to believe than what the facts suggest.

But ranting about it is pointless. You can see which world view has more appeal – the rational or the New Age – by looking at any mainstream book store. At Meadowhall, Ottakar's has three cabinets of Mind, Body, Spirit including such topics as 'Afterlife psychic phenomenon', 'Angels, faeries and spirits',

'Divination and predictions' and 'Magic and ritual'. There is just one shelf of philosophy. Over at Waterstone's, there are ten shelves on Mind, Body, Spirit, against half a shelf of philosophy. I think I now understand better why such ways of thinking are still so widespread in modern, educated England. But this is one aspect of the national philosophy which I think is plain wrong. The world is indeed a strange and mysterious place, but not because of any hidden causal order or deeper purpose. The mystery is largely in the operations of the human mind, a strange organ capable of creating its own vision of reality with little regard to how the world really is. There is no clearer example of that than English metaphysics.

8

Our Cup of Tea

*View from my front bedroom at
Flash Lane, Bramley, Rotherham, S66*

One of the main reasons I wanted to live in an Everytown, rather than simply observe the workings of the English mind from a distance, is that the way people think and the world view they embrace needs to be understood as a whole. The behaviour of the English abroad, for instance, would be incomprehensible if you didn't know how they lived for the rest of the year. Mindsets, like diets, form organic wholes: just as a full English breakfast cries out for a cup of tea and *spaghetti alle vongole* for a glass of wine, so conservative communitarianism, illiberalism, comfort, convenience and hefts all form part of the same philosophical package.

To see this, I needed to immerse myself in all aspects of mainstream English life as fully as possible, which meant setting the radio to the nation's most popular station, Radio 2; only reading the best-selling newspapers, the *Mail* and the *Sun*; and watching solely box-office number ones at the cinema and top-rating programmes on the television. (My cultural diet was more rigorously mainstream than my gastronomic one.)

Rotherham's own artistic legacy reflects the populist tastes that invite derision from the cultural cognoscenti. Duggie Brown, the Chuckle Brothers and Paul '*Hi-De-Hi!*' Shane are four sons of the town who made their names on the northern club circuit before hitting the big time on television. In 1989 Rotherham also gave the world Jive Bunny, whose annoyingly catchy medleys got aunts and uncles dancing embarrassingly at weddings all over the country. And that's pretty much it (apart from former Conservative Party leader William Hague). But before dismissing Rotherham's artistic legacy, consider that *Hi-De-Hi!* was one of the most successful television comedies of its day, and Jive Bunny was only the third act ever to have three consecutive number

ones with their first three singles. If you dismiss these achievements, you dismiss the tastes of mainstream England. And that is
something many people who are otherwise keen to avoid conde-
scension find very easy to do. If there's one thing that will smoke
snobbery out, it's taste.

Consider, for instance, the most popular songs now played at
weddings and funerals. The matrimonial top five is 'You're
Beautiful' by James Blunt, 'Angels' by Robbie Williams (also
popular at funerals), 'Everything I Do' by Bryan Adams, 'The
Power of Love' by Jennifer Rush and 'I Will Always Love You' by
Whitney Houston. For funerals, it's 'Goodbye My Lover' by Blunt
again, 'Candle in the Wind' by Elton John, 'Bridge over Troubled
Water' by Simon and Garfunkel, 'You'll Never Walk Alone' by
Gerry and the Pacemakers, and 'Spirit in the Sky' by Norman
Greenbaum. My first reaction when I read this was not to think
how bad the songs were, but to cringe at the thought of going to
a wedding or funeral where one of these tunes was played. But if
I try to justify this, I'm lost. For instance, I would probably not
mind at all if someone chose something more obscure, but no
better. The cringe factor appears to come mainly from the fact that
these songs have been tainted by ubiquity and become empty
clichés. It is as though the mere fact that they are so popular means
that any emotions they stir must be shallow or ersatz. And that is
precisely what reveals my own snobbery. What I really don't like is,
I think, that people don't care that sincerely loving these songs
marks them out as part of the 'herd'. Indeed, that may even be one
reason why they are chosen for such events in the first place: they
are songs everyone knows, if not loves. The mark of a philistine is
that he does not care how much of what he likes is popular, while
the mark of the snob is that he does. The snob, however, would
probably claim that it is the other way around.

It would be easy to dismiss mainstream England's tastes in art
and culture as unsophisticated, and therefore inferior. But if you

are to take their beliefs and opinions seriously, as I wished to do, you have to get over the snob factor and consider the popular aesthetics, as well as the popular ethics and metaphysics. Given the list of what mainstream England tends to go in for, that can be quite a challenge. The most popular books of recent years have been *The Da Vinci Code* and the Harry Potter series. The populist National Television Awards gave *Dr Who* three gongs for best drama, actor and actress. *EastEnders* was the best soap, Ant and Dec were best entertainment presenters; '*Millionaire*' as it is simply known was the top quiz, Sharon Osbourne won the award for best expert (I'm not sure if Professor Robert Winston was in the running); *Big Brother* was the best reality show and *The X Factor* the best entertainment show. All these selections were reflected in the top viewing ratings these programmes achieved.

When people visit a London theatre, they are more likely to see the kind of long-running musical the critics disdain, such as the inanely plotted Queen musical *We Will Rock You*, than the latest Pinter revival. This is not because they think Ben Elton's magnum opus is a searingly intelligent dissection of the menace lying beneath civilized society, but because it's much more fun and accessible than watching two people talking about cornflakes before being verbally terrorized by a couple of strangers. A woman I met who saw *We Will Rock You* when she had a weekend in the capital acknowledged the plot was silly and 'just an excuse to play loads of Queen songs', but it was a spectacle and as a Queen fan she really enjoyed it.

The nation's favourite artist is Jack Vettriano, who is loathed by the art world and knows it. He told the *Mail*, 'I am an outsider, in so far as I do not have one connection in the art world. I taught myself to paint in a back room and maybe some critics think that is a bad pedigree. But so be it. The trouble is I think their feathers are very ruffled because, regardless of what they say, the public love what I do.'

That pretty much sums up the powerlessness of our cultural elites. The unwashed masses do persist in liking the wrong things. What's worse, they actively deride much 'serious' art as a waste of time and money. The *Sun* knew its readers would be on its side when they reported that 'Barmy health care bosses have blown an incredible £9 million on hospital ART in just TWO years', a figure which 'would pay the annual salaries of 415 nurses'. Actually, most such money came from funds specifically for the arts, so the comparison is pointless, even if claims that such installations are therapeutic are somewhat dubious. The key point, however, is not the rights and wrongs of the specific case, but the way in which spending money on art can be portrayed so obviously as a bad thing. As Keeley, 19, from Kent, said in the incisive *News in Briefs* section – a short sentence or two from a page three girl to show she has as much brains as she does clothes on – money should not be spent on 'pointless sculptures'.

I know that some people will object to the catalogue I have assembled of examples of the popular aesthetic. They will claim that I have deliberately presented a lowbrow picture when, in reality, plenty of 'ordinary people' like high art, and those who don't probably would if they were given a chance. As a way of defending Everyman, however, I think this is fundamentally misguided. Rather than accept what all the evidence shows are the most popular cultural experiences, this argument distorts the facts to show that apparent ignoramuses really do like what the cultural elites say they should like after all. That does not strike me as respecting the aesthetic tastes of the English mainstream.

So how could we set about a more honest assessment? The key is to realize that if the charge against the English public is that it doesn't like enough high art, the case should be dismissed very swiftly indeed. For one thing, much high art is intellectually demanding, requiring a thorough schooling in the history and tradition of the art form from which it emerges, a keen inherent intelligence, or both. So unless the average IQ rises by thirty-odd points and we all spend several years studying all the arts seriously, most high art is always going to be a minority pursuit. This may strike some as harsh and elitist, but actually people have little problem accepting their own limitations. People will often say things like 'I don't understand it', 'It is a bit obscure for me', or 'I can't follow it'. Put these statements into the third person, however, and you'll be accused of being elitist and snooty: 'They don't understand it', 'It is too obscure for them', or 'They can't follow it'. We've got very bad at accepting that not everyone is equally able to do everything, even though this implies no moral judgement. If I don't know what the hell's going on in a Stockhausen composition and you don't know what's going on in Kant's *Critique of Pure Reason*, that doesn't make me a better person than you or vice versa, and nor should it make either of us better than someone who doesn't understand either.

I think that most people can more or less accept that. After all, there are very few people who are so cultured that they fully appreciate all the arts. Most notably, very few people read poetry these days, and no one will think you stupid if you're not one of them. Not liking high art may be acceptable, but what brings out the cultural snob in people is liking 'low art'. What really gets the goat of the cultural elites is not that more of the masses don't read Orwell, it's that so many love *Big Brother*.

But are the most popular cultural products really so risible? I don't think so. For instance, I read *The Da Vinci Code* on holiday in Mallorca and thought it was brilliant. I've heard others 'confess' the same thing, but they always insist on qualifying their praise with something like 'It's terribly written, of course', 'Pure junk, of course', or, as Professor Michael Wheeler, the curator of a cash-in exhibition at Winchester Cathedral put it, 'Good for nothing' as literature, though 'Good as a white knuckle narrative'. The book is allowed as a guilty pleasure, like a Big Mac, as long as you publicly acknowledge that you know it's not that great *really*. If you do insist on saying something intelligent about it, it should be about its cultural or semiotic significance, and not about any intrinsic merit it may have. So, for instance, you might point out that Brown has tapped into what I described earlier as the folk metaphysics, and the way in which that draws us to things which suggest, as Langdon puts it in the novel, that 'The chaos of the world has an underlying order.' Or, as he thinks later, and Brown even italicizes it: '*Everyone loves a conspiracy.*' This ability to plug into the collective mindset should be seen as a sign of authorial skill, not a failing or accidental merit.

In any case, it would be a mistake to write off the success of *The Da Vinci Code* in only those terms anyway. *The Da Vinci Code* is above all a masterful piece of storytelling. It is accused of being formulaic, but actually it's formally quite complex and innovative. The back story spans centuries and involves numerous characters as well as a wealth of the now notorious historical detail, not all of which is nonsense. There are also at least four parallel and intertwined narrative threads, yet despite all this weight, the story begins with action which never lets up, and it all takes place over twenty-four hours. Every one of the 105 short chapters ends on a cliffhanger, and each one is the product of the internal logic of the story, not of ad hoc devices to keep things going. It's a remarkable technical achievement to pull this off, and the book's success is partly because readers are responding to this and recognizing that it is far superior to most genre thrillers.

You might grant all of that but still dismiss the book as a minor work on various other grounds. First, it is received wisdom that the book is 'badly written'. What does this mean? For example, characters are thinly drawn stereotypes. The bad guys say things like 'excellent', like Monty Burns in *The Simpsons*, when they hear good (evil) news. To provide an excuse to let the readers in on some crucial information, people say things like 'But first I want you to tell me everything you know about the priory of Sion.' But all that is good about *The Da Vinci Code* depends on it being written in a non-literary style. The pace and plotting require that nothing is slowed down by complexities of character or literary longueurs. The use of stereotypes is what allows the book to crack on at breakneck speed.

There are other ways in which people try to claim that any merit *The Da Vinci Code* might have is shallow. Cynics say it flatters our intellects by dealing with history and great art in a facile way. But take away the derogatory adjectives and it is hard to see why what is being claimed is a bad thing. The book deals provocatively with history and great art, and the fact that the story is fiction makes us constantly wonder how much is true. It makes us want to look at the *Mona Lisa*, *The Last Supper* and the history of Christianity with fresh eyes. How many books can say that?

Still, people will find more objections. Isn't this an example of craft not art? That's just an empty put-down. If the implication is that craft is just mechanical and a matter of application, that's just wrong. Most writers of literary fiction couldn't craft a thriller like this no matter how hard they tried. Craft should be respected. Top craftspeople are as rare and talented as top artists, and most artists need to practise their skills as much as any artisan.

A final objection might be that art has to be more than just entertainment. This 'higher purpose' argument is highly dubious and John Carey demolishes it with characteristic vigour and clarity in *What Good Are the Arts?* It is romantic tosh to think that people leave a Mahler concert better people than when they came in. The old cliché that Nazis enjoyed their Wagner is no less true or pertinent for being an old cliché. You could even argue that things we enjoy purely for their own sake and not for any moral or intellectual benefits they confer are in some ways superior, since they are valued as ends rather than as mere means. In any case, operagoers and intellectuals enjoy good food and wine and see them as much a part of the good life they lead as the arts they enjoy, even though steak tartare is neither a moral nor intellectual pleasure.

So I would have to conclude that *The Da Vinci Code* does what it does very well and any attempt to belittle it by pointing out the things it doesn't do is simply snobbery, which is tied in with the suspicion that great art can never be so readily accessible. There also seems to be a false assumption that the ease with which something can be appreciated reflects the ease with which it could be produced, as though a literary novelist could toss off a good historical thriller in a weekend.

Once you stop comparing popular art with high art and assess it on its own terms, it is not difficult to see just how good a lot of it is. Indeed, I found very few highly popular books, films and television programmes to be bad, and most were actually pretty good. This is a decent strike rate, considering that no one enjoys every play they go to, or every novel they read.

For instance I saw seven out of the thirteen films that topped the UK box office charts during my stay. None were bad and some were excellent. Tim Burton's *Charlie and the Chocolate Factory* was a wildly inventive, funny and twisted movie, which nonetheless managed to be genuinely very moral. *Pride and Prejudice* was an excellently executed and faithful adaptation of a book generally considered to be a classic. *Wallace & Gromit: The Curse of the Were-Rabbit* was hilarious, ingenious and stamped with its creator's distinctive voice. These are the Dickenses of our day: genuinely popular entertainments which can only be denied the credit they deserve as artistic achievements if we rule a priori that the popular and accessible must be too lightweight to be great art.

Other chart-toppers were enjoyable without being of the same quality, but the same goes for a lot of art and performances.

I don't think that someone who goes to a bad piece of devised theatre is showing greater taste and aesthetic sensibility than someone who goes to a good, entertaining film. The movie *Serenity*, for instance, is a terrific piece of kick-ass storytelling. And although it's not deep, it doesn't lack intellectual content. One of its main themes is the morality of using ends to justify means, which it deals with quite subtly, questioning crude utilitarian justifications without taking an absolutist line. It also deals with the dangers, and needs, of being a 'true believer': highlighting the balancing act of realizing that without conviction we are lost, but too much of it makes us dangerously blind. I'm not saying the film is the profoundest treatment of these issues ever, but it certainly handles them better than some fringe theatre productions or literary novels, and it entertains you a lot more along the way.

Like *The Da Vinci Code*, *Serenity* uses clichés, but again only to enable it to move with the required pace. Without them it might become too hard to follow, especially in the fantastic opening reel, which sets up the scenario in a pacey, original way, giving us just enough of exciting scenes that could easily have been stretched out too thin, and cutting them together in a way that intrigues and takes the story on, and us with it. So why then did the *Guardian*'s critic Peter Bradshaw say 'It really is great' but then award it just three stars? Because with popular art, there is always a difference between great and really great, or, in this case, between really great and *really* really great. It is never accepted wholeheartedly for what it is, and is never worthy of too much praise.

As for the other chart-toppers I saw, *The Fantastic Four* was great fun, *In Her Shoes* was gently amusing and engaging, while *The 40-Year-Old Virgin* was both funny and sweet. The masses may not appreciate Kiarostami, Almodóvar or Riefenstahl (one more against the argument that great art is morally improving), but they won't watch just anything. The most popular popular art is usually pretty good.

It's not just popular art that is of a high standard. I haven't heard anyone try to claim that *Big Brother* is art (although had Damien Hirst created it as an installation that would have been more than possible), but nonetheless, to dismiss those who watch it as voyeuristic cretins is far too hasty. For one thing, the show is popular not only with readers of the red tops. The *Guardian* and *Observer* printed more words about the celebrity version of the programme than the *Mirror* and *Sunday Mirror*. Furthermore, the *Times/Sunday Times*, *Daily Mail/Mail on Sunday* and *Independent/Independent on Sunday* all gave the show more coverage than the *Sun/News of the World*. And, although up to 10 million people watched it, it seems most of the 50 million who didn't, loathed it. Almost everyone I talked to about the programme thought it was puerile, stupid rubbish.

And that's what it looked like to me when I first tuned in and observed a group of uninteresting, self-absorbed, shallow, vain people who never had any interesting conversations. They were both too frivolous and too serious: their interests and thoughts were on nothing of any substance, but they treated their petty squabbles and rivalries as seriously as kids in a playground. Evidence of their stupidity abounded. Craig came out with one line Ricky Gervais couldn't script. Talking about the chat show he'd like to have, he said, 'It'd be fun but also with depth to it, like a cross between *Jerry Springer* and the *Vanessa* show.' On another occasion the deadpan voiceover explained that the housemates had to write and perform a play about key moments in the house. 'Big Brother asked the housemates to choose a genre for their play. They chose "arguing".' For those who thought the 18–25 core demographic of *Big Brother* were all out to 'make poverty history' and 'save the planet', *Big Brother* is a harsh reminder that most people of all ages prefer 'gossip' to big issues, the personal to the political. Just as the *Sun* has few pages on real news and several on the love lives of the famous, so *Big Brother* is a politics-free zone.

However, if you manage to get over your initial repulsion and stick with it, the back-biting, alliance forming and unpeeling of layers of personality do become fascinating. There is something addictive about this kind of thing, which probably helps explain the popular fascination with soaps and celebrity gossip. You want to know what happens to people, even if they are nothing to you. Even if, as in the *Big Brother* house, you find none of them really likeable.

I certainly found one of the main rewards of watching *Big Brother* was forming hypotheses about what people were really like or what they were thinking and then seeing if these were right. For instance, Irish 'babe' Orlaith had been threatening to walk out and had been crying a lot, but most of the housemates said she was just an attention-seeker putting on an act. So when one week when she was up for eviction she said she would walk if she wasn't evicted, they just didn't believe she was sincere. In an otherwise very dignified exit, the person who was eventually booted out, Kemal, laughed at the idea of Orlaith quitting as preposterous. But I believed her, so when she did in fact quit, I was chuffed to be right. And I think many people play similar games with themselves watching the programme. Everyone likes to think they are good judges of character and *Big Brother* gives us an opportunity to test it.

There is an evolutionary hypothesis for why we find this compelling: we have evolved to be empathetic, socially curious beings who need to know how others are thinking to protect ourselves. Reality TV gives us the chance to test and hone our skills in a way which scripted dramas and soaps cannot, since writers often sacrifice genuine human nature for dramatic expediency. However, although the curiosity that draws us to programmes like *Big Brother* has an adaptive advantage, it is arguably not entirely suited to the modern world. These skills and instincts emerged in cultures where you could and needed to understand only a relatively small number of people. But now, with modern media, there is no natural brake on our curiosity about others and these natural desires are indulged to an excessive extent. It is like the way we evolved to stuff ourselves with fat and sugar because for most of our history, we needed to store up calories when we could. Now fat and sugar are plentiful, that instinct is bad for us. So the desire to understand how others' minds work has become insatiable in a society that exposes the lives of so many people in the media. But the desire to observe people and understand how they tick is not in itself objectionable, and this is surely what is so fascinating about *Big Brother*.

By the last few weeks of the series, I was totally hooked. I found myself fearing that *Big Brother* was a terribly misanthropic force, exposing the weakness of human nature. Craig and Makosi were bitching all the time about how other people were sly and bitchy, demonstrating the depressing truth that people are often unwitting hypocrites. And like the psychologist Stanley Milgram's classic experiments, the programme also showed how badly people are prepared to behave if they are given the right incentives by those in authority. On one occasion, Big Brother kidnapped Makosi and put her in a suspended cage, and then offered each housemate in turn a treat, to be paid for by Makosi spending a further thirty minutes locked up. All said yes (Kinga to fags, Craig to pizzas and burgers, Anthony to beer) apart from Eugene, who said no and was also quite distraught, not knowing if Big Brother was playing a double-bluff trick. But instead of being humbled by Eugene, Craig bitched about him being upset, probably because to admit Eugene had been honourable would have showed up his own selfishness. At times like these I sometimes shouted at the screen.

But there are also reasons to be heartened. In general, when the public voted, it punished deceitfulness, nastiness and lying.

The better behaved were saved. In that way, the programme taps into people's innate sense of justice, which is one reason people care so much about who gets evicted. So despite the narrow concerns of the viewers, they are following a basic moral compass. Not that it points infallibly in the right direction, of course. For instance, in all six series of *Big Brother*, the first housemate to be evicted was female. As for winners, three were male, one a woman and one a male-to-female transsexual. Internationally, at the time I was watching the programme there had been 52 male and 39 female winners. The misogyny of a society that judges women more harshly than men is evident in the voting.

The 2005 result was encouraging but imperfect. The final came down to two men: Eugene, the honourable, upright geek; and Anthony, the vacuous pretty boy who managed to steer clear of most of the political battles and bitchiness. The only thing I found objectionable about him was his attitude to women, but as we'll see, that's society's norm. When it came to the crunch, looks triumphed and Anthony Hutton walked out the winner. You could take as the moral of the story that the English have a basic grasp of decency and justice, but that both men and women tend to prefer a vacuous man's man to an interesting anti-bloke.

Given how much the series gives you to pick over in terms of right and wrong, human psychology and group interaction, it's just snobbery to say that people who watch it are mindless idiots. People who follow the show are just fascinated by their fellow human beings, and that, rather than artistic merit, is the perfectly good reason why *Big Brother* is so popular.

While the attractions of Dan Brown, *Big Brother* and blockbuster movies all turned out to be understandable and justified, I struggled to make sense of the large adult readership of the Harry Potter books. I read the first one and though it was clearly a very inventive and witty children's book, I couldn't see why so many adults loved it; so much, in fact, that such adult-orientated collectables as 'an authentic recreation of the famous wizard's wand' for £25 or a porcelain Hedwig Owl for £195 are sold in large enough quantities for their makers to advertise them in glossy flyers in best-selling Sunday papers. It's not like Philip Pullman's *His Dark Materials* trilogy which is richer and more complex than many adult novels. Nor is it like films such as *Shrek*, which operate at two levels to give both parents and children plenty to enjoy. Nor are the grown-ups who read it confined to the generation of 'kidults' – people in their twenties and thirties who continue to indulge in childlike pleasures. I met many much older people, who otherwise subscribe to the Pauline doctrine that when you become a man, you put away childish things, yet read J. K. Rowling.

The appetite for infantile indulgences seems insatiable in England today. For instance, Woolworths aims one-third of its Hallowe'en lines at adults. One feature of the Harry Potter books suggested a reason for this. J. K. Rowling's books are often said to be highly derivative. For the children who read them, this is irrelevant, since to them it must all seem quite fresh. For adults, however, this may be part of their appeal. There is a familiarity to the myths and stories that makes reading about them an undemanding, reassuring pleasure. Whereas any adult novel will deal with relationships, trouble and strife, the trials of Harry have no counterpart to real adult life. The escape is therefore total. And the very formulaic nature of the stories provides familiarity, with the novelty purely in the details. It's about enjoying the different safely, because it is contained within the bounds of the familiar. That should ring a few bells. Comforting familiarity, safe stimulation and undemanding difference are the characteristics of life as a holidaymaker rather than a tourist. And perhaps that's why I have trouble understanding the Harry Potter phenomenon: I still hanker for the life of a tourist.

There were other aspects of popular taste which my inner

snob was less inclined to stay quiet about. Despite the best efforts of Ikea, for example, chintz is still big. When guests come round, there are still plenty of people who will put their cakes on doilies on elaborate cut-glass stands and use a silver slice to cut them. But despite the Hyacinth Bucket stereotypes, most do not do so to put on airs and graces but because they like to. Do the fans of classic plain white crockery really have better taste or have they just learned that this is what their peers judge to be more tasteful? Given what is considered sophisticated changes with fashion, the answer is surely the latter. Was it not fashion that led households everywhere to strip and varnish wooden floors, and then carpet over them once too many of the hoi polloi followed suit?

We love to look down on people's taste in homes. Alain de Botton was hardly being controversial when he laid into the 'Barratt Boxes' typical of new builds. I don't much like them either, but the one I lived in on Flash Lane was comfortable enough. His critique is just another example of highbrow disdain for popular taste. 'One of the reasons people don't protest more about how ugly many new houses look is that no one is supposed to know what is beautiful,' he told the *Guardian*. The possibility that people don't find the houses ugly at all and that they are not stupid for doing so doesn't seem worth entertaining. Pete, for instance, loves his bungalow and thinks the houses on the development it sits in are fabulous. Most people can't afford to live in characterful period homes, which often need a lot of work to make them comfortable. They get what they can afford. Their priorities may not always be quite right. Although average new house sizes have not fallen over the last twenty-five years, they are getting more cramped as people cram in en suite showers, utility areas, playrooms and studies. But it's not obvious that more space and fewer features is the better bet. Most people who suspect it is, including myself, are probably not having to make the same hard choices about what kind of family home to get within a tight budget.

Similarly, I was initially astonished by the couple who wanted to put UPVC double glazing in a listed cottage, but couldn't because of planning restrictions. On reflection, however, I thought our commitment to energy efficiency must be very shallow if it can be trumped by the desire to preserve a period feature. People are very selective about what original fittings they think must be retained. It is not usually considered cultural vandalism to install central heating, plumbed baths and inside toilets in properties that didn't originally have them.

Although I find portraying the 'common man' as more 'real' than his bourgeois counterpart to be romantic drivel, examining popular taste did make me come to appreciate a refreshing lack of pretension. Of course, popular tastes are shaped by fashions and the media, but then elite tastes are shaped by more local trends and fashions too. It is simply impossible to divorce cultural preferences from the social contexts in which they arise and are maintained. If you're going to compare the 'authenticity' of people's preferences I think you need to look at how free people feel to simply like what they like. And on that score, I think the university-educated culture vultures lose out. They often have a sense of awareness of, and concern for, what's in and what's not that is positively adolescent. Anything you admit to liking or disliking threatens to reveal something unflattering about you. In contrast, one of my hosts would happily play CDs of popular arias and songs by Classic FM favourite Katherine Jenkins, oblivious to the fact that many Radio 3 listeners would think them naff. If I'd told her as much, I imagine she might well have felt hurt, but it wouldn't have affected her own enjoyment of the music. In contrast, many of more 'sophisticated' taste are constantly aware of how acceptable or outré their preferences are, which is why all those who liked *The Da Vinci Code* have to add a ritual qualifier admitting it's rubbish.

This makes it hard to keep up with the cultural elite. For instance, one moment burlesque is sexist, reactionary kitsch, the next it's 'primarily a form of satire', as dancer Angie Pontani put it. I thought I saw one example of this constant need to be one cultural step ahead at the Edinburgh Festival when I met two writers who both claimed to love the much derided film *Sex Lives of the Potato Men*. One had seen it six times and claimed it was in his top three all-time films. They claimed that they didn't enjoy it ironically, which is just as well, since irony was by that time out, and sincerity was in. So how does one get the sense of cultural superiority one used to get from irony? Consciously or not, I thought these guys were getting it from being sincere about things people would not believe you could be sincere about. Call it post-ironic perverse sincerity. I might be being unfair to these people, who were perhaps just being sincere without any hyphenations, but very often you get a competitive sense among such people that what you like will say something about you, and you want to make sure it says something at least interesting. It needn't even be a matter of what you like, but how you like it.

Look at what is actually enjoyed at such cutting-edge cultural smorgasbords as the Edinburgh fringe, however, and it's impossible to make a case for its superiority over more popular taste. For instance, I saw one show that was the very parody of a fringe act: *Jonny Woo's Night of a Thousand Jay Astons*, 'a drag lip-synch musical about the alleged slutty one from Bucks Fizz.' I thought it was very funny for about half an hour, but sixty minutes was stretching it thinner than a footballer's wife, being little more than a series of lip-synch routines to a ropy back catalogue. But everyone else seemed to love it, and many in the audience had seen it several times. Fans insisted that it was crammed with great tunes, which seemed to confirm to me that post-ironic perverse sincerity really was in. Never before had the unpretentious enjoyment of *We Will Rock You* appealed more.

If you want evidence of the hollowness of the notion of good taste, do what many people of all social classes do and visit a stately home. I went to Chatsworth House in Bakewell, Derbyshire, a fine country house which stood in for Pemberley in the *Pride and Prejudice* film. Chatsworth is very grand and so are its 105 acres of gardens. But what is there to really admire inside? An early version of what would now be called chav chic: an OTT, tasteless display of wealth. It reflects the passing fashions of its day, when, in the aftermath of the Renaissance, antiquity was in. Hence ceiling frescos and statues are often of Greek and Roman themes, with a bit of Egyptian thrown in. There is little aesthetic reason for this, it was just what every duke who wanted to stay ahead was doing. Nothing is left plain that can be decorated, especially intricately, since fiddly work is labour intensive and so demonstrates how wealthy you are. Visiting Chatsworth may seem like a cultured thing to do, but most of us are simply gawping at the scale and expense of it. We laugh at the Americans who say out loud 'Gosh, to think the Duchess of Devon-shire actually slept in this room!' but isn't that what we're thinking, and what makes it interesting? Indeed, isn't one of the most common comments when people walk around these places, 'Can you imagine actually living here?'

The interior of Chatsworth displays no more signs of good taste than the house I walked around in Rotherham in which the owner had themed several rooms after an era in English history: Edwardian, Georgian or Victorian. In both I saw nice things and tacky things, and in both I saw too much for my liking. Yet one would be sneered at as evidently tasteless while the other would be enjoyed as a remarkable example of seventeenth-century culture.

My defence of the popular aesthetic could be seen as disingenuous, since I haven't changed my own tastes. I still tend to prefer independent films to Hollywood movies, though a good blockbuster always has its place. Nor have I decided to decorate my home with Royal Doulton plates or ordered tickets for a Ben Elton musical. But that would miss all my points. I'm not saying the tastes of the English Everyman are better than those of the more self-consciously cultured. I'm not even claiming that he or she would not do well to give a bit more time to some of the more 'arty' stuff they tend to dismiss. Nor am I denying that a great deal of popular culture is pap. All I am saying is that a lot of what the masses do enjoy has real merit, not in a patronizing sense, but in one that demands respect, whether it's your cup of Earl Grey or not. And I'm also saying that a great deal of what passes for good taste has no more merit at all, and is often valued more for what it is supposed to reveal about its admirers than for its intrinsic value.

The best of popular culture should be seen as part of our culture as a whole, not inferior to or separate from it. If we are to criticize the majority of English people, it should not be for liking what they do, but for confining themselves to those parts of the cultural landscape they are familiar and comfortable with. All echelons are capable of this narrowness, but there are some reasons for thinking that the conservative instincts of the mainstream make it more prone to miss out than those who at least in theory are committed to enjoying culture wherever it is found, regardless of how familiar it is.

I think these conclusions tie in with what else I've discovered about the English philosophy. As elsewhere, the beliefs and opinions of the English do add up to a philosophy that is more coherent and more worthy of respect than is often thought. That doesn't make the mainstream entirely right, not least because it tends to take too narrow a perspective, but it does mean that we should be more careful to ensure that any disagreements are not merely unwitting expressions of snobbery.

That most judgements about culture are exactly that, is, I think, proven by the fact that most people only have a very shallow knowledge and understanding of most art forms. For instance, I don't know many people who are truly knowledgeable about painting. Most will certainly take in a museum or two if visiting a foreign city. They will also have a favourite artist, own a print or two, and probably know a few random bits of art historical information, such as the meaning of chiaroscuro. They might even venture some opinions as to the relative merits of the Uffizi and the Prado, as if they were in a position to judge. The inhabitants of Everytown are no different. The main difference is that the latter are not self-conscious about the right way to talk about art.

Johnny, for example, was a big admirer of Rubens, and though he recognized Van Gogh had great talent, 'let's be honest, Justin, some of his pictures could have been painted by a kiddy.' Pete, who like most of his generation left school at sixteen, liked Rubens too, but went more for English painters like Gainsborough, and the equine painter George Stubbs. 'Stubbsy – he were shit hot. *Shit* hot.' But Pete could also tell you that Stubbs sometimes painted his horses inaccurately, with all four hooves off the ground at the same time. Many of us flatter ourselves that our appreciation of art is more subtle, because we don't use such adjectives as 'shit hot'. Even if we're right, we should be prepared to accept that if people simply allow themselves to enjoy what they enjoy, they will tend to choose the better over the worse from exemplars of the art forms they do appreciate, and that only prejudice and ignorance stop us from seeing the merits of many best-selling novels, top-rated TV shows or blockbuster movies.

9

Ladies and Gentlemen

Keith and Teresa Bury, Maltby, Rotherham

One of the most interesting studies I came across while in S66 concerned the sex lives of the British. One in four men admitted to having had sex with prostitutes, while one in five women owned up to an extra-marital affair. And 37% of males and 13% of females had at least one homosexual experience that resulted in orgasm. More than eight in ten of those interviewed agreed with divorce. But the most interesting aspect of the survey was when it was conducted: it was a Mass Observation study from 1949. The only statistics which would make you suspect that it was not conducted last week concerned marriage: only 68% of males and 50% of females had engaged in premarital sex, and one in three brides was pregnant on her wedding day.

Time and again I had been given reason to believe that English attitudes have not changed as much as we might think. But surely attitudes to sex and gender have altered radically. Growing up in England in the early eighties, it certainly seemed as though we were quite far down a historic road of change that would soon reach its inevitable destination. According to the then standard version of history, sexual liberation took off once safe and widely available contraception divorced sex from repro-duction. Gay liberation was becoming a reality and homophobia would surely soon become as unacceptable as racism, if not com-pletely eradicated. Women's liberation had been following a linear narrative, starting with the suffragettes, through the rise of women in professions and positions of power, due to arrive some time in the not distant future with full equality. Part of this process included the requirement that women should not be treated as sex objects, which meant any indication that a man found a woman attractive was inappropriate in almost all contexts. Back then, the media was heralding the arrival of the 'new man', the latest stage in the evolution of human gender relations. New men were not afraid to show their emotions, they would never wolf-whistle at a woman and they would be caring and considerate, not macho and aggressive.

Looking at England today it is comical that anyone should have believed such things. As the 1949 study suggests, the fundamentals of sexual behaviour remain the same over generations, which is hardly surprising. What is less obvious is that traditional sex roles would be so resistant to change. The progressive story assumed that equality would mean men and women becoming more similar: in stereotypical terms, men would soften up and women would toughen up. But what actually happened was that people rebelled against this and traditional gender roles have become reaffirmed more aggressively than before. This process began under the cover of irony: the magazine *Loaded* launched the fightback with the strapline 'for men who should know better'. But it was never truly ironic, merely knowing: some people won't like this, but we don't care. Boys will be boys and girls will be girls. It was ever thus and ever shall be.

So how do the English see the sex differences, and how does that colour the relations between them? Despite the talk of increased equality, the facts suggest that most people remain firmly wedded to their traditional roles. Recent research at the University of Bristol has shown that although they take time off around the birth of a child, fathers soon revert to working just as many hours as their childless peers. Nor do they want it any other way. While there are nearly 200,000 house husbands, in the *Daily Mail*'s words 'Only 2.1 million women of working age now choose domestic life'. The use of that 'only' says it all. This is a country where a supermarket can advertise that 'Asda mums really do pocket the difference' and their potential customers don't even blink at the assumption behind it.

In Everytown, the acceptance of traditional sex differences

and roles is so deeply embedded that it is a simple fact of everyday life. Down at the House of Steel, one of the sponsors regularly gave an advertiser their plug by saying, 'So ladies, if you want to lose a stone for that Christmas party, give Slim FX a call . . .' One time he added, 'Apparently Slim FX is for men too – I can't believe that!' Over at Wigan's corporate hospitality suite, they had a Miss Wigan Athletic and young, skimpily dressed cheerleaders who the MC sends off with a 'You've made an old man very happy' quip, before going on to tell some jokes about his wife.

Among the generally older drinkers at The Travellers traditional roles are even more marked: wives are rarely seen in the pubs but often found outside, picking their husbands up or dropping them off. One said of his wife – one of the few to regularly come in for a drink – that she was not interested in politics when the conversation turned that way. Johnny also quipped that she was bored and asked, 'Shall we talk about knitting or embroidery?' She didn't appear to take any offence. This seems typical of the area. As a novice driver I went with a mechanical question to a neighbour and I was told by the woman, 'I do the driving and leave all that stuff to him.'

Among men, women are still discussed largely as the kind of sex objects feminists used to complain about. For instance, I was advised early on to go down to The Masons on a Sunday night because of the 'totty'. One of the two guys who told me this phwoared at the memory and noted, 'I tell you, you could stand your pint in some of their tits.' How old was this totty? I asked them. Generally between 18 and 25. And how old are you two? Late thirties and early forties. And these young girls go for middle-aged men, do they? 'Sometimes you get lucky.' This isn't untypical and the men in question weren't Neanderthals. Even driving to the races with Neil and Andy, they ogled and leered at the totty on parade outside, making passing comments such as 'Fuckin' 'ell, I wouldn't mind riding her'.

If the sexes have come closer together in England, it has not been by adopting the most desirable characteristics of the other. Men's hairdressers on Friday afternoons are now as full of people preening themselves for the weekend as women's are. One in four men look for specific brands when they shop, a similar proportion to women. Young women are now just as likely (or perhaps more so) to get drunk and throw up as young men. They also go to football matches wearing replica tops.

Both our top-selling national newspapers reinforce traditional gender roles in different ways. In the *Sun*, it's an unapologetic boys-will-be-boys, tits-out-for-the-lads thing. So, for instance, it sees nothing prehistoric in its 'Bot Idol' competition, 'a sizzling new crusade to find the girl with Britain's best BOT'. As for page three, it celebrated its thirty-fifth birthday in 2005, and got readers to vote for all their all-time favourite. 'Here's our top 20 . . . yes, we know it's 10 . . . do the maths.'

Sometimes the gender differentiations are more subtle. It is well documented, for instance, that the media loves it when victims are young, female and attractive, such as Davinia Turrell, 'the girl in the mask' who survived the 7/7 bombings. In other reports the *Sun* often mentioned that female victims were pretty or beautiful, as though that made it all worse. Of course, whether or not men were handsome was not noted.

The *Mail* is less raunchy, of course, but still it keeps each gender in its place. It jumps on any news that might show that women's liberation has had disastrous consequences. Once it claimed that 'Men who opt out of going to work in favour of running the household and looking after children may be putting their health at risk', since an American Heart Association study showed house husbands were 'almost twice as likely to have a heart attack as men who work'. It also loves stories like 'Abortion pill is a danger to women' and 'Trauma of abortion can last five years', even though the report in question identified the source of the trauma as the circumstances that lead to the decision to abort, such as financial problems, unstable relationships and mental illness, not the abortion itself. The *Mail on Sunday* also reported, 'Registrars warned on bogus gay weddings', even though, in fact, the warning had been about bogus weddings of all sorts.

The *Mail* also likes ladies to be feminine, and saw nothing to lament when it reported that Phillippa Stewart had become the first Oxford student to reach the finals of Miss England, a competition few back in the eighties thought would still exist in 2005. Even our elite universities think it's great that women can be judged on their looks. Oxford issued a statement saying, 'Everyone at the university is extremely proud of her achievements.' And I'm sure her achievements were exactly what the judges looked at the longest.

Stewart cropped up in a 'glamour shoot' for the *News of the World* shortly afterwards, and her look was much more Rotherham High Street than Oxford Quad: straightened blonde dyed hair, plenty of make-up and sultry posing. Still, she had clearly picked up some advanced post-feminist theory at Oxford: 'Some say it is sexist,' she opined, 'but it should be seen as a celebration of the female form.' Interesting use of the definite article that: the only female form that is celebrated is a stereotypical thin, young, busty one. The actual female forms of the vast majority of women are rarely celebrated.

For the unvarnished view of how many men see women, you need to look at the hugely popular men's magazines. The best-selling men's monthly is *FHM*, which sells nearly 600,000, considerably more than *Cosmopolitan* or *Marie Claire*, or the best-selling music monthly *Q*, which has a circulation of well under 200,000. The top weekly is *Nuts*, which sells just under 300,000, slightly more than its rival *Zoo*. Anyone tempted to dismiss the world view reflected in them as marginal should bear these figures in mind.

Media debates have tended to focus on whether magazines like *FHM* and *Zoo* are pornographic, but this misses the point. They are not porn: they are much worse. Pornography may well be objectionable, but it is at least obviously a transgressive fantasy that does not pretend to present a model for actual sexual relations. *FHM*, in contrast, presents itself as reflecting what normal men like and want from normal life. As such, it informs readers' views on reality much more than porn ever could. But in this reality, no women appear who are not a male fantasy, always up for it and in many ways. For example, in 'Girls on the sofa' they interview groups of real women at clubs. All are clearly 'mad for it'. None give dull answers to questions such as 'Do you like to vary sex locations?' and 'Would you invite a "plus one" into your bed?' One answer, from Gabby (18), reads, 'As long as I was a bit drunk and having a good time, I'd be happy to have extra guys – and girls – in my bed.' By using real people this is projecting an image of what the ideal life of a young man can actually be. What's more five of these girls are 18, two 19, three 20 and one 23: many are barely legal. Is it any coincidence they have the youngest girls they can get away with?

The message is that this is just 'how lads are', and the evidence seems to be that young women now simply accept that. There is no shortage of people volunteering for *FHM*'s 'High street Honeys' competition, in which ordinary girls compete to show they're as hot as the top models. The look of girls out for a night on the town is also straight out of the pages of these magazines: plenty of cleavage, fake tan, and straight, blonde-dyed hair. Young women are conforming to the image of how men's magazines think they should look. They will even buy copies for their fellas, as a woman at Birmingham airport did. 'It keeps them quiet, doesn't it?' the cashier said knowingly to the buyer. *Zoo* even ran a competition to 'win a boob job for your girlfriend'.

Plenty of girlfriends would jump at the prize. One survey

suggested that two-thirds of British women would like to have some form of cosmetic surgery, with breast enlargements the most popular option. Making yourself a sex object is now seen as such a natural thing to do that the mainstream seems to think it is positively admirable. For instance, the Rotherham edition of the *Sheffield Star* reported on 'young Rotherham model Holi b', an 18-year-old (barely legal again) who only launched her career a few months before but was having lots of success. This success, which the paper was celebrating, included being a finalist in *Maxpower* magazine and a '*Maxpower* live babe' at a competition at the NEC. She was also a finalist in the centralbabe.com contest. That website warned that it contained material of an adult nature and you had to be over 18 to enter, but actually that was a tease – there was not even a nipple in sight. But still, all the girls posed just like *FHM* taught them to, in their best here-to-please stances. The point is the *Star* reported it as though Holi was on her way to being something really good, not entering a sleezy, demeaning profession. That's because to suggest it is demeaning marks you out as a prude or an old-style feminist.

Feminism has retreated further than where it was when I grew up. The battle to liberate women from the tyranny of having to look appealing to men has been crushingly lost. Another poll, for instance, showed that over half of all women believe that if they had better looks and a better body, they would have a better career. And the depressing truth is that they are probably right, since both sexes have internalized the looks-based value system: in the survey, 78% said other women are more critical of their weight and shape than men. Only 2% felt happy with their body, with 95% saying they felt unhappy about their body on a daily basis.

As for the need to conform to men's expectations, this is now absolute. The women who are celebrated are precisely those who claim to enjoy doing what, by some fortunate coincidence, men want. When *Big Brother* contestant Orlaith got her page three shoot, she said, 'I've always wanted to do this. It's an honour.' Of course it is. What woman would think otherwise? Likewise, the *News of the World* reported on ITV's official 'soap-babes' 2006 calendar, featuring hotties from TV soaps. 'Tina [O'Brien from *Coronation Street*] is usually quite shy but she loved posing for this.' In the same issue, there were previews of the British University Babes 2006 calendar including remarks by 19-year-old Selina Soopramanien, who said, 'I'm a real girlie girl and I like my men [plural, of course] to be just that – men. My ideal bloke has to know exactly what to do in the bedroom so I could just submit and be swept away by passion.'

Male-fantasy lesbianism is also portrayed as amazingly popular among heterosexual women. In the same piece, Rebecca Claire (20) is shot 'girl-on-girl'. It was a real thrill for her, of course. 'I've never been up close with a girl like that. But I loved it! . . . There's nothing more enjoyable than getting naked with a good-looking girl.' Lesbianism is great, just as long as it's of the kind that titillates men and allows them the promise of joining in. Otherwise, it's a joke. *Zoo*, for example, once advertised a 'lezzer' picture special in which they promised 'no dungarees'. The *Sun's* Mel and Becky also apparently enjoyed a lesbian affair which provided a good excuse to snap them together. It also allowed them to rate lesbian couples, in which top marks went to the ones most men would like to see at it, and low marks went to 'butch' types. Male homosexuality, however, rarely gets this kind of positive coverage, because male heterosexuals don't find it arousing.

While attitudes to sex roles are at least consistent and straightforward, attitudes to sexual behaviour are a bewildering mass of contradictions. Most puzzling is the fine line between being a goer or a slag, liberated or a slut. Often this manifests itself as plain hypocrisy. For instance, the *Sun* complained of *Big Brother* contestant Orlaith that she 'has flashed her false boobs every day since arriving in the house in a blatant bid to win the male vote'. Coming from a newspaper that flashes its often false boobs every day on page three in a blatant bid to win the male vote, this was a bit rich. And when Orlaith left the house, the paper signed her up to do exactly what they had been complaining about in the paper. So what is acceptable behaviour for a woman who wants to get attention? How can she be sexy without being slutty? The answer is perhaps that it is not for her to say. At any moment, it might be decided that she has gone too far.

The *Sun*, for instance, ran a story in which it said, 'The dangers of promiscuous sex are made terrifyingly clear today.' On another occasion it published research that may or may not be flawed, but that doesn't matter: the point is how it reacted to it. The paper reported it as 'shocking new research' which showed that a quarter of 16–24-year-olds wait less than a fortnight before sleeping with a new partner, and more than half 'sleep with a fella' within a month. Yet its sister Sunday, the *News of the World,* reported shortly afterwards that 'rampant glamour girl Abi Titmus last night made her most shocking confession yet – she resisted the urge for FIVE WHOLE WEEKS before finally bedding new love Lee Sharpe!' So what's shocking here, waiting a month to consummate a relationship or not waiting a month?

In another issue of the *Sun*, columnist Fergus Shanahan argued that teenagers 'get pregnant because they can't resist the relentless peer pressure on teenage girls that says you've got to have a boyfriend, and if you've got a boyfriend you've got to jump into bed with him. Boys and sex are cool and if you don't conform you're a loser.' The same paper's front page proclaimed 'Ashes hero [Pietersen] pulls Caprice' and 'Wa-hey for Hollywood! Keeley's Hepburn Strip', trailing a two-page raunchy *Breakfast at Tiffany* inspired glamour shoot, as they call it. That looks to me like sending out the messages Shanahan says are causing the problem.

This kind of confusion, however, can have very serious

consequences that can work against both sexes. For instance, what are we to make of this small incident in *Big Brother*? The eventual winner Anthony won a 'date', which involved going into the diary room alone and being given food, drink, seductive music and small talk. Anthony played along as though it were a real date, having a laugh. At the heart of the date was, of course, booze. At one point he said to Big Brother that she was trying to get him drunk, adding that usually that was his technique. His comment echoed that of someone in The Travellers one Friday who said, 'You can take your pick of the girls at this time of night because they're too pissed to care.'

Sometimes it seems that I am the only person in the country who thinks this kind of attitude is pernicious. 'If we didn't get drunk, no one would ever get together,' as one person somewhat overstated the point. But we're not talking about the loosening of English reserve here, we're talking about trying to get girls drunk in order to get them into bed. Imagine Anthony had said that his usual technique was to put Rohypnol or ketamine in a girl's drink. Of course, there's a difference, but the basic dynamic is the same: you drug the woman to lessen her capacity to resist. Sure, a woman can always turn down a drink, but once she is at a certain level of drunkenness, her ability to make these choices sensibly is greatly reduced.

A young man learns that it is normal to have to get a girl very drunk before she'll have sex with him. At the same time, he is also expected to realize that there is a line that should not be crossed between consensual sex and date rape. But how is he supposed to see this line when it is so frequently blurred by alcohol? Young men and women learn that waking up one morning with someone, not sure exactly what you did the night before, is a rite of passage to be laughed about, not a rare aberration. Is that rape? If so, we are a nation of rapists. A woman who says no may be able to be made to say yes, or perhaps not say anything at all, by being plied with drink. Is this consensual sex? If it is, then it is under-standable if people are unable to judge at precisely what point a woman is too drunk to consent and it becomes rape. Far from trying to excuse date rape, I'm suggesting it is even more preva-lent than it seems to be, and that many of the social norms make us complicit with it. If we bring young men up in a culture that encourages them to see women as potential sexual partners whose resistance can be eroded by alcohol, at some point many of them will overstep the mark too.

Evidence of this confusion came in a report by the Forensic Science Service for the Home Office, which investigated 1,000 cases of alleged Rohypnol-assisted rapes over three years and found that not one involved the use of the drug but 65% of those tested had taken alcohol, illegal drugs or both. Given that such accusations would only usually be made when the woman did not remember what happened, it seems likely that in many such cases a woman feels that she has been violated, but the circumstances of the rape are so close to that of a typical drunken shag that from the man's point of view, nothing wrong happened at all.

However, perhaps the oddest thing about modern attitudes to sex is that they totally invert the historic relationship between offi-cial fact and reality. Until quite recently, everyone was at it and no one talked about it. Now everyone is supposed to be at it, and everyone's talking about it, but really, we're not doing it that much. Survey after survey shows that we don't have sex that often, or for very long. A survey by bedmaker Silentnight, for instance, showed that sex is only the fourth most popular bedtime activity after sleeping, reading and watching TV. A more sober study published in the leading medical journal, *The Lancet*, sug-gested that the average Briton has sex once a week and that over a lifetime the average number of sexual partners was seven for women and thirteen for men, suggesting either or both were lying. These results have been confirmed by other serious studies.

These are hardly results which suggest we are an England of randy, rampant sex fiends.

It's easy to miss this dour reality because fatuous polls suggesting the opposite get reported all the time. Polls like the Great British Sex Survey are online and self-selecting, so are skewed by the fact that most people who take part do so for a laugh or to boast. But even this showed that the most common popular answer for the number of sexual partners people have had is between two and five, selected by 34%. Given that we're supposed to be jumping into bed with people all the time, this is a pretty low figure.

What then are we to make of the overall picture of gender relations and sexual behaviour? We seem to be wedded to traditional stereotypical roles in which men have the upper hand, defining how women should be, and finding their demands largely met. This is not because women are idiotic and subservient but because the majority must like being traditionally feminine as much as men like them to. The narrative of 'oppression' is therefore somewhat simplistic, but not redundant, for it does still seem to be the case that men being men and women being women favours those with the Y chromosome more.

Our self-image is of a nation free of all sexual repression, happily indulging our lusts in guilt-free, easy encounters. Forget legends of lusty Latins – Europe's largest sex shop is in Rotherham. But when it comes to actually having sex, we're much more conservative. We don't have sex very often and not with that many people. And we'd do it even less if we didn't get drunk so often.

Is this good or bad news? The most benign interpretation is that the old feminists were wrong. Their mistake was to try to defy human nature. 'Boys will be boys' is not a feeble excuse but a reflection of reality. Freed from the misguided politically correct shackles of how we ought to be, we have simply reverted to type and are happy with it. And that includes young women who are mystified by suggestions that their appearance and behaviour is to please men. They do it to feel good about themselves. Of course, feeling good about yourself is in part due to feeling attractive, but isn't that normal? Every animal wants to attract a mate. And let's not forget that traditional views of gender can oppress men too. We moan about the pressure on women to be feminine, but what about the pressure on men to be masculine? As for the mismatch between the amount we talk about sex and the amount we do it, who cares? The point is that we do talk about it, celebrate it and feel easy about it. Sexuality infuses many of our thoughts and the way we react to people, whether we care to admit it or not. That's why we talk about it a lot, even if we do it rather less.

But I find it hard to be so sanguine. Yes, some earlier feminists did overstate the extent to which gender differences were mere social constructs. But human behaviour is determined by a mixture of nature and nurture, and the pendulum has swung from overestimating the importance of nurture to complacently accepting the inevitability of nature. The result is that the old analysis of women's disadvantaged status in society is now more valid than ever. The argument that women just like to look 'feminine' to feel good about themselves is wafer thin when survey after survey shows that almost all hate their bodies and the way they look, from an alarmingly early age. In the face of these facts, arguing that current attitudes are good for women is perverse. The fact that the status quo is not entirely good for men also misses the point, as this is just what progressives would argue too. Nevertheless, the current state of affairs does suit men more than it does women. As an example, think of acting, where it is true that being good looking is an advantage for both sexes. But it is also very clear that 'unconventional' looks are far more acceptable for men than women.

As for attitudes to drink, sex and consent, if you try to defend them by saying that getting drunk is just how we woo, then it is hard to avoid the conclusion that fundamentally we are as sexually repressed as we ever were. If we were truly liberated, then getting drunk to get laid would be an aberration. After all, Italians rarely get drunk, yet they don't seem to have much trouble copulating.

The harsh truth is that we are not yet at ease with sex. Our relationship with it seems to be somewhat like our relationship with food, which should not surprise us. The thin line between the sexually free and the dirty slapper reveals a nation which can't quite make up its mind whether sex is good or dirty and settles for the compromise that usually it is both. Like binge drinking and binge eating, to let go we seem to need to let go entirely, erasing our inhibitions with alcohol. The Protestant puritan still lurks in the back of our minds, telling us sex, like food and drink, is not something that should just be accepted as part of life.

I wouldn't want to say the current situation is all bad news, especially from a historical perspective. Homosexuals and unwed parents are accepted more than ever, and, officially at least, we accept that sex is a natural thing for consenting adults to do for nothing other than their own pleasure. In many ways, there has never been a better time to be a sexually active English man or woman.

However, the retreat of feminism is worrying, if entirely consistent with England's conservative communitarianism, in which we all have our place and role. The trouble with the reversion to highly traditional gender roles is that they are ultimately constraining for both sexes. We don't have the freedom to be ourselves if everything around us says that to be normal, men must behave in this way, and women that. And it is certainly worse for women. Men are beginning to report more anxieties over their looks and bodies, but the weight of oppression falls much more heavily on women than men, as national newspapers and lad mags reflect. Feminism needs yet another new wave, one that is much more realistic about the tendency of 'boys to be boys' and 'girls to be girls' but which can work with that, not against it. The 'new feminism' heralded by Natasha Walter was meant to do just that, but nearly a decade after the publication of the movement's eponymous book, it has failed to turn the tide. But unless something does change, women's liberation will mean nothing more than the equal right to get pissed and succeed on men's terms.

10

Down with the Youth

*Me ready for a night on the town
styled by George at Asda*

My first striking image of Rotherham's youth came through the window of a number 2 bus as it was pulling out of the Interchange. A teenage girl was sitting on a bench, mouth clasped tightly to that of a boy who was leaning over her, using his left foot on the bench to stabilize himself. She had her arm draped loosely around his neck, and in her right hand a cigarette smouldered. Then, without opening her eyes or interrupting her snog, she stretched out with her right arm and tapped the ash from the end of her fag.

A gap of around ten years is usually sufficient for your juniors to turn into aliens. Decades before you think you're old, you start to notice that you're no longer young. I realized this when I went into a hip Manchester record store and not only didn't recognize half the artists, I didn't understand the categories. Of course, that was the whole point. Youth is always reinventing itself in order to keep the fogies out.

Sometimes their behaviour simply baffles their elders. One Saturday night there was a car smash at the Cross Street junction, visible from my house. A couple of guys down the pub walked past it around midnight, and they saw a young lad filming it on his mobile phone. A copper came over to him and said, 'If you want to see something fucking gruesome, I'll take you down to the fucking morgue. Now wipe that off.' None of them could understand why anyone would want to capture an accident on camera. But I had some sympathy: instantly sharing whatever happens to you with your mates is natural to the young lad's generation, no more ghoulish than talking about what you saw down the pub later, which the older lot did, of course.

But despite such differences and the incomprehension gap they open up, are the nation's young people really any different to the generations that preceded them? In Rotherham, the powers that be certainly hope for 'A New Beginning', the title of a song written and performed mainly by primary school children of the Get Sorted Academy to launch the Rotherham Renaissance master plan. As a symbol for the initiative they chose 'Baby Katy', whose face smiles out on the promotional literature. The hope that the next generation will get it right is one we perhaps have to cling to, in spite of the evidence. Old mistakes are repeated and new ones made. One contemporary folly is that, partly out of an overzealous desire to keep them safe, children spend too much time indoors in front of the television. Teenagers spend on average two hours a day watching TV and two and a half months per year staring at some kind of screen. However, since most households watch 25 hours of television a week, it's not clear who is in a good position to tell them off. An Ofcom study also showed that 73% of 8–15-year-olds have a TV in their bedrooms. This is one reason why there are around 1 million obese children in the country.

A less noticed mistake of the moment is a serious confusion as to whether we want kids to be kids or little adults. Ideas of what it means to be young or an adult have become so stretched as to lose all meaning. One survey showed that on average people believe youth ends when you're 49. The middle-aged are down with the kids, but the kids don't want to be kids anyway. Children are being made to look like little adults from a remarkably young age. On a bus, I once saw a toddler so young she barely had any hair, yet she was wearing an adult-looking gold ring. When I went to get my hair cut in Wickersley, a boy who was not yet big enough to sit in the chair without his mum was being given a wet-look spiky finish, as though he were one of the lads getting ready for a night on the town. Popping around to a neighbour's I saw what I at first thought was a woman sitting in a chair having colouring put into her hair. It was actually an eleven-year-old boy.

It's the Baby Gap effect: parents are discovering the fun of dressing up their children in clothes they think are hip, so the vast majority of children of all ages are clad in logoed gear from as early as they can remember. Should we then be surprised that 78% of children say they love shopping and the average ten-year-old can remember 300 to 400 brand names?

This is even more serious when you consider that dressing children as adults inevitably sexualizes them, as does dressing adults sexily for children. For the 2005 Blue Peter Christmas special, presenter Zoe Salmon, in the words of the *Mail on Sunday*, was 'pictured frolicking in a bikini that leaves precious little space for her Blue Peter badge'. But that's now what the audience expects. People like the girl who looked about ten walking around the Rother Valley Country Park with her parents wearing a pink jacket with 'bitch' emblazoned on it are far from unusual. Parents and even schools largely accept such things as normal. I opened a copy of the *Rotherham Record* one week to see a picture of some Year 8 (12–13-year-old) pupils at Maltby comp who 'put on a dance festival to raise funds for local charities'. They were dressed like the fabled totty down The Masons on Sunday: skimpy tops, short skirts, and one with fishnet stockings. The sexualization of youth has gone very far if this can be printed without even raising an eyebrow. But of course if an adult man were to even express a sexual interest in someone of that age he would be considered a pervert. It's as though we accept it is normal for the young to be sexy but not for people older than them to notice.

Every now and again, however, something catches the eye to make us wonder if we're going seriously wrong. For many parents it's when they see what their little angels are reading. The average age of a *Cosmo Girl!* reader is 14.5, while *Bliss*'s readership is girls aged 13 to 18. Between them they sell over 400,000 copies. These magazines are full of articles on boys and sex, and although

it is true that the details are often very informative and responsible, the general effect is to encourage girls to become sexualized
mini-adults as soon as possible. One month *Cosmo Girl!* was
giving away a free 'sexy top' while *Bliss* had a free 'sexy dress'.

Perhaps it is because little shocks any more that we barely
notice when things might be inappropriate. The woman with her
young child wearing a FCUK T-shirt was not an unusual sight,
though she would probably tell her daughter off if she used the F-
word. Likewise, it is hard to see how adolescents can be expected
to be sexually restrained when exhortations to lack of restraint
appear in the most family-orientated of locations. The old pier at
Cleethorpes, for instance, has been converted into a nightclub,
Pier 39. Overlooking the packed family beach, they spread out a
huge banner advertising their Wednesday club night: 'Get laid.'
(Their website also promises that you can 'Get drunk for free with
our fantastic Champagne giveaways! These include loads of fun
games . . . Roadcone [sic] Challenge – can you drink a whole
bottle of champagne through a roadcone? Or take part in the
Champagne train – the more you drink, the more you get!')

Assuming that, despite all this, childhood does still exist, what
dreams of an adult future do these proto-citizens have? According
to one typical survey, ten-year-olds think the very best thing in
the world is having money and being rich, followed by being
famous. Other surveys suggest boys want to be footballers and
girls models, with pop stars quite high up the ratings for both
sexes. Perhaps it was always thus. But people today are more
media-aware than ever before. They are used to being recorded
and photographed and hence have a feeling that being famous is
not something exotic, as it was in the golden age of Hollywood,
but really something anyone can be. And in many ways they are
right. In a recent *Celebrity Big Brother*, one contestant, Chantelle,
was put in the house because she wasn't famous, with the task of
fooling the other Z-list celebs into thinking she was in a girl

group, which she did. Chantelle marked the end of a progression from people being famous for doing something, to being famous for being famous, to being famous for not being famous.

The extent to which fame is on people's minds was highlighted in *Big Brother*, in a now notorious scene (which seems the right word, despite the supposed veracity of the drama), in which one of the contestants, Makosi, told selected housemates that she thought she was pregnant. This gave new impetus to an interminable 'did they or didn't they' debate in the tabloids which followed Makosi's swimming pool clinch with fellow contestant Anthony. Makosi and her confidante demonstrated how many who aspire to fame have an almost instinctive sense that everything, even the most intimate details of your life, is a commodity to be sold to audiences. In the *Big Brother* house, people rarely look straight into the cameras. But when Makosi dropped her bombshell, her eyes flicked up to one of them, as though she knew she was performing for the world. More than this, her friend Vanessa's first reaction was to say 'You'll be the first person ever to get pregnant on *Big Brother*!', seeing this most personal of events in the most public of terms. When the philosopher George Berkeley said 'To be is to be perceived' he surely didn't have this in mind.

Perhaps children have always wanted to be rich, famous and grown-up too soon. The difference now is that we offer them more opportunities to succeed. Instead of telling them adulthood can wait, we send out a message that they are indeed just like us, by a combination of doing childish things ourselves and giving them the trappings of adult life. That is, until they do something we don't approve of and then, rightly puzzled, they complain that we're treating them like babies. All this may well alter the nature of childhood, but it doesn't fundamentally alter the national mindset. Indeed, it might even help to reinforce it, since by passing on our adult attitudes and aspirations so young, we plant the roots of the adult English philosophy even deeper.

It's hard to be sure, because once they become consenting adults, young people move around in packs and tribes, and it is just not possible for someone approaching forty to casually mix with them as you can with people older than yourself. They only emerge with their own kind, and the very idea of talking to someone older seems weird.

Talking to various people of different ages, however, a consensus emerged about the stages people move through as they grow up. Kids start by meeting and drinking in the streets. Then they graduate to going down The Masons and clubbing. They then pair off and marry, and 'When they have kids the shutters go down.' That's why I didn't see many people in their thirties or forties anywhere other than in supermarkets. As one put it, 'They work hard and they holiday hard.' The annual break is the only time many people get to relax at all, which perhaps in part explains why holidaymaking is preferable to tourism. Only when the kids are older do people go out again, which is why over-fifties provide the core for things like Maltby Tennis Club and the Dearne Valley Ramblers.

The under-age drinkers' hypothesis certainly seemed right. Tennis in Coronation Park in Maltby was usually played with boozing teens in the background, and you often saw groups of youths heading down the road with bottles and cans in plastic carrier bags. The impression is backed up by a website that would horrify respectable parents everywhere, called knowhere.co.uk. It lists 'hook-up spots': 'That hallowed spot where everyone hangs around with their mates dreaming of the time when they can get into the pubs or clubs – a bench, a corner: you name it.'

In S66 I discovered that the Tanyard gets the most recommendations, even though it's in the supposedly nicer end of the district. 'The Tanyard shopping precinct is the best place in Wickerlsey for anyone between the ages of 10 and 16. The best time is around 7 p.m. when all the cider youths come out to play!!!'; 'the tanyard in wickersley (but expect to get beat up by someone with a mullet)'; 'The Tanyard at Wickersley outside Willis. They by White Beast (White Cider), wripp the lable of and get bladdered. There all a bunch of beast drinking youff dreaming of red yova's (Nova's).' (I don't understand that last one either.)

Still, there are plenty of other places to meet if that doesn't appeal. Also 'Friday nights at the REC on FLASH LANE – BRAMLEY is brilliant night out for youths. They go down there to congrigate and drink white shite.' This is a reference to White Lightning, a cheap, strong (7.5% ABV) cider beloved of teenagers and winos everywhere. 'Sorby Way at Wickersley is full of Yoofs who drink beast and 20/20. The Rec at Bramley is full of scrubbers from bentley road who get pissed out of their heads.' If they haven't done so by now, expect the *Mail* to launch a crusade to 'close down this vile website now'. Their readers would at least be right to worry that their own children may well be among the keenest participants in these hook-ups. A survey by Ipsos MORI suggested that teenagers from affluent homes were actually more likely to drink than their less privileged peers, and that although they start later, by the time they're 14 or 15, girls are out-boozing boys.

The rise of female drinkers aside, wasn't it always thus with teenagers? At the moment we're in that part of the cycle where drinking seems to be at a peak, but drug use has actually gone down among 16–24-year-olds. If binge drinking is brought down, I wouldn't be surprised to see drug use go back up again. Young people will always take risks in search of highs of one sort or another. When I was at school, people used to buy bottles of Woodpecker cider, because it was sweet enough to pass for a soft drink, but cheap and alcoholic enough to get you moderately sloshed. People would talk about getting drunk, but the truth is that most could hardly afford enough to lighten the head. All that is new is that today they use the web to spread the word, rather than write 'meet at the rec satadays at 8 if u wont 2 get pissd' on toilet walls, although, actually, they still do that too.

There are plenty who say that kids today have no respect for their elders and are out of control, and there are enough feral youths ready to reinforce that impression. At the Maltby Co-op and Coronation Park they keep the customer toilets locked because kids kept vandalizing them. But all generations have a habit of seeing the worst in the ones that follow them. For instance, the *Sun* once made its cover story about a 'six-mad' 'jobless yob aged just 20' who 'has fathered six children by six different women' . . . 'and yes, you're paying for it'. Yet in a side bar, getting much less attention, was the 'gymslip mum, 16' who gave birth mid-GCSEs, even taking some papers in hospital, on the day she gave birth to Ebony (who is white as the driven snow). Mother Hannah said, 'I might be a teenage mum but it doesn't mean you have to be a failure.' Deputy Head John Topping was rightly supportive: 'She has had an extremely challenging time in her young life but has continued to work hard and seek advice from staff and student colleagues.' The yob is held up as the prime exhibit, and Hannah a mere curiosity.

However, sometimes subjective experience does have an impact that brute facts cannot justify. On one ramblers' walk, for instance, I was talking to a pensioner who was complaining about how the streets didn't feel safe any more. I tried to argue that people's fear was out of all proportion, and that in fact your chances of being attacked as a pensioner are very slim: young men are more likely to be set on than any other sector of the population. But even as I was saying this, walking along an old disused railway line, three boys aged about ten appeared and started shouting questions at us and telling us to watch out because trains were coming. They weren't being nasty, just rude, disrespectful pests. I told them we weren't on a sponsored walk, we were walking for fun, and were having a conversation. After more petty annoyances, my septuagenarian companion gave them a short 'in my day' speech in which he told them you should say 'excuse me' if you want to interrupt people. They just looked at his muddy sandals and said, 'Your feet are a mess.' They then moved off, swearing and calling him an 'old codger'.

Prompted by a remark earlier in our conversation about how no one challenges this kind of bad behaviour any more, I guiltily made an effort to make them realize they were out of order. I had noticed that they were all wearing tracksuits with the name of their club on it (Ravenfield YBC, as I recall). So I asked what was on their backs, as a warning that we might report them to their club. One of the boys replied incoherently, 'Read it yourself, you deaf cunt.' He then weakly lobbed a stone in my general direction. It's then I realized that it's no good saying, 'Don't worry, grandad, they're not going to attack you.' The decline of civility and growth in threatening behaviour makes vulnerable people understandably afraid. In the same way, when my companion moaned about the lack of visible police on the streets, I found myself saying the usual stuff about how a copper on the beat won't stop a crime as a result of his routine patrols for on average eight years, which is true. But again this missed the point: reassurance does matter, and clamping down on low-level misbehaviour – the clip-round-the-ear effect – does contribute to this. And it's also true that we are less likely to tell children off ourselves. An ADT/TNS survey asked the question, 'If you saw a group of 14-year-old boys vandalizing a bus shelter, would you intervene?' Only 34% of Britons would, compared to 40% or more of the French and Dutch, around half of Spaniards and Italians, and 64% of Germans.

All this might well be true, and it explains why people are not necessarily wrong to worry about declining levels of respect among children. But that still doesn't mean that kids in general are out of control. It's just too easy to tar them all with the same brush. Similarly, we seem to be far too easily shocked by tales of teen copulation. A study by Christian Research, for example, showed one in ten children had had sex by the age of 14 and that 22% had done so by the time they were 17. Shocking? Well, I think the fact that 78% of children don't have sex until they're 17 or older suggests that they are rather a restrained lot, given how many messages they get from the media that having it off is the duty of every red-blooded man and woman. Perceptions of pre-teen life seem to be right in many respects, but too pessimistic overall.

What of older youths, those who are over 18? What was their life of pubs and clubbing like? To get some idea, I clearly needed to go out 'binge drinking'. Not that this promised to be fun. A poll of 18–30-year-olds found that 36% of young women said they had been victims of sexual assault after getting drunk; 27% of the women and 16% of the men said they had been arrested or cautioned by the police; 19% of the women and 14% of the men had been injured because of an accident after getting drunk; almost half of the young women questioned said they did not eat a meal either before or during a 'big night out'; almost one-third said they drank too much because they had had a bad day or week; and 31% said they got drunk to make them feel more confident. The youth of today sure know how to enjoy themselves.

But before I could go out, I needed some glad rags. Where could I get kitted out? The answer came to me in a queue in Edinburgh. In front of me were three very chic, posh girls, one wearing some kind of pashmina/shawl/poncho hybrid, sunglasses perched on her head, puffing on a Marlboro Light. Another wore jeans with weird fake fur stuff sticking out from under the bottoms. A female steward came along the queue to check our tickets. One of the girls said to her, 'Those are really nice trousers.

Where did you get them?' 'You're going to laugh,' she replied, 'Asda!' They didn't laugh. They didn't say anything. They were aghast to discover that they actually said they liked something so common. But they are out of step: thrift chic is in. Primark is the new Prada, Asda the new Armani. Asda is now the leading UK clothes retailer by volume, while Marks & Spencer, despite tales of its long decline, is still number one by value.

So clearly I would have to get my disco trousers at Asda. Guessing what would pass for hip in Rotherham isn't easy but I bought a black shirt with tasteful thin blue and white vertical stripes, ideal for wearing untucked with my black trousers, subtly patterned with barely noticeable blue lines, and some black moccasins. The whole outfit cost £42. My game companion bought a truly horrid turquoise blue pleated dress with a gaudy sewn–in silver waist band. With some glam gold high heels her bill came to £25. Five items, £67.

This was actually for my second attempt at a big night out. Because that's not the sort of thing a bloke knocking on forty does by himself unless he's looking to pull or be punched, I was relying on willing visitors for company. However, on the first attempt, my American companion found the experience so excruciating that she felt compelled to quit after about an hour. I thought the English hen weekend she had recently been on had prepared her for it, when in reality it had simply used up all her tolerance and anthropological curiosity.

We had headed for Rotherham town centre's binge-drinking zone, where a police car was already parked up a side street, ready for Friday's fun and frolics. My friend had picked a more or less random bar called Tryst, which felt part pub, part nightclub: it had an upper bar and lower, bigger one with dance floor and DJ.

You could almost smell the hormones as the lads circled in hunting packs and the lasses paraded for them. They were almost all dressed in very revealing, leg- and cleavage-emphasizing clothes, wearing make-up as though the amount you put on indicated just how worth it you were. Many danced in look-at-me ways, raising their arms above their heads and sometimes wriggling up against each other in that girl-on-girl way the lad mags love. The boys, in contrast, were generally standing around in groups, staring at the girls, drink in hand, heads keeping rhythm like not particularly funky chickens. Whereas the women looked as if they had spent hours getting ready, the blokes looked more casual, though the style was just as regulated and studied: short hair messed-up-with-gel, with untucked shirts or T-shirts of a trendy calibre. It was classic meat-market stuff: boys and girls, in separate groups, girls on show, men inspecting. There would be some bids made for the goods later. As my American friend predicted, some of the boys would start dancing badly behind a group of girls as their first approach. From the outside, an anthropologist would most definitely say that almost everything about the way the women dress and behave is designed to 'sell' themselves to potential suitors, who are also behaving just like buyers in a market. But this is mainly a game: if it were normal for such evenings to end with people picking up new sexual partners, then the average number of such partners people had would be far higher than it actually is.

The whole ritual confirmed that the setback for old-style feminism described earlier is not confined to older generations. If anything, the young conform to gender stereotypes more willingly and fully than their elders. Yet the women would say they were doing this for themselves because they enjoy it. Both would be right. The women do enjoy attracting a mate, not just for the mating but also because it makes them feel good about themselves. They also like to provide the bosom-shaped bait for the men to bite on: most women prefer to be sought and not to do the seeking (or at least to seek in such ways that make the man feel as though he is the hunter and not the hunted). But the terms of the exchange are weighted against the women. It is they who have to make the effort and look appealing: the blokes – though better 'groomed' than some previous generations – have much less to do. You could say that the girls have the power to reject advances, so they wield ultimate power. But this is the right of veto, not to negotiate what gets put on the table. What's more, because it places physical attractiveness at the heart of the evening, it is bound to harm the self-esteem of those who see themselves being constantly overlooked in favour of their 'hotter' friends. They can learn to compensate, however, by simply being more upfront. Girls soon learn that most men find it very hard to say no to the offer of any kind of action, and so if you don't have the kind of looks that turn heads, just flaunt what you have got to offer more.

That may be sobering and depressing, but then reality often is. This is the way people behave because it's what they want, not merely because they are brainless pawns in a game of sexual politics. A world in which the sexes know their roles is at least a more straightforward one to deal with. I for one certainly wish that we weren't quite such a feral bunch, and I know enough men and women who manage to opt out of the game to know that we shouldn't think everyone must always be like this. But at the same time, when you see people behaving more or less as they have done for most of human history, it would be naive to think it can all be swept away by a theoretical recognition that this is not terribly empowering for women, or dignified for either sex. Some see it that way, but the vast majority do not.

As a game to play its attractions are obvious, but its appeal as a spectator sport is limited, so this first night on the town was cut short. However, my second attempt was with a northern lass who was able to enjoy the experience as a nostalgic throwback to younger days. Going shopping for glad rags was therefore an essential part of the entertainment, even though George at Asda is not quite Top Shop.

This time we had chosen our destination more carefully: we were on our way to Rotherham's premier nitespot, Liquid + Diva, two clubs in one. The first thing I noticed inside was that it was stylishly done out, felt spacious and the bars looked straight out of adverts set in hip nightclubs. If this was indicative of what is now the norm, clubs have certainly improved on the dank cellars of my youth.

Unlike some city clubs where cool rules only in the sense that the rules are so strict it's not cool at all, here people seemed basically to be out for a good time and didn't much care about what other people thought. Still, we were pleased to see our outfits blend in pretty well. Pointing out people wearing 'my shirt' became a favourite game, and when one noticed us, we compared. 'Nah, not the same,' he said, in good humour. My friend even scored a bullseye, spotting someone wearing the exact same dress as her. Clothes shopping at supermarkets no longer marks you out as poor.

Lined up in the fridges behind the bars were so-called alcopops such as WKD, Smirnoff ice and other bottled mixes. The most popular drink by far was WKD Blue. We ordered one but couldn't even get close to finishing it. It tastes like fizzy bubblegum. But it contains caffeine and taurine, which combined with the sugar and alcohol makes it essentially a delivery mechanism for drugs that will get you through the night. It serves exactly the same function as sweet cider used to, or even worse, snakebite and black, a notorious mix of lager, cider and blackcurrant cordial that was every youth's preferred way to get hammered. It was considered so lethal that many pubs refused to serve it, recognizing that if you ordered it you had only one intention – to get drunk – and that if you succeeded, which you surely would, you'd probably follow it by throwing up. The equivalent while I was in S66 was called a turbo shandy: a sweet, green mix of half a pint of lager and a bottle of WKD Blue.

Young people have always found ways around the problem that while they want to get drunk, their palates find traditional alcoholic drinks hard to take. The only difference is that now the brewers are solving their problem for them. Surprisingly, however, most alcopops are only around 4% alcohol, so although it may seem that the drinkers are getting through them, each bottle is the equivalent of just a half pint. Maybe that's why the brewers have managed to make ordering a shot or two to accompany them de rigueur. Some of the stuff they're coming up with is as vile as it is successful. One brand I saw in many pubs and clubs was Corky's Vodka Shots, foul-looking 'shooters' with flavours such as white chocolate, chocolate orange, coconut and butterscotch. It's the fastest-growing brand on the market – with year-on-year sales up 287%. It's sweet and it's alcoholic. Short of making chips that are 5% proof, what more could a young Englishman want? The brewers' success probably just means people are taking longer to 'graduate' from sweet drinks to 'proper drinks', like ale or whiskey.

Overall there was nothing at all to suggest young people were more decadent than when I first went to nightclubs. If anything, the atmosphere was more civilized than was typical in Folkestone clubs of my youth. As the evening wore on there were some signs of alcohol-induced tension. I must have knocked one girl because she gave me a no-blink stare of death, but the closest I got to trouble was when ordering some drinks. The time before the barmaid had ignored me for ages, serving people who had clearly been waiting less time. So when this time she just turned straight to me, I took my chance and ordered. Being English, I was aware that I had breeched queuing etiquette and so tried to explain to the guy next to me what had happened last time and why there was no point in trying to get her to serve in order. He replied, 'Well, you could have told her I was first. It's just common decency, isn't it?' I apologized. The younger generation can't be all bad if my edgy encounter involved me getting gently told off for being rude.

Security was very impressive. One person was bundled off the floor efficiently by bouncers before anyone could see what the problem was. When I took my bottle to the dance floor I was courteously told to remove it for safety reasons. A bouncer was also looking over cubicle doors in the loos, obviously looking out for drugs.

Even when we finally got to leave, coming up for 2 a.m., people were showing signs of inebriation to a lesser or greater degree, but no one looked horribly pissed. But then, when we were in the lobby, someone from the staff came through trying to get some security. 'The membership desk,' he said and gestured as though to indicate a glass had been shoved in someone's face. Sure enough, a few moments later a guy with his top off was led out, blood coming from his face, saying, 'Who bottled me? Who bottled me?' Another guy followed, held by the throat, though someone else was saying, 'It wasn't him.'

Assuming that the incident was what it seemed, and not an accident, how, if at all, should that have coloured my perception of the evening? 'It was all good natured,' I might say, 'oh, apart from the glassing.' The trouble is that, as Kate Fox has pointed out, young men plus alcohol has always equalled violence in this country. That is a deep-rooted problem of our culture which is not going to change in a hurry. But if anything, attitudes to such violence have shifted, and people are less willing to tolerate it. The managers of the club certainly knew that. 'I don't want him leaving looking like that,' said one of the security staff of the bleeding man. Incidents such as these can cost licences.

Drinking seems to have changed in two ways. One is that women are doing it too. That is a concern if you think it's bad behaviour in the first place, but since most people seem to think there's nothing wrong with men getting bladdered, focusing on women drinking is just hypocrisy. The second difference is that concentrated drinking zones have emerged in town and city centres as drinking joints have clustered ever closer together. Go back forty-odd years and most boozing would be done at a local. This change has made it much more common for groups of drunk young men to bump into other groups they don't know and for sparks to fly. It may well be a serious issue for local authority licensers, but again, it doesn't suggest that anything fundamental has changed. Even the racial profile of the city centre pubs and clubs seemed remarkably old-fashioned: black and Asian faces were rare, and the few we did see were generally together.

Nor is there any sign that the clubbers won't make essentially the same progressions to home and family as their parents and grandparents did: 80% of 16–25-year-olds expect to marry and have children, 82% believe family is important and 92% yearn to buy their dream home.

The future of the traditional English philosophy therefore looks pretty secure. Such changes as have occurred do not run deep. We need not worry about the decline of values in youth, but neither should we be filled with a new hope that they will radically change the future. As *FHM* put it, 'No matter how grim life gets, you'll always have beer, curry, football . . . and sex. Well, you may not *have* it, but you can always read about it right here.' I hate to say it, but on that score *FHM* shows it understands the English mind better than most high-brow publications.

11

The End

Roche Abbey, nr Maltby,
Rotherham, December 2005

It had been coming almost as long as I'd been there. The first sign of the festive season in S66 came on 9 August, when I saw the first 'CHRISTMAS BOOKINGS NOW BEING TAKEN' banner outside Ye Olde King Henry. Soon after, a similar sign went up outside the Hellaby Hall Hotel. That may seem early, but by late November Ye Olde King Henry was already fully booked for Christmas lunch. Christmas may come but once a year, but it likes to stay as long as possible.

Christmas and New Year for me meant the end of my time in Everytown. Then it would be back to Bristol and all the trappings of pseudo-bobo living: Fairtrade organic cappuccinos that cost £2, restaurants that source local seasonal ingredients, independent cinema, Fresh and Wild as well as Sainsbury, ideas festivals, harbour festivals, music festivals, chip shops that sell calamari, a full-time professional theatre, a nationally acclaimed arts centre, jazz in styles that post-date the war.

I got a sneak taste of my old future life when I had to move most of my stuff back to the south-west after the house I had been living in was finally sold. I was lucky that I was offered a room in someone else's house, who didn't even want any rent for it. Others would have offered too. Everyday kindness is often overlooked, but it makes a big difference. I had seen plenty of it here. The move itself depended on another act of generosity. I had not had my licence long enough to hire a van myself, but Neil offered to drive one down to Bristol, and return with it by himself while I sorted things out. This he did at a constant 69 mph, convinced as he was that the bastard police would fine him if he dared exceed the speed limit.

Arriving back in Bristol, I soon got a reminder of one of the main differences between life there and in S66. Unloading outside my flat, I passed a woman from downstairs who had been one of my neighbours for a year. I don't know if she even recognized me, but we didn't indicate any familiarity to each other. Such a response from my Bramley neighbours would have been inconceivable.

Yet after Neil went and I'd done some unpacking, I went out with a friend and soon felt a real lift from being back in the city I chose as my home. Yes, it had been a good six months in Rotherham and yes, I had met nice people. But life there just does seem grey, drab and colourless compared to the variety on offer in the city. The fundamental similarity, however, is that both me and my S66 friends want to live where we fit. In Everytown, the tailoring is close fitting, whereas I prefer something baggier and more accommodating. But it's still a question of cutting your cloth to fit your jib, and for all my talk of greater choice, adventurousness and so forth, I am as much of a type as anyone else. This really hit me in an unavoidable way when I was in North London with some time to kill. I had not had lunch, it was getting on for 4 and I craved something Italian. I settled on Carluccio's café where I had some olives, a porcini lasagnetta and a glass of red wine. In between mouthfuls I read some of *True Brits*, a book about eccentric English traditions. As I was finishing up, another single man of around my age came in and sat a few tables down. He too had some olives before his main course arrived and he also read a book. The myth of my own individuality was shattered yet again. I can argue for the superiority of my own choice of life if I like, but I should not pretend I am a rugged individual to Everytown's sheep. We all find our hefts.

I was only in Bristol for a day or two, however. I had to get back to Bramley to see my time through. By that point I had the feeling that another few weeks wasn't going to significantly alter my understanding of the English philosophy. The last month was more than anything an opportunity to see whether it did all really fit together and add up. It was not one I grasped as eagerly as I might have hoped, however, since I spent most of December with a rotten cold. Prior to this I hadn't been sick for ages, but this one was a real nasty bugger. I wondered whether this had anything to do with my adopted lifestyle. Perhaps being more English had literally made me ill.

A trip to Hull for a writing job provided one opportunity to get some perspective on the journey I'd been on. I had been following the progress of Justin Irwin, a north London-dwelling charity executive who had given up work to try to qualify for the World Darts Championship. Now, at the New Walton Club – a working men's club – he was finally playing in the qualifiers for the Professional Dart Players Association World Championship finals.

When I first saw him play it was at the Hampshire open in Southampton in the spring. That was a real culture shock for me: an overwhelmingly white, male working-class environment in which beers and cigarettes were the main fuel. Tattoos were the norm and many players wore gaudy nylon shirts emblazoned with their nicknames: Dale 'The Artful Dodger' Newton, The Muffin Man, Martin 'Silver Burch' Burchell, The Thriller, Smack-On Rooney, John 'Old Stoneface' Lowe, Steady Eddie, The Wizard, Peter 'Snake Bite' Wright. But now the environment felt quite natural to me, even though it was still not my locale of choice. Who knows how much I had been able to understand the English mind, but at least it was no longer utterly alien to me.

Justin got an unlucky draw against Simon Whatley, a former world championship quarter finalist, ranked about thirty-five in the world. He did creditably, throwing the only maximum 180 I saw all day, but he still lost. He had enjoyed his own immersion in a much purer working-class world than that of Everytown. We both seem to have appreciated the lack of bullshit, pretension and lifestyle competitiveness that goes with professional city life.

But not enough, however, to embrace it as our own. This is where I have to be more honest than those gushing television anthropologists who talk of how wonderful life in so-called primitive tribes is and how much we have lost in our modern ways, yet base themselves in that depraved West and take its pay cheques. My own choice between two less extreme options rested on the issue of limits: to get the benefits of a more typical English life, you have to be prepared to live in the ways that foster the communitarian conservativeness it depends on. I'm just too fixed in my individualistic ways for that.

I'm also too fixed in my gastronomic ways. Not living in my own place during my final weeks meant I cooked less. This gave me the excuse to try some popular 'dining solutions' I had hitherto managed to avoid. For instance, opposite Morrisons there was a McDonald's which had a drive-thru. I had never been to one of these in my life and when I pulled up at the ordering hatch, I had even managed to miss looking at the menu. It didn't need to be prominently displayed because most people know exactly what they want already.

I felt as if I was on a factory assembly line, which in a sense I was, as the process is based around them assembling your meal as easily as possible. At window one you order – veggie melt deli sandwich on brown please, and small fries. At window two you pay and are handed a little bag with condiments – or in my case a couple of serviettes. Then at window three you collect, except that because deli sandwiches are cooked to order I actually had to pull into bay one and wait for it to be brought to me, which it was, very quickly.

So what did I do next? I could have taken it home, I guess. But that would have been delayed, not instant, gratification. So I pulled up in the car park to eat it, sitting in the seclusion of my own car, with views of other cars, munching on bland mass-produced fast food which I had got without leaving my vehicle. It seemed grim, but there was a constant flow of vehicles while I sat there chewing. If food is fuel, which for the English it still primarily is, then this was the ultimate delivery mechanism.

Another type of food I hadn't eaten for ages, and not at all in S66, was a frozen ready meal. So I tried a new-fangled Birds Eye SteamFresh meal. 'Steaming is an excellent way to retain the *fresh flavour and goodness* of food,' I learned from the packet. 'That's why our chefs have created New Birds Eye SteamFresh meals to gently steam in the microwave, *using succulent and tender ingredients* for a delicious and satisfying meal.' They made it sound so tempting. I had bought salmon with penne pasta and a dill sauce, and the salmon was actually wild. Carrots and broccoli were an odd addition but it all helped to make for a more balanced meal. And the ingredients were actually largely gunk-free. It tasted fine, but I couldn't see why you'd eat them regularly. The flavours of these things are crude and become less appealing the more you eat them. Nutritionally it was 335 calories, 1.5% fat, 6.4% protein, 9.9% carbs, of which 1.9% sugars. Eating convenience food does not necessarily mean eating junk: that's just what we often choose.

Other than frozen meals and drive-thrus, takeaway options in Maltby were limited. I had already become an expert on local chippies. Bramley's was run by a Greek family. I once asked them if they'd do any Mediterranean specialities – some calamari, perhaps? The woman laughed at the suggestion. But there are only so many chips you can eat, so I tried the inevitable Indian takeaway. After a few, I was beginning to tire of every dish tasting the same when I passed it one evening to find that it was locked up. A handwritten sign said that it had shut for refurbishment. But the official council notice next to it revealed it had been shut down because of an infestation of rodents serious enough to pose a risk to health. I sighed at the thought that yet another prejudicial stereotype – the dirty Indian takeaways where you can't trust what goes in the curry – appeared in real life without me looking for it. Only the other week the *Advertiser* had reported of another Indian in the town centre that had been shut down for similar reasons. Once again I was reminded that people may generalize too widely, but very few of their fears and anxieties are not based on some kind of truth. It's what you make of the truth that matters.

Nevertheless, with their value of toleration, the English can on the whole be trusted not let their fears and prejudices get out of hand. For instance, Diwali lights had been put up in a central Rotherham street and no one seemed to mind. Anyone can do what they like as long as it doesn't threaten 'us'. There was even one encouraging sign of how, given time, cultures can mix without anyone even noticing. In the market, the traditionally British and all-white Whiston Brass Brand played 'Mary's Boy Child', a Negro spiritual.

The benign side of a culture which values toleration but not integration also manifested itself when I went to get my hair cut at a barber's which I had been observing since I had arrived and which I had only ever seen Asians use. Funnily enough, however, when I went in, there was another white customer in a chair. Still, it felt like a community centre for Asian men, several of whom came in, sat around, smoked and chatted without having haircuts. Newspapers and posters on the wall appeared to be in Urdu, as was the conversation, though the fasting calendar was bilingual. My barber didn't seem keen on small talk with me but chatted happily to others in his language. I eventually asked what the (clearly light-hearted) debate they were having was about. He leaned in and whispered in my ear, 'Dirty talk.' Then, 'He is asking what it tastes like downstairs.' Another pause. 'He says cheese. What do you think?' Funnily enough, I wasn't that keen to offer my opinion. However, I did find this oddly reassuring. Of course, all around the world, in any culture, you find blokes being blokes, boasting and talking dirty. It's not very edifying but it does suggest that beneath the surface differences, people are just people, and their reluctance to mix and integrate with people they perceive as different is not a gesture of hostility. We should worry less about integration. Who cares if a barber's has an almost exclusively Asian clientele, just as long as when a white customer does come in, they are happy to cut his hair?

But still the nation was agonizing over the place of its minorities, and toleration was being stretched by the perception that Englishness was under siege. These fears were exploited by the papers who went mad for stories about politically correct councils banning traditional Christmas celebrations. Even the Archbishop of Canterbury seemed to get caught up in the *Mail*- and *Sun*-induced paranoia. 'This year there seems to have been even more stories about the banning of Christian images and words by silly bureaucrats,' he wrote in the *Mail*, failing to point out that more stories does not necessarily mean more cases, and that most of the stories turned out to be spurious anyway. If reasserting England's allegedly Christian values means allowing people like the Archbishop to pontificate even more, then that is one more reason to oppose it.

The *Rotherham Advertiser* joined in the frenzy. It reported that the local council was 'under fire as carols are axed'. The actual facts are that previous Christmases had seen carols, recorded at Rotherham Minster, piped around the town centre to create a festive atmosphere. This year there were none, but instead the council had programmed more live carols and brass bands. But still, the paper duly talked up the story as being about traditions under attack, giving space to a 'local activist' – who writes a lot of letters to the *Advertiser*, including one on an unrelated topic published that week – Marlene Guest from Kimberworth Park: 'I know it is because they don't want to offend non-Christians,' she said, with certainty. 'I think it is appalling because they are chipping away at our religion, tradition, culture and way of life we have cherished for centuries.' I read this and then took a look at the council's main leaflet for festive events, titled 'Get ready for Christmas in Rotherham'. The word 'Christmas' was everywhere and among the events listed were several in Rotherham Minster, including Advent Songs of Praise, the Christingle service, nativity service, carols by candlelight, midnight mass on Christmas Eve and both holy communion and family Christmas communion. In other words, all this talk of political correctness gone mad had gone mad. But it did reflect the Zeitgeist sense of the indigenous English culture being under threat, a sense that is not going to be diminished by making people feel obliged to mix and integrate more than they want to.

The build-up to Christmas continued to gather pace. The number of houses with elaborate external light displays was truly awesome. Who can begrudge people who work 48 weeks a year in this grey country a little excess during the darkest month? But there does seem to be a price paid for all this heightened jollity. The concentration of the big displays seemed inversely proportionate to wealth: Maltby's poorer former local authority houses were done up the most. Once someone giving me a lift even took a detour to admire all the various lights on show. She liked the big outdoor displays, some of which were described as pretty, others as fun. But it also made her think that her own more modest line of lights around a bush just didn't compare. There is an element of competitive consumption to this which makes Christmas a bane. No wonder an estimated 2.4 million people were still paying off debts they ran up the previous Christmas.

Christmas certainly seems to get bigger every year, but maybe that's just because mine gets smaller. The living rooms of my neighbours were highly festive; one sported a Rudolph taller than the kids. Plenty would turn their noses up and say that the typical English home at Christmas is tacky, but it's not meant to be tasteful. It's for the kids.

Various groups I had been involved with had their festive

dos. The Dearne Valley Ramblers had their Christmas lunch at The Rockingham Arms in Wentworth. For £7.50 we got the world's smallest prawn cocktail, turkey that must have been reared in baking trays to keep it within budget, trimmings, a tiny slice of Christmas pud with brandy sauce, and instant coffee. But I would take that over a fine feast that priced half the members out. It reminded me that the English disregard for the quality of their food is largely a matter of disinterest, and that this is hardly a sin.

One guy on the walk before the meal provided another example of the English desire to see order and patterns in the randomness of life. He told me he always wins raffles. He tells people, 'I'm going to win', and they don't believe him. But in the Christmas raffle (included in the meal price), in which there were almost as many prizes as tickets, he didn't win as much as a cracker. Nor did he at another group's Christmas lunch the day before. People will always look for patterns, ignoring any evidence that suggests there are none.

The last Wednesday jazz night before Christmas at The Horseshoes was also a bit of a party. Regulars brought food to share and donated raffle prizes, so there was a wide selection of sausage rolls, meaty sandwiches, quiche, cake, and some cheese and biscuits. A fine spread is a wide spread. People piled up their plates but still didn't get close to finishing it.

One of the regulars complained that the music at Christmas party night is never as good as usual. Too much 'having a bit of fun'. One woman was allowed her annual chance to sing and though she did so with great enthusiasm, once a year seemed about right to me. There was also a 'New Orleans-style' parade, which wasn't actually a parade because there was no space to move. Rather, the band got their parade gear on (sailors' caps, and, er, that's it), the drummer strapped on his bass drum and they all stood up. But the key ingredient was the ladies who brought decorated umbrellas. A good dozen or so all stood up and worked their way towards the front, spinning their brollies and bopping roughly in time with the music. This is a British adaptation of the New Orleans tradition of the parade band leader having an umbrella, and my friend finds it embarrassing. Then, of course, came the raffle, where numerous bottles of wine and big tins or boxes of chocolates such as Quality Street, Roses and Cadbury's Miniatures were snapped up.

Also in the run-up to Christmas came the TV evening of the year: the showdown between the live finals of *Strictly Come Dancing* and *The X Factor*. They went head-to-head at almost identical times, and both had an early evening final followed by a prime-time results show. About 23 million saw both shows, getting on for half the country. And, as I had learned to expect, the *Sun* reported 'Bookies take £3 million in bets on who'll win.'

It was more reinforcement of what I had come to believe: little fundamental has changed over recent generations, and our entertainment culture remains rooted in the traditional working-class model of a big night out, even when it's spent in. Here we were in 2005 watching updated versions of timeless classics: *Opportunity Knocks* with more glam and bigger prizes, *Come Dancing* with celebrities and more glitz. The main difference was that they had perfected the formula, which both programmes followed. In both results shows we started, after some tension, by finding who had come third, then the last two performed one more time before the final vote, in which the public decided. And the stakes were higher than in the old days too: *Strictly* raised £1.5 million for Children in Need; the winner of *The X Factor* got a £1 million recording contract. They even showed the single going into production live straight after the result. It was the bookies' favourite for the Christmas number one, even though they didn't yet know who would sing it. And, of course, the bookies were right. Before the final result, we were shown films of 'what they've been through' and 'what it means to them' so the emotion is really ramped up. Things aren't what they used to be: they're just bigger and better versions.

For Christmas itself, however, I got out of the way of my kind saviours, who even offered to share their family Christmas Day with me. A big part of me thought 'great for the book!', but I felt this would overstep the decent boundaries of hospitality, so I took a cottage just outside Sheffield with a friend. For Christmas Day, however, it just had to be The Travellers for lunch, where we had booked for the second sitting. When we arrived, the first lot of diners had all gone, which was surprising, especially since it turned out they were running about 30 minutes late. But I shouldn't have been surprised. The English are very bad at long, lazy lunches. The puritan in them can't see the point of hanging around longer than it takes to get the food down you.

It didn't feel like The Travellers at all. None of the evening regulars were in for a drink, and their bar had been taken over for food. The meal itself was the basic carvery with knobs on, charged triple, which is fair enough, because staff costs are much higher on Christmas Day. But what I noticed most of all were the signs of social unease on several of the nearby tables. It was as though the people weren't used to either sitting around a table and eating, eating out formally, or both. One table next to us hardly exchanged a word throughout. On the other side, a couple and a daughter (I can't presume to say 'their') were largely quiet but got there in the end. Given that Yorkshire folk are a chatty lot this seemed especially odd. It is as though the situation was not just unfamiliar but actively unsettling, perhaps a little too different.

There was snow in the Peak District before we left the cottage, and of course our return to the outside world on 27 December had to be shopping at Meadowhall. We were late. A record six out of ten stores opened on Boxing Day and, as the *Sun* put it, 'Three million Brits went on a £5 billion sales spree.' It was sale time, and the English poured out onto the streets as though being deprived of shops for two days had sent them into consumerist cold turkey.

The papers continued to run true to form, with the big two playing their smiley cop, miserable cop double act. The *Sun* knows that Christmas is a feel-good time and led with a story about the Tsunami one year on, quoting 'the angel of the beach' Tilly Smith, 11, who said 'It wasn't death that won the day . . . humanity triumphed.' The *Mail*, however, knows that there is no holiday from anxiety and insecurity. Its front page screamed GREAT BOGUS BARGAIN SCAM, giving stressed sale shoppers more to worry about, while we were also given a STAY HOME WARNING AS SNOW HITS and found out about PETROL PUMPS RUNNING DRY. Bah humbug.

More snow offered the chance to be reminded of how rural England remains. I took advantage of the scenic white blanket and walked the short 7.5 mile version of the waymarked Maltby circuit, which takes in fields and villages such as Hooton Levitt, Carr, Brookhouse, Laughton-en-le-Morthen, as well as Roche Abbey. It was a beautiful walk in the crisp air under clear blue skies, and all on the doorstep of one of Rotherham's most deprived areas. Yet few others were walking, though a good number were sledging on the slopes at the back of St Bartholomew's Church.

And, then, finally it was New Year's Eve. Not everyone came out to toast in 2006. Good, miserablist *Mail* reader that he is, Neil hates to see his local full of people who never usually come out and so stayed in. Andy also stayed at home with his family. It made me realize that what I had been thinking of as a single group of friends was really a loose coalition of overlapping alliances. But this is surely what any apparent community is: a series of networks. If there are enough of them, and they overlap, you have what we can call a community, but it's never homogeneous. The so-called decline of community is no more than a loosening of these networks. The idea that we have lost anything more singular is a myth. Even if everyone did know of everyone else, they disliked or didn't much care for many of them.

Reg and Pete did come out, as did a few others, and as it was a special night, we took Pete's traditional New Year's Eve tour of the village, starting at The Master Brewer, a pub I hadn't been to. The Brewer felt more like a solidly working-class pub than The Travellers. It seemed everyone was smoking, women were dolled up to the nines, a gang of young girls were all dressed up as bunny girls. It reminded me that the Everytown I had come to know was not in any way extreme, that I could easily have gone for grime and grit, and that anyone who thinks the England of this book represents only the working-class end, not the mainstream middle, doesn't know the half of it.

I found myself back where I had started: in a pub, with something that looks like racism. Only this time, the joke (told by someone I didn't know) really was racist. I think I can tell the difference better now, but the joke was a reminder that although the majority may not be deeply prejudiced, a sizeable minority are. The point is neither to confuse the two, nor excuse them all.

One person I chatted to in the pub ran a vocational training company, which gives skills and opportunities to young people who have neither. He provided a good example of how unsocialist traditional working-class Labour voters are: everyone thought his work was pointless crap. Reason number one was that it was largely paid for by European money which is taxpayers' money, i.e. our money. Number two, the people the money is spent on are work-shy wasters. So much for the solidarity of the proletariat. But, number three, what really riles them is that he makes a very good living out of it, as do many chief executives and senior managers in public services. When you consider that Andy earns £12k a year filling vending machines, you can see why they find these high salaries repugnant.

There was some kind of minor mêlée in The Brewer, so we headed off. We couldn't go into The Ball, because they had a dinner dance on. I caught Pete looking through the window, his usual intense stare transformed into something more ponderous, less certain. What he saw were people in what was until recently a rough pub, dressed in black tie, sitting at table dining. There were no familiar faces: at £40 a throw this was mainly a gathering of the village's new money, the people who didn't usually come out at all. It was as though Pete was getting a glimpse of another world which was going to come and take over his. If he could have looked into their minds, however, I suspect he would have seen that this new world is much like the old one with more money and pretension.

Not that the old world has passed yet. Next stop was Bramley Working Men's Club. It was 11.30 on New Year's Eve, and in the concert room they were calling bingo. Big fun in Little England. But time was short, so it was only a quick one there before heading to The Travellers for midnight. The other bar was full with mainly twentysomethings and their disco. But our bar was subdued. Many people actually left twenty minutes before midnight, to see in the New Year in front of their own televisions, I'd guess. People pay a lot to buy their homes and make them comfortable: it leaves them with less cash and inclination to spend as much time in the pub as previous generations. Reg was among the early leavers, so when New Year came, it was me, Pete, a couple of others, and no big song and dance, even though it was now also Pete's birthday.

By 12.45 that was it. Farewell to S66, not exactly with a whimper, but not a bang either. I was leaving with too many thoughts and not enough order to them. What you have been reading is a retrospective attempt to make sense of it all. I left convinced that my main challenge was to do justice to the people I had met, some of whom I had come to call friends, without glossing over their faults and my strong disagreements with some of their beliefs and opinions. That, fundamentally, is the task of all intellectual inquiry about people: to try to see the strongest case for why they believe and do what they do and still be able to scrutinize it and disagree if necessary. (The same could be said for international relations.) That is the only way to be both humane and intellectually honest. I'm not convinced I've always managed to be both, and sometimes trying your best is not good enough.

So as I drove off the next day, I didn't have a neat summary of what I'd learned. I could sum it up later. In the mean time, it felt more as though I had tuned in and had come some way towards being able to look at the everyday and see in it a reflection of the way the English mind thinks. Had I really cracked it? Listen to what the universe is trying to tell you. As a last sop to the English gambling obsession, I had bought a Lucky Dip Lotto ticket for the New Year's Eve draw, even though I had never won yet. 7, 16, 33, 36, 48, 49. Checking the numbers at the service station I found I had won £10. Maybe it was an omen: at last I had really hit the small time.

Epilogue

The English Philosophy

Colin Newey, Bramley, Rotherham

It was August 2006, over seven months since I had left Everytown. I was returning to S66, this time not by train but in my M-reg Vauxhall Corsa. It was to be its last decent run before I sold it. Much as I had enjoyed joining the car-owning majority, for a city-dweller like myself it had become an expensive luxury, not the necessity it is for most of my fellow countrymen.

Between leaving and returning I had been able to sift through my experiences and findings and now I felt I was in a position to be able to tentatively sum up the philosophy of the English people. And, perhaps surprisingly, I had found that it could be broken down into the standard categories of academic philosophy.

First, there is epistemology and metaphysics: what there is and how we know about it. Like our leading scholarly philosophers, we are a nation of empiricists who are more trustful of experience than we are of detached reason. But we are too willing to accept the apparent evidence of our own senses and experience, and fail to take seriously the possibility that we could be fundamentally and systematically mistaken about how we perceive things. Hence the high regard placed on 'common sense' which is often little more than unquestioned, inherited assumption. This approach leads us to see patterns and purposes in nature which are no more than artefacts of random, purposeless events.

Second, there is ethics. As reputed, 'fair play' is central to our ideas of right and wrong, but, contrary to official proclamations, this does not necessarily mean playing by the rules. Giving and getting your due is what counts, and since human beings have a tendency to self-serving bias, in practice this means hardly anyone thinks they aren't due at least a bit more than they've got.

Ethics is not just about right and wrong, its also about the best way to live, and, like Aristotle and Epicurus, we seek happiness and pleasure. But our Protestant, puritanical past has not been left behind, and when it comes to the pleasures of the flesh, we don't seem able to enjoy them fully as simple, natural goods. Instead, we binge and purge. Food is fuel and filling up at a good price is valued over quality. Nor are we very good at savouring our meals: we eat quickly, in front of the television, or on the go. We feed our faces then diet, and when we drink alcohol we tend to down too much too quickly. Our fascination with reading and talking about sex hasn't stopped it being a bit dirty, and it is sometimes impossible to tell where we draw the line between liberated sexual enjoyment and lewd behaviour. It seems we cannot help thinking that everything that is good is also bad, and we can't quite believe that the two need not go together.

We are a nation of hefted holidaymakers who believe in finding what we like and sticking to it. We then, quite naturally, become concerned to maintain our status within that setting. For many who see themselves as working class, this leads to conspicuous consumption, if the opportunity arises, but little anxiety. For the self-identifying middle classes, however, status is the cause of some insecurity. The reason there is so much fear in the *Daily Mail* is because its readership is all too aware of how close it is to the 'lower' social orders its families have escaped from. Like Agent Starling in *The Silence of the Lambs*, they have a Hannibal Lector whispering in their ears, reminding them that they are only a few generations away from 'poor white trash'. On one level they probably sense that their attitudes are largely shared by the groups they seek to distance themselves from. We are not primarily individualists. We like to stand out, but only as high-status individuals within the group, not genuine individualists who have rejected the group's values.

Our political philosophy is linked closely to this. We are conservative communitarians who believe that rights and privileges are derived from membership and commitment to English society, and are not equally applicable to all, irrespective of family history or current behaviour. This makes us illiberal, because it means we do not believe that principles such as right to fair trial or life have to be maintained at all costs: rights can be forfeited or suspended. We are tolerant of those who want to live differently in our midst, but only if by doing so they do not threaten to become so numerous or vocal as to change the fundamental character of English life for the majority.

Ethics and politics also meet in our attitudes to sexual difference. The argument that women should have equal rights before the law may have been won, but there is now little sense that women are being systematically discriminated against on the basis of underlying sexist assumptions in society. Most people believe, rightly, that men and women are generally different. But this has led us to complacently embrace once more traditional sex roles that were challenged in the sixties and seventies. Fat is no longer seen as a feminist issue, and the desire to look 'good' has become seen as something all women naturally want to do. Social norms have distorted whatever truth is in this insight so that almost every woman is now unhappy with her appearance. If feminist thinking is to advance again, it must take on the lesson that most people want men to be men and women to be women, in ways that traditionalists will recognize.

The popular aesthetic is not one that can be summed up in a number of neat principles, but then high culture has also defied numerous attempts to define what makes something a work of art and in what its value rests. Nevertheless, the best examples of popular culture do have real merit, and if something is very popular, there are usually good reasons for its success. What blinds admirers of high culture to this is perhaps that such hits are of course highly accessible, and that a certain stern view that really good art should be difficult still prevails, as does an elitist sense that what too many people like can't really be that good.

This English philosophy is extremely resilient, despite the many superficial signs of change since the Second World War. Despite increased wealth, the dominant culture is working class in character, and despite their mysterious fashions, the young English look set to preserve our philosophical tradition for future generations.

So when I arrived back in S66, it no longer felt strange but comfortably familiar. By chance, when I turned on the television, I caught the slapstick routines of Rotherham's own Chuckle Brothers, purveyors of old-school comedy for a new generation. Clubland lives on. In the *Rotherham Advertiser*, Marlene Guest had another letter printed. 'We are struggling with human rights laws that have made a mockery of justice,' she wrote. I wondered if she would be writing in protest when this book comes out.

The paper also reported that race-related incidents had risen 25% in the year to March 2006 compared to the year before, under the headline '7/7 backlash'. But Councillor Shaukat Ali was still talking an upbeat message about community relations, saying that the rise was a result of increased awareness, not more actual incidents. The report is an example both of the ongoing problem of race relations in the country but also of the dominant desire not to bring things to a head. Few seem keen on either confrontation or real engagement, but want to try mutual toleration for as long as possible.

There is also more fuel for people's fears, with reports of a shooting in Thrybergh which left a man seriously injured, reminding me that although people may worry too much, they don't fret about crime and disorder for no reason.

There were some changes. The Rotherham Renaissance plan was moving along slowly, causing pain in the short term with the hope of gain in the long run. The Imperial Buildings had been closed for refurbishment and the All Saints' Building down the road was set for demolition or renovation soon, which would force the town's only bookshop out. Its owner and his colleague had been expecting this for a long time. Indeed, at Christmas, their pessimistic appraisal of the town centre's prospects had led to me to ask if it was a coincidence that they had both *Grumpy Old Men* and *Is It Just Me or Is Everything Shit?* on such prominent display. My quip was a little unfair though: they only complain so much because they care. Like Marlene Guest, Shaukat Ali and the English majority, they have an attachment to their locality which is what makes a sense of community possible.

Perhaps the most seismic change was that Reg had finally delivered on the promise he made to me when I first met him and stopped going to The Travellers. Among middle-aged and older drinkers at least, yet more new managers at The Ball had seen it rise into the ascendancy, while The Travellers declined. Change does happen slowly, although it's hardly an overturning of the old order when people move from one heft to another on an adjacent, very similar field.

Although I felt I did now understand England better, I would not like to presume to have got it entirely sussed. Attempting to sum up the national philosophy is in many ways an absurdly ambitious project. I hope to have got a lot right, but I know I will have got many things wrong, and the problem is I don't know which part of my hypothesis is which. In some ways, I don't much care. If the value of intellectual inquiry about our fellow humans is to be found solely in getting the right answers, then a great deal of it is a waste of time. But it is always worth maintaining an open attitude in which we seek to understand those around us. Hence any value my project had would be entirely negated if it ended with the delusion that I now had the answers. This is just a start.

I was reminded that human beings always retain the capacity to surprise when I went to visit Pete, who was convalescing after open-heart surgery. I took Andy, having discovered that although they drank together a couple of times a week, Andy had never been to Pete's house in his life. In fact, the idea of doing so seemed so weird to him that he had not yet seen him weeks after his operation. That partly reflects the nature of male friendship, which can be extremely compartmentalized. But it also reinforced the sense I had on New Year's Eve that communities are not homogeneous, but networks of overlapping alliances, concentrated sufficiently to provide an illusion of oneness.

I caught up with almost everyone I saw regularly and it felt good to be able to come back here and be able to drink and chat with such a friendly, decent set of men. My time among them had changed me; I had acquired a greater respect for what I had previously seen as dull, stifling provincial English life. If ever I was tempted to see my more individualistic lifestyle as somehow superior, I should remember that it is in fact parasitic on these more settled communities. Flitting about would be much less satisfying if there weren't places like this I could go to and find more cohesive communities to ease back into. Nor would it be much fun going to ethnic restaurants or foreign countries if they had all become so cosmopolitan as to make them indistinguishable. If no one put down roots, the forest of society would simply be washed away. Liberal individuals need conservative communitarians more than they would like to admit. Despite my failure to identify with England and my disagreements with its philosophy, my country is like a troublesome family I cannot and should not disown.

The English in Numbers

Self-identifying working class in 1964: 65.7%
Self-identifying working class in 2005: 58.2%[1]

National daily paper readers: 60–70%
Local newspaper readers: 80–84%[2]

Percentage who believe immigrants should learn English: 82[3]
Percentage of British Muslims who believe immigrants should learn English: 90[4]
Percentage of British Muslims who believe western society is decadent and immoral and that Muslims should seek to bring it to an end: 32[5]

Mixed-race marriages in the UK: 2%[6]

Percentage who disapprove of homosexuals in high office: 39[7]

Average annual cost of keeping a new car on the road: £5,539
Average annual mortgage repayment: £5,112[8]

Average number of trips per year to shopping centres: 61[9]

Proportion of school children who have a packet of crisps in their lunch box every single day: two-thirds[10]
Number of cookery books owned by Britons: 171 million
Number of cookery books never used: 61 million[11]

Number on a diet at any one time: 10 million[12]

Average cost of a family holiday: £3,000[13]

Amount gambled on the 2006 football World Cup: £1 billion[14]
Amount gambled annually on The National Lottery: £5,000 million[15]

Americans who believe in God or a higher power: 91%
Britons who believe in God or a higher power: 67%[16]

Percentage who believe the national identity should be based on Christian values: 72[17]

Number of housewives: 2.1 million
Number of house husbands: 200,000[18]

Percentage of women who feel happy with their bodies: 2[19]

Average frequency of sex: once a week
Average self-reported number of sexual partners for men over a lifetime: 13
Average self-reported number of sexual partners for women over a lifetime: 7[20]

Average amount of time teenagers spend watching TV: 2 hours a day[21]
Average amount of time households spend watching TV: 25 hours a week[22]
Percentage of 8–15-year-olds with a TV in their bedrooms: 73[23]
Number of obese children: 1 million[24]

Average number of brand names a 10-year-old can remember: 300–400[25]

Percentage of Britons who would intervene if they saw a group of 14-year-old boys vandalizing a bus shelter: 34
Percentage of Germans who would intervene if they saw a group of 14-year-old boys vandalizing a bus shelter: 64[26]

Percentage of 18–30-year-old young women who have been victims of sexual assault after getting drunk: 36[27]

Proportion of binge drinkers: one in four[28]

Percentage of 16–25-year-olds who expect to marry and have children: 80[29]

Number of people at Christmas still paying off debts they ran up the previous year: 2.4 million[30]

Notes

1 ESRC study by Anthony Heath, John Curtice, Gabriella Elgenius and Jean Martin
2 European Journalism Centre, www.ejc.nl
3 BBC poll, 10/8/05
4 BBC poll, 10/8/05
5 YouGov/*Daily Telegraph*, 23/7/05
6 2001 census
7 BBC News Online, 18/7/05
8 RAC & Abbey National Research, 2006
9 *Daily Mail*, 13/10/05
10 *Guardian*, 11/1/06
11 *Guardian*, 14/2/06
12 Mintel, BBC News Online, 5/11/04
13 *Guardian*, 31/8/04
14 William Hill, www.puntersrealm.com
15 The National Lottery Commission, www.natlotcomm.gov.uk/ CLIENT/content.ASP?ContentId=24
16 ICM/BBC, www.bbc.co.uk/1/hi/programmes/wtwtgod/default.stm
17 BBC poll, 10/8/05
18 Office of National Statistics, *Daily Mail*, 13/10/05
19 *Top Santé*, reported in the *Sun*, 4/8/05
20 *The Lancet*, vol. 358, no.9296, 1/12/01
21 British Dietetic Association, press release, 1/6/06
22 British Audience Research Board, www.barb.co.uk

23 Ofcom, *Guardian*, 3/5/06
24 British Medical Association, www.bma.org.uk/ap.nsf/Content/Child Obesity
25 The National Consumer Council, www.nec.org.uk/ protectingconsumers
26 The *Economist*, 13/5/06
27 LM Research/the Portman Group
28 BUPA/Wellness
29 Face, *Guardian*, 28/5/06
30 One Advice, *Guardian*, 19/12/05

Notes

p. 9 *Rotherham, like England, is much less urban than you might think. UK 2005* (HMSO, 2004), National Statistics' official yearbook, classifies 79% of England as 'agricultural', and 21% 'urban and other' (p. 279). Rotherham Borough Council claims 70% of the borough is rural.

p. 12 *As Michael Collins put it in his biography of the working class.* Michael Collins, *The Likes of Us* (Granta, 2004), p. 110, G. K. Chesterton quoted on p. 77, from *Heretics* (Bodley Head, 1905)

p. 12 *in London 29% of the population is from an ethnic minority. Social Trends* (Palgrave Macmillan, 2005), pp. 10–11

p. 18 *a burglar alarm (like a quarter of homes in England).* The English House Condition Survey, 2004. Exact figure is 27%.

p. 19 *Most WMCs are affiliated to the CIU: the Working Mens Club and Institute Union, which was founded in 1862.* The Working Mens Club and Institute Union, www.wmciu.org.uk

p. 24 *The proportion of the population who identify themselves as working class has remained more or less constant.* Data available in the British Social Attitudes Survey, www.britsocat.com. Prof. Anthony Heath of Oxford University has been conducting comparative work over time for the ESRC's Identities and Social Action programme, www.identities.org.uk.

p. 25 *as historian Tristram Hunt sees it. Tristram Hunt: The Rise and Demise of the Middle Class*, Channel 4, first broadcast 17/7/05

p. 26 *Take, for instance, the famous advice column Dear Deidre.* Dear Deidre: *Sun*, 24/10/05

p. 27 *'I am white, middle-class, love my wife and adore traditional TV sitcoms. So why does the BBC hate me?'* Quentin Letts: *Daily Mail*, 15/7/05

p. 29 *Over three-quarters of the UK adult population go to pubs.* Kate Fox, *Watching the English* (Hodder & Stoughton, 2004), pp. 88, 253

p. 32 *the UK murder rate.* Paddy Hillyard, Christina Pantazis, Steve Tombs, Dave Gordon and Danny Dorling, *Criminal Obsessions: Why Harm Matters More Than Crime* (Crime and Society Foundation, October 2005)

p. 32 *twice as many murders per head of population in Scotland as there are in England and Wales.* One recent Home Office study showed the murder rate in Scotland to be 2.2 per 100,000 of population, and only 1.1 in England and Wales. This ratio has been pretty constant over recent years.

p. 32 *why the English lost the Battle of Hastings in 1066.* Peter Haydon, *Beer and Britannia: An Inebriated History of Britain* (Sutton Publishing, 2001) p.8

p. 33 *the definition of binge drinking.* BUPA/Wellness study, reported in the *Daily Mail*, 27/10/05

p. 33 *from 64% men and 36% women to 58% men and 42% women.* Report by research agency TGI, BBC News Online, 19/11/05

p. 37 *two-thirds of Britons live within five miles of where they were born.* This stat has been cited in *Prospect* magazine; 'Post-Multiculturalism and citizenship Values', talk by Yasmin Alibhai-Brown to the Immigrant Council of Ireland, 11/12/03; and in *Porcupines in Winter: The Pleasures and Pains of Living Together in Modern Britain* by Alessandra Buonfino and Geoff Mulgan (Young Foundation, 2006). Although the original source of this has proved elusive, there is plenty of other research that suggests it is at least closer to the truth than might be supposed.

p. 37 *Local commercial radio attracts 25 million listeners a week.* RAJAR (Radio Joint Audience Research Limited) figures for quarter ending March 2005.

p. 37 *Wolverhampton's* Express & Star *sells just under 180,000 copies.* European Journalism Centre, www.ejc.nl

p. 39 *The most important ingredients for happiness.* Prof. Mansel Aylward: quoted in the *Daily Mail*, 1/9/05

p. 39 *'big seven factors affecting happiness'.* Richard Layard, *Happiness: Lessons from a New Science* (Penguin, 2005)

p. 40 *Washing machine ownership is now nearly universal.* National Statistics Online, data for 2004

p. 52 *tube travel was still down.* Official Transport for London figures, quoted at www.thelondoncommuter.com/ tubeNews.htm

p. 53 *a 77% drop in the number of people in the Central London Congestion Charging Zone on the day of the bombings.* Footfall figures: SPSL, reported in the *Guardian*, 12/7/05

p. 53 *21% admitted that they would change 'plans'.* Populus poll, www.populus-limited. com

p. 54 *60% agreed with the capital sentence. Mail on Sunday*, 10/7/05

p. 56 *The town's ethnic minority population is only 3.1%.* Latest reliable figures are from the 2001 census and put the UK ethnic minority population at 7.9%. More recent estimates suggest that has risen to 8.7%.

p. 56 *47% of all Britain's ethnic minorities live in London.* Statistic cited in *Guardian* leader, 1/8/05

p. 57 *The Slovenian philosopher Slavoj Žižek provided a warning about misinterpreting what jokes mean.* Žižek repeats himself endlessly, but my source was an interview I conducted with him for *The Philosophers' Magazine*, issue 25, 1st quarter 2004.

p. 59 *Many young Asians in the town would talk about 'Paki' shops.* On the discussion boards of www.muslimyouth.net one contributor even wrote, 'actually 2 be hon3st i dont consider paki 2 be a derogatory term anymore . . . way i see it is that i am a paki.'

p. 63 *61% believe that 'our laws should respect and be influenced by UK religious values'.* BBC News Online, 18/7/05

p. 63 *mixed race marriages are on the rise.* 2001 census

p. 64 *75% of immigrants there did not have a Spanish friend.* *Metro* (Valencia), 24/2/06

p. 65 *90% of Muslims thought immigrants should learn English.* Published 10/8/05, full of challenging findings, http://news.bbc.co.uk/1/hi/uk/4137990.stm

p. 67 *monolithic 'Muslim community'.* Amartya Sen, *Identity and Violence: The Illusion of Destiny* (Penguin, Allen Lane, 2006)

p. 69 *13% of British Muslims thought the 9/11 attacks were justified.* David Goodhart: *Guardian*, 15/7/05

p. 69 *13% of British Muslims still considered the London bombers to be martyrs.* Populus survey for *The Times*, 4/7/06

p. 69 *a poll of British Muslims published three weeks after the 7/7 bombings.* *Sun* poll, 23/7/05

p. 70 *'Western society is de   cadent and immoral'.* YouGov poll, *Daily Telegraph*, 23/7/05

p. 70 *'Muslim women taking on modern roles in society'.* Pew Global Attitudes survey, published 6/7/06, http://pewglobal.org/reports/display.php?ReportID=254

p. 70 *'parts of this country don't feel like Britain any more because of immigration'.* BBC poll, 10/8/05, ibid.

p. 71 *putting council services under intolerable pressure.* Slough Council: 'Immigrants "swamping" council services', *Daily Telegraph*, 28/6/06

p. 79 *'British people's right to say what they think'.* *Daily Telegraph*, 27/7/05

p. 80 *white English people have no monopoly on being illiberal.* BBC poll, 10/8/05, ibid.

p. 80 *'It must be remembered that a working man . . . is seldom or never a Socialist in the complete, logically consistent sense.'* George Orwell, *The Road to Wigan Pier* (Penguin, 1962)

p. 82 *52% want to 'limit freedom of speech'*. BBC poll, 10/8/05, ibid.

p. 87 *fair cooperation is actually the norm.* Evolution of cooperation: Matt Ridley's *The Origins of Virtue* (Penguin, 1997) provides a clear introduction into the evolutionary basis of cheating and cooperation.

p. 89 *39% disapprove of homosexuals in high office.* BBC News Online, 18/7/05

p. 98 *a quarter of household expenditure.* Car running costs: RAC survey for third quarter 2006, www.racnews.co.uk; mortgage costs: Abbey National Research, cited at www.in2perspective.com, 14/6/06

p. 100 *'the best perpendicular church in the country'*. Pevsner quoted by Rotherham Minster's website, www.rcti.org.uk/allsaints.php

p. 105 *Cinemas now actually make more money from the stuff they sell you than they do from tickets.* See 'Munching at the Movies', a report by *Screen Digest*, April 2005, www.screendigest.com. The headline finding is 'Concessions account for a quarter of all revenue in UK cinemas but half the profits.'

p. 107 *'Intolerance of groups is often, strangely enough, exhibited more strongly against small differences'* Sigmund Freud, *Moses and Monotheism* (1939)

p. 112 *what would a competent judge choose?* John Stuart Mill, *Utilitarianism* (1863)

p. 118 *David Hume . . . was a famously corpulent gourmand.* Roderick Chisholm, *The Great Infidel: A Life of David Hume* (John Donald, 2004)

p. 118 *a packet of crisps in their lunch box every single day. Guardian*, 11/1/06

p. 121 *virtually no reference to the daily experience of most English people.* Jeremy Paxman, *The English* (Michael Joseph, 1998); Roger Scruton, *England: An Elegy* (Chatto & Windus, 2000)

p. 121 *'Little minds are interested in the extraordinary; great minds in the commonplace'* Elbert Hubbard, *Thousand and One Epigrams* (1911)

p. 121 *half of all British households don't even have a dining table they regularly use.* The 50% claim was made in the *National Post*, 5/7/03. Joanna Blythman, in *Bad Food Britain: How a Nation Ruined its Appetite* (Fourth Estate, 2006), makes the lesser claim that one in four British households no longer has a table that everyone can eat around.

p. 122 *the 'informal dining' sector.* Awards announced in December 2005 issue of *Management Today.*

p. 127 *171 million cookery books owned by Britons. Guardian*, 14/2/06

p. 128 *Britons are Europe's biggest consumers of ready-made meals.* Datamonitor survey, reported in *Metro*, 11/11/05

p. 128 *76% of men and 73% of women did not eat the recommended five portions.* *Guardian*, 9/1/06

p. 128 *The top food brands in the UK by sales value.* Annual survey conducted by TNS for *Marketing* magazine, reported in www.marketresearchworld.net, 24/8/06

p. 131 *Slimming is a national obsession.* Mintel study, reported in BBC News Online, 5/11/04

p. 131 *Atkins Nutritional went into bankruptcy.* *Daily Mail*, 2/8/05

p. 132 *suggesting that scientists had finally found the key to permanent weight loss.* *Observer Food Monthly*, March 2005

p. 132 *growth in the food sector.* TNS worldpanel survey, reported in the *Guardian*, 16/8/06; quote from director Edward Garner.

p. 135 *a survey on why people lose weight.* Survey by TNS for Zocor Health-Pro, reported in *The Times*, 5/11/06

p. 142 *Spain remains Britain's number one holiday destination.* ABTA Travel Statistics and Trends 2005, published June 2005

p. 142 *the Balearic Islands are the most popular areas.* Reported in both the *Independent* and the *Guardian*

p. 143 *For most people, their annual trip is something they spend months planning and looking forward to.* Average holiday cost: £2,725 according to the *Guardian*, 31/8/04

p. 145 *98% thought that Britons let the country down in the eyes of foreigners.* www.carrentals.co.uk survey of parents, *Sun*, 22/7/05

p. 159 *5.5 million people attended race meetings in 2003.* www.prospects.ac.uk, accessed 30/7/05; statistics cited from an independent Business In Sport and Leisure (BISL) study.

p. 159 *Official government statistics.* *UK 2005* (HMSO, 2004), p. 271

p. 159 *Brits had bet around £1 billion on it.* This figure was widely cited as the expected total value of bets, and according to bookmaker William Hill, expectations were met; www.puntersrealm.com

p. 159 *the biggest growth areas have been 'football . . . financial spread betting and "novelty betting"'.* *Economist*, 14/7/05

p. 160 *The National Lottery, on which we bet nearly £5,000 million a year.* The National Lottery Commission figures for year to 31 March 2006, www.natlotcomm.gov.uk/CLIENT/content. ASP?ContentId=24

p. 171 *Only a small minority are seriously religious.* ICM survey for BBC News 24's *Faith Day*, 14/10/06, http://news.bbc.co.uk/1/hi/uk/4434096.stm

p. 171 *69% identify themselves as Christians.* Survey in January 2004 by ICM for the BBC's *What the World Thinks of God*, http://news.bbc.co.uk/1/hi/ programmes/wtwtgod/default.stm

p. 172 *a country which 69% believe has an essentially Christian national identity, and which 72% believe should be based on Christian values.* BBC poll, 10/8/05, ibid.

p. 172 *a premonition dream which over half of us claim to have had.* Reader's Digest poll, as reported by BBC News Online, http://news.bbc.co.uk/1/hi/uk/5017910.stm

p. 172 *a ghost sighting, which one survey suggested 13% of us have experienced.* YouGov poll, October 2004, www.yougov.com/ archives/pdf/OMI040101073_1.pdf

p. 173 *our memories are terribly unreliable.* Bugs Bunny and Disney World: study done by Jacquie Pickrell and Elizabeth Loftus; their main paper in this area is 'The Formation of False Memories', *Psychiatric Annals* 25, 1995, 720–25

p. 175 *an ability to attribute powers of cause and effect to things in the world.* Lewis Wolpert, *Six Impossible Things before Breakfast: The Evolutionary Origins of Belief* (Faber and Faber, 2006)

p. 176 *The majority are, as another BBC survey on belief concluded, not religious in any specific way.* Survey cited in Joan Bakewell, *Belief* (Duckworth, 2005)

p. 177 *a public obsession with astrology.* Mass Observation study: Michael Collins, *The Likes of Us* (Granta, 2004)

p. 185 *Consider, for instance, the most popular songs now played at weddings and funerals.* Sun, 5/11/05

p. 186 *'the public love what I do'.* Jack Vettriano, *Daily Mail*, 29/10/05

p. 188 *'Good for nothing' as literature.* Prof. Michael Wheeler on *The Da Vinci Code*: *Guardian*, 24/4/06

p. 190 *A final objection might be that art has to be more than just entertainment.* John Carey, *What Good Are the Arts?* (Faber and Faber, 2005)

p. 193 *the show is popular not only with readers of the red tops.* Media Guardian, 30/1/06

p. 197 *Woolworths aims one-third of its Hallowe'en lines at adults.* Woolworths spokesperson quoted in the *Sun*, 31/10/05

p. 198 *We love to look down on people's taste in homes.* Alain de Botton: quoted talking about his book *The Architecture of Happiness* (Hamish Hamilton, 2006) in the *Guardian*, 26/4/06. The phrase 'Barratt Boxes' is not de Botton's own. The rather better 'Turkey Twizzlers of Architecture' is.

p. 198 *Their priorities may not always be quite right.* Royal Institute of Chartered Accountants study, cited in the *Daily Mail*, 13/8/05

p. 200 *one moment burlesque is sexist, reactionary kitsch.* Angie Pontani: quoted in the *Observer*, 2/5/04

p. 206 *the sex lives of the British*. Mass Observation study: data reported in *Little Kinsey*, a BBC 4 programme broadcast on 5/10/05; see http:// news.bbc. co.uk/1/hi/magazine/4293978.stm

p. 207 *fathers soon revert to working just as many hours as their childless peers*. Research led by Dr Esther Dermott at the University of Bristol, reported in BBC News Online, 24/8/06, http://news.bbc.co.uk/ 1/hi/uk/5280838.stm

p. 207 *there are nearly 200,000 house husbands*. Data from the Office for National Statistics, cited in the *Daily Mail*, 13/10/05

p. 209 *One in four men look for specific brands when they shop*. Report by the Future Foundation, cited in the *Sun*, 3/8/05

p. 212 *two-thirds of British women would like to have some form of cosmetic surgery*. Report by *Top Santé* magazine, reported in BBC News Online, 8/8/01, http://news.bbc.co.uk/1/hi/health/1480597.stm

p. 212 *both sexes have internalized the looks-based value system*. Women's discontent with their bodies: report by *Top Santé* magazine, reported in the *Sun*, 4/8/05

p. 213 *'I'm a real girlie girl'* Calendar girls, *News of the World*, 9/10/05

p. 214 *the relentless peer pressure on teenage girls*. Fergus Shanahan, *Sun*, 7/10/05

p. 216 *65% of those tested had taken alcohol, illegal drugs or both*. Forensic Science Service report: toxicological findings in cases of alleged drug-facilitated sexual assault in the United Kingdom over a 3-year period by Michael Scott-Ham and Fiona C. Burton, *Journal of Clinical Forensic Medicines*, vol. 12, issue 4, August 2005

p. 216 *A more sober study published in the leading medical journal, The Lancet, suggested that the average Briton has sex once a week*. *The Lancet*, vol. 358, no. 9296, 1/12/01

p. 217 *OuEurope's largest sex shop is in Rotherham*. The branch of Pulse and Cocktails was heralded as such when its opening was announced, BBC News Online, 3/3/03

p. 220 *it has failed to turn the tide*. Natasha Walter, *The New Feminism* (Virago, 1998)

p. 223 *Teenagers spend on average two hours a day watching TV*. British Dietetic Association study, press release, 1/6/06

p. 223 *most households watch 25 hours of television a week*. Broadcasters' Audience Research Board, see www.barb.co.uk

p. 223 *73% of 8–15-year-olds have a TV in their bedrooms*. Ofcom study: reported in the *Guardian*, 3/5/06

p. 223 *there are around 1 million obese children in the country.* British Medical Association, www.bma.org.uk/ap.nsf/Content/ ChildObesity

p. 223 *people believe youth ends when you're 49. Daily Telegraph,* 7/9/05

p. 224 *78% of children say they love shopping.* Ed Mayo, *Shopping Generation* (The National Consumer Council, 2005); see www.ncc.org.uk/pro-tectingconsumers

p. 225 *what dreams of an adult future do these proto-citizens have? What 10-year-olds Want,* by Luton First, published 19/12/05, see www.lutonfirst.com

p. 228 *although they start later, by the time they're 14 or 15, girls are out-boozing boys.* Ipsos MORI poll, reported in the *Observer,* 9/7/06

p. 228 *drug use has actually gone down among 16–24-year-olds. Economist,* 1/9/05

p. 229 *The yob is held up as the prime exhibit, and Hannah a mere curiosity. Sun,* 29/8/05

p. 230 *my companion moaned about the lack of visible police on the streets.* Chances of beat bobby stopping crime: a regularly cited statistic, repeated by Richard Best, director of the Joseph Rowntree Housing Trust, *Guardian,* 7/3/01; Hamish McRae in the *Independent* actually claimed that 'Statistically the chance of a police officer on the beat being within 100 yards of a crime was something like once in every 70 years', 2/2/05

p. 230 *'If you saw a group of 14-year-old boys vandalizing a bus shelter, would you intervene?' Economist,* 13/5/06

p. 231 *What was their life of pubs and clubbing like? Anatomy of a Big Night Out,* report by LM Research for the Portman Group

p. 232 *thrift chic is in.* Asda and M&S lead the way: 'Supposedly secret sales surveys' carried out by Taylor Nelson Sofres, a retail research agency, reported in *Economist,* 23/9/04

p. 236 *It's the fastest-growing brand on the market. Publican,* November 2004

p. 238 *80% of 16–25-year-olds expect to marry and have children.* Survey by youth marketing agency Face, reported in the *Guardian,* 28/5/06

p. 241 *a book about eccentric English traditions.* J. R. Daeschner, *True Brits* (Arrow Books, 2004)

p. 247 *An estimated 2.4 million people are still paying off debts they ran up the previous Christmas.* Study by debt consultants One Advice, *Guardian,* 19/12/05